The King and His Courts

THE ROLE OF JOHN AND HENRY III IN THE
ADMINISTRATION OF JUSTICE, 1199–1240

The King and His Courts

THE ROLE OF JOHN AND HENRY III IN THE
ADMINISTRATION OF JUSTICE, 1199-1240

———◆◆◆———

RALPH V. TURNER

Cornell University Press, ITHACA, NEW YORK

First published 1968

Library of Congress Catalog Card Number: 68–24775

PRINTED IN THE UNITED STATES OF AMERICA
BY KINGSPORT PRESS, INC.

FOR MY MOTHER

Thelma Smith Turner

Acknowledgments

The encouragement of many people made it possible for me to complete this study. A list of them all would be far too long, for it would include almost all my associates for the past seven years. But some of them must be singled out for recognition.

I wish to acknowledge my great debt to the late Sidney Painter, who first guided me in the study of medieval English history, to Professor Joseph R. Strayer of Princeton University, and to Professor John W. Baldwin of the Johns Hopkins University. Other members of the history department at Johns Hopkins and at the University of Arkansas have offered me invaluable encouragement and advice. The Johns Hopkins University provided fellowships which enabled me to begin this study, and the Florida State University provided financial aid for further research in the summer of 1965. Ohio University made available funds for the typing of the manuscript. The staffs of the Public Record Office and the Institute of Historical Research in London were most helpful. My debt to my typists, Mrs. Betty McCord at the Florida State University and Mrs. Norma Riggle at Ohio University, must be acknowledged too.

To all these people, I wish to express my thanks.

RALPH V. TURNER

Ohio University
December 1967

Contents

Abbreviations

Beds H.R.S.	Bedfordshire Historical Record Society Publications
Bracton	Henry de Bracton, *De legibus et consuetudinibus Angliae*, ed. G. E. Woodbine (4 vols.; New Haven, 1915–1942)
Cal. Chtr. Rolls	*Calendar of Charter Rolls* (6 vols., Public Record Office; London, 1903–1927)
Cal. Pat. Rolls	*Calendar of Patent Rolls, Henry III* (6 vols., Public Record Office; London, 1901–1913). The first two volumes are actual Latin transcripts, not calendars, and are abbreviated as *Pat. Rolls.*
Close Rolls	*Close Rolls of the Reign of Henry III* (14 vols., Public Record Office; London, 1902–1938)
Court of King's Bench I	*Select Cases in the Court of King's Bench,* Vol. I, ed. G. O. Sayles (Selden Society, Vol. LV; London, 1955)
Court of King's Bench IV	*Select Cases in the Court of King's Bench,* Vol. IV, ed. G. O. Sayles (Selden Society, Vol. LXXIV; London, 1955)

CRR   *Curia Regis Rolls,* ed. C. T. Flower
                                   et al. (14 vols., Public Record Office;
                                   London, 1922——), and unpub-
                                   lished rolls preserved at the Public
                                   Record Office

Dial. de scac.   Richard fitz Neal, *Dialogus de scac-
                                   cario,* ed. and trans. Charles Johnson
                                   (Nelson's Medieval Classics; Lon-
                                   don, 1950)

Dict. Nat. Bio.   *Dictionary of National Biography*
E.H.R.   *English Historical Review*
Exc. e rot. fin.   *Excerpta e rotulis finium in turri
                                   Londinensi asservatis, A. D. 1216–
                                   1272,* ed. Charles Roberts (2 vols.,
                                   Record Commission; London, 1835–
                                   1836)

Flower, *Introduction*   C. T. Flower, *Introduction to the
                                   Curia Regis Rolls* (Selden Society,
                                   Vol. LXII; London, 1944)

Foss, *Judges*   Edward Foss, *A Biographical Dic-
                                   tionary of the Judges of England
                                   from the Conquest to the Present
                                   Time 1066–1870* (London, 1870)

Glanville   Ranulf de Glanville, *Tractatus de
                                   legibus et consuetudinibus regni
                                   Anglie, qui Glanvilla vocatur,* ed.
                                   and trans. G. D. G. Hall (Medieval
                                   Texts; London, 1965)

Holt, *Northerners*   J. C. Holt, *The Northerners: A
                                   Study in the Reign of King John*
                                   (Oxford, 1961)

Law Qtrly. Rev.   *Law Quarterly Review*
Lincs Assize Roll   *The Earliest Lincolnshire Assize
                                   Rolls, 1202–1209,* ed. Doris M. Sten-
                                   ton (Lincoln Record Society, Vol.
                                   XXII, 1926)

Northants. Assize Roll   *The Earliest Northamptonshire As-
                                   size Rolls, 1202 and 1203,* ed. Doris

M. Stenton (Northamptonshire Record Society, Vol. V, 1930)

Note Book   *Bracton's Note Book,* ed. F. W. Maitland (3 vols.; Cambridge, 1887)

Painter, *King John*   Sidney Painter, *The Reign of King John* (Baltimore, 1949)

Pat. Rolls   *Patent Rolls of the Reign of Henry III* (2 vols., Public Record Office; London, 1901–1903)

Pleas before King   *Pleas before the King or His Justices, 1198–1202,* ed. Doris M. Stenton (Selden Society, Vols. LXVII–LXVIII; London, 1948–1949)

Pollock and Maitland   Frederick Pollock and F. W. Maitland, *The History of English Law before the Time of Edward I* (2d ed., 2 vols.; Cambridge, 1898)

Powicke, *Henry III*   F. M. Powicke, *King Henry III and the Lord Edward: The Community of the Realm in the Thirteenth Century* (2 vols.; Oxford, 1947)

Proc. Br. Ac.   *Proceedings of the British Academy*

Proc. without Writ   *Select Cases of Procedure without Writ under Henry III,* ed. H. G. Richardson and G. O. Sayles (Selden Society, Vol. LX; London, 1941)

RCR   *Rotuli curiae regis,* ed. Sir Francis Palgrave (2 vols., Record Commission; London, 1835)

Richardson and Sayles, *Governance*   H. G. Richardson and G. O. Sayles, *The Governance of Mediaeval England from the Conquest to Magna Carta* (Edinburgh, 1963)

Rolls for Glos., War. and Staffs   *Rolls of the Justices in Eyre for Gloucestershire, Warwickshire and Staffordshire, 1221, 1222,* ed. Doris M. Stenton (Selden Society, Vol. LIX; London, 1940)

Rolls for Lincs and Worcs.	Rolls of the Justices in Eyre for Lincolnshire (1218–19) and Worcestershire (1221), ed. Doris M. Stenton (Selden Society, Vol. LIII; London, 1934)
Rolls for Yorks	Rolls of the Justices in Eyre for Yorkshire in 3 Henry III (1218–19), ed. Doris M. Stenton (Selden Society, Vol. LVI; London, 1937)
Rot. de lib. ac de mis.	Rotuli de liberate ac de misis et praestitis, ed. T. Duffus Hardy (Record Commission; London, 1844)
Rot. de obl. et fin.	Rotuli de oblatis et finibus in turri Londinensi asservati, ed. T. Duffus Hardy (Record Commission; London, 1835)
Rot. lit. cl.	Rotuli litterarum clausarum in turri Londinensi asservati, ed. T. Duffus Hardy (2 vols., Record Commission; London, 1833–1834)
Rot. lit. pat.	Rotuli litterarum patentium in turri Londinensi asservati, ed. T. Duffus Hardy (Record Commission; London, 1835)
Sanders, Baronies	I. J. Sanders, English Baronies: A Study of Their Origin and Descent, 1086–1327 (Oxford, 1960)
Trans. Royal Hist. Soc.	Transactions of the Royal Historical Society
Wm. Salt Soc.	William Salt Archeological Society, Collections for a History of Staffordshire

The King and His Courts

THE ROLE OF JOHN AND HENRY III IN THE
ADMINISTRATION OF JUSTICE, 1199–1240

Introduction

For this, then, the king is made and elected, that he might do justice to everyone, that the Lord might be in him, that he might make judgments of his own will, that he might sustain and defend what he has justly judged, because if it is not he who does justice, peace can easily be brought to an end and it is useless to make laws and do justice unless it be that there is someone to keep the laws.[1]

Medieval English political thinkers from John of Salisbury to Henry de Bracton recognized that the king was the fountain of justice; they considered the giving of justice one of his most important duties. All students of English legal and constitutional history are aware of the attention that Henry II devoted to this obligation. Henry so greatly expanded the scope of royal justice by his assizes that the *curia regis* became not simply a court for disputes between his great tenants-in-chief, but a court of ordinary resort for pleas of the crown, proprietary actions, and possessory assizes open to all his free subjects. The old county and hundred courts and courts of private jurisdiction were bypassed in many instances; and the beginnings of a common law in England can already be discerned. This expansion of activity by the *curia regis* necessitated the establishment of specialized branches to speed the administration of justice. In the course of the twelfth century, as the task of governing England grew more complex, some of the offices of the *curia regis* tended to "go out of court"; that is, they were removed from the king's personal supervision. The exchequer early splintered off from the unspecialized *curia regis* to develop into an autonomous financial office

---

[1] Bracton, II, 305, f. 107.

with its own customs and procedures; the chancery, a permanent secretariat, later followed it. So too, during the late twelfth and early thirteenth centuries, other offshoots of the *curia regis* developed to hear the greatly increased number of pleas. These common law courts included the justices of the bench at Westminster, the itinerant justices sent on eyre throughout the kingdom, and the court *coram rege*, held wherever the king might be.

The fact that each of these three courts was known as a *curia regis*, although only one of them actually followed the king, raises an important question: To what extent were the royal courts subject to the king's will? It is possible that the royal courts had become, like the exchequer, a branch of the *curia regis* with a settled routine that did not require the monarch's constant supervision, but it is also possible that the king was active in the day-to-day administration of justice. Today two authorities in English legal and constitutional history, G. O. Sayles and H. G. Richardson, maintain that Angevin government was an "impersonal monarchy" in which the justiciar exercised a greater responsibility in judicial administration than did the king. One of the major themes of their version of English history is the wide powers wielded by the justiciar,[2] but their theory must be tested by a study of the ruler's role in justice. The problem is perhaps most clearly stated by A. J. Carlyle:

The history of mediaeval society constantly impresses upon us the conviction that the real difference between a barbarous and a civilised political system lies in the fact that the latter has an almost automatically working administrative and judicial machinery, while the former is dependent upon the chance of the presence of some exceptionally competent and clear-sighted individual ruler.[3]

In this work, I hope to determine to what extent England had developed "an almost automatically working . . . judicial machinery" and to what extent it still depended upon "the chance of the presence of some exceptionally competent and clear-

[2] Richardson and Sayles, *Governance*, esp. chap. 8, "The Structure of Government in the Twelfth Century," pp. 156–172.

[3] R. W. and A. J. Carlyle, *A History of Mediaeval Political Theory in the West* (New York and London, 1903–1936), III, 31.

sighted individual ruler" during the period from 1199 to 1240. The selection of this period, which includes the reign of King John (1199–1216) and the early years of King Henry III (1216–1240), has been dictated largely by the availability of sources, always a problem for the medievalist. Although the common law courts originated under Henry II, and enrollments of pleas heard by the royal justices probably began in 1166, no plea rolls date from his reign. Some surviving plea rolls date from the reign of King Richard I, but the first complete series begins with the reign of King John. Because of a lack of sources, then, no study of royal intervention in the courts is possible before 1199. If plea rolls from earlier reigns survived, King John's reign would still promise a fuller picture of the monarch's judicial activity than the reigns of his father and brother. There had been an absentee government in England during Henry II's last years and during Richard's entire reign, when much of the supervision of government fell to the justiciar. When John received the crown, he was determined to govern the kingdom with the vigor his father had shown in his early years; and following the loss of Normandy in 1204, he remained in England as the actual head of the government.

The choice of 1240 as a terminal date is more arbitrary. Since Henry III was only a boy in 1216, the government was in the hands of a regency council until he came of age, and not even then did he play a prominent role in the government. To find him taking an active part in judicial affairs, it is necessary to extend the study into the period of his personal rule, which did not begin until 1232. The years 1232–1240 provide a fair sample of the work of the courts after the young king assumed power. Excerpts from the plea rolls are available in *Bracton's Note Book*, which also contains useful marginal comments on certain cases.

In addition to the simple matter of availability of sources, there are other reasons for concentrating upon the reigns of John and Henry III in a study of the relations between the monarch and the courts. The controversial nature of King John's judicial activities itself suggests a second question about the courts: How much did John rely upon his courts, and how much did he follow "due process of law" in his dealings with his subjects? He was regarded by many of his contemporaries as a tyrant ruling according to his own will rather than according to the law, as a true king should. An examination of court cases should make clear the extent to which John submitted to the law in dealing with his subjects. Did he ever proceed against his enemies by instituting litigation in his own courts? Could persons with grievances against their ruler gain a hearing there? Then, there is the question of the quality of justice given in the royal courts of King John. John's work in the judicial sphere has long been overshadowed by his more publicized arbitrary seizures of land, extortions of money, and ruthless harrying of his enemies. But today few historians would deny that he played an active role in the administration of justice, devoting prodigious amounts of time and energy to judicial problems.[4] There is less certainty, however, about the results of this devotion, and few scholars believe that it brought any benefits to his subjects. Bryce Lyon summarized traditional opinions of John's judicial activities when he wrote:

John often forbade his small council to hear a case unless he was present; under him justice was swift and frequent but it suffered often from his arbitrary and unscrupulous methods. He respected neither custom nor procedure and seemed to settle each plea upon the basis of his own whim. His law was virtually prerogative law.[5]

---

[4] E.g. Sir Cyril Flower in *Introduction* remarks that, "like his father, King John took an active interest in the course of justice" (p. 497). In *From Domesday Book to Magna Carta 1087–1216* (*Oxford History of England*, Vol. III, 2d ed.; Oxford, 1955), A. L. Poole writes, "Yet King John—and it is remarkable in a man of so unstable a character—had a genuine and even a conscientious interest in the administration of justice" (p. 429). Doris M. Stenton expresses a similar view in her Raleigh Lecture on History, "King John and the Courts of Justice," *Proc. Br. Ac.*, XLIV (1958), 111, where she says, "The most striking fact which is revealed is the continuing close supervision by the King of his judges' work in the courts." Even F. W. Maitland acknowledged John's interest in justice, though he was not sure that this represented any genuine respect for the law: "King John liked to do justice, or what he called justice" (Pollock and Maitland, I, 170).

[5] *A Constitutional and Legal History of Medieval England* (New York, 1960), p. 281.

Doris M. Stenton, on the other hand, has taken a favorable view
of King John's judicial activity: "In the long view it may well
appear that in the matter of judicial administration King John
deserves credit rather than blame." [6] It is indeed true that John
often wished to hear pleas himself, but it is not certain whether
his interest in the courts worked to the detriment or
benefit of the parties involved. He could certainly influence the
course of justice when he chose. John may have regarded the
common law courts as useful instruments for implementation of
his policies, and he may have interfered in their operations for
his own ends; or he may have looked upon them as a lucrative
royal monopoly, selling a commodity—justice—that had to be of
good quality in order to sell. How much the king did influence
the work of justice can be determined only by an analysis of the
cases recorded in the plea rolls.

The administrative records of John's reign confirm many of
the despotic acts that his contemporaries cited in accusing him of
tyranny, as J. E. A. Jolliffe has shown in his *Angevin Kingship*.[7]
Frequently the plea rolls for the years of John and his son Henry
III corroborate these arbitrary actions. In most cases the evidence
is offered merely incidentally and not as the chief point at issue,
for few were bold enough to seek justice against the king in the
king's own courts. Yet it should be remembered that the king
had other, more effective instruments for harrying his victims.
The king's forests were outside the jurisdiction of the regular
courts and were governed according to his personal will. Offend-
ers against forest law were punished solely "at the king's
pleasure." [8] The exchequer was a court for royal financial matters operating under its own law, and its operations could bring
ruin to unlucky crown debtors. The king's autocratic actions
taken through these courts must have had some effect upon the
courts of justice which a study of their operations will reveal.

Of course, the tyrannical nature of John's rule brought forth
the reaction by the barons that resulted in Magna Carta. The
Great Charter included twelve chapters dealing with the admin-

---

[6] "King John and the Courts," p. 127.   [7] London, 1955.
[8] *Dial. de scac.*, pp. 59–60.

istration of justice. Chapter 40, with its promise that the king would not sell, deny, or delay right or justice for anyone, constituted an indictment of John's earlier administration of justice. The range of other judicial provisions extends from such technical details as how often itinerant justices should be sent to the counties to take the assizes (chapter 18 of the original issue) to the great principle enunciated in chapter 39: "No free-man shall be arrested or imprisoned or disseized or outlawed or exiled or in any way destroyed, neither will we set forth against him nor send against him, except by the lawful judgment of peers and [vel] by the law of the land."

The judicial chapters of Magna Carta suggest a third question which a study of the royal courts in the early thirteenth century should seek to answer: How successful was the attempt by the barons to reform the administration of justice in the king's courts? It must be discovered whether the royal justices of Henry III were any less submissive to the king's will. According to F. M. Powicke, Henry III's biographer, the king continued to take part in the work of his courts. Powicke points out that "the royal letters reveal the persistent co-operation between king, judges, and the members of the council both as a source of legal definition and as the highest court in the realm. Henry, like his father, was an active participant in these discussions and judgements." [9] A comparison of the judicial activities of the monarchs before and after the issue of the Great Charter should help to clarify the question of Henry's judicial activity. The answer is complicated by the fact that the monarch was a minor in the years immediately following Magna Carta. The functions of the ruler were exercised by a regency council composed of men in sympathy with some of the aims of the baronial rebels. This council was active in the sphere of justice in the years before 1227, when Henry declared himself to be of age. An examination of the plea rolls during his minority should reveal how seriously the legal clauses of the Charter were taken by the young king's council. And an examination of the rolls from the early years of Henry's

[9] *Henry III*, p. 333.

personal rule, 1232–1240, should show any changes that took place once he was free of his council's control.

The functioning of the royal courts in the early thirteenth century, then, raises three fundamental questions: To what extent was such functioning automatic and to what extent was it under the monarch's personal supervision? What was the nature of King John's judicial activity—a genuine attempt to improve the working of the courts or a mere tampering with them for his own ends? Was there any difference between the standard of justice in the royal courts before Magna Carta and the standard of justice after its issue?

To answer these questions, the first place to turn is to the judicial records, the plea rolls, for the reigns of John and Henry III. The first surviving rolls of the central court at Westminster date from the time of King Richard, and the first rolls of the court *coram rege* appear in the reign of King John. The rolls down to the end of Henry III's reign have been collected at the Public Record Office under the common title *"curia regis* rolls," although the keepers of the rolls have disentangled them and have separated those which represent proceedings before the king from those which are proceedings of the bench at Westminster.[10] The *curia regis* rolls through 1232 have all been published; excerpts of rolls after that year can be found in *Bracton's Note Book* and in *Placitorum abbrevatio, Richard I–Edward II.* Also kept in the Public Record Office are the assize rolls, records of pleas heard before the itinerant justices. Excerpts from these rolls have been printed by various county record societies.

Since the royal clerks often recorded the pleas in brief and stereotyped form, their descriptions of the cases need to be supplemented if the significance of royal intervention is to be recognized. Here the remarkably complete administrative records kept by the medieval English monarchs are of use. The earliest surviving chancery enrollments of royal charters, letters close, and

---

[10] On the composition of the plea rolls, see C. A. F. Meekings, *List of Rolls and Writs of the Court Coram Rege Henry III* (typescript, 1957, in Literary Search Room, Public Record Office, London); Flower, *Introduction,* pp. 18–19; and Lady Stenton's introduction to *Lincs Assize Roll,* pp. xxviii–xxxii.

letters patent date from the reign of King John. These rolls are particularly useful in casting light on possible reasons for the king's special interest in an action that otherwise appears quite ordinary. The pipe roll, the record of the exchequer, may reveal that one of the litigants had offered a fine to obtain the king's special consideration, or it may indicate that the other litigant was in debt to the king and did not enjoy his favor. The close rolls and patent rolls may record instructions sent by the king to the justices concerning actions coming before them. Also, many suits were ended by a compromise between the two parties, and the final concords were carefully recorded. Many of these records —the "feet of fines"—have been preserved and published. Sometimes the king had a hand in effecting the compromise, and the final concord reveals his role.

Once the plea rolls have shown that the king did play a part in a proceeding, and once the administrative records have shed further light on his activity in the case, it is necessary to evaluate his role. It may be shown that he acted in accordance with custom or that he interfered with ordinary procedures. His interference may indicate a desire to facilitate the administration of justice, or it may be an arbitrary tampering with it. To evaluate the king's role, it is essential to know what was the usual procedure in the royal courts, and also what was the substance of the law. For this purpose two legal treatises written during the period are invaluable. The book attributed to Glanville, *De legibus et consuetudinibus regni Anglie,* reveals the law and procedure of the royal courts at the beginning of the period under consideration—the end of the twelfth century. Bracton's *De legibus et consuetudinibus Angliae* does the same for the close of the period—the middle of the thirteenth century.

Using these sources, I propose to study the king's role in the work of his courts of justice in the thirteenth century. Many have written of John, Henry III, and justice without consulting the cases before their courts. Careful consultation of the plea rolls, noting individual cases which concerned the king in some way, is the only way to evaluate his role properly.

1

The Three Royal
Courts of Justice

The medieval English kings took a threefold oath at their coronations. One of the promises that they made was to administer justice equitably to all men.[1] Certainly medieval political thinkers considered the monarch's obligation to render justice to his subjects one of his essential duties. In the view of Henry de Bracton, writing in the thirteenth century, the king was the judex ordinarius of the realm, and his duty *primo et principaliter* was to judge.[2] According to Bracton, the king would decide all cases himself were he able; but since such personal attention was obviously impossible, he had to appoint judges delegated to share his task.[3] The need for royal judges was especially urgent by the time of Henry II, whose legal innovations greatly increased the amount of litigation in the royal courts, and whose vast Continental domains kept him away from England for long periods. Henry and his successors tried a number of experiments in judicial organization as they attempted to ensure justice to their subjects. By the middle of the thirteenth century, when Bracton wrote his treatise on the laws of England, there were three judicial branches of the *curia regis*:

For he has several courts, one before himself, that is in the royal hall, and chief justices who terminate cases pertaining to the king himself,

---

[1] See Percy Ernst Schramm, *A History of the English Coronation*, trans. L. G. Wickham Legg (Oxford, 1937), pp. 195–196, for Richard's and John's coronation oaths.

[2] Bracton, II, 304, f. 107.

[3] *Ibid.*, p. 306, f. 108; Pollock and Maitland, I, 514–515.

and the cases of all those resulting from complaint or by reason of privileges or franchise. As, for example, if it be someone who ought not to be impleaded except before the king himself. He has also a court and justices remaining *in banco* who take cognizance of all pleas of which they have been authorized to take cognizance, and without authorization they have neither jurisdiction nor [power of] coercion. He also has justices who are itinerant from county to county, sometimes to hear all pleas, sometimes for something special, for taking assizes of novel disseizin and mort d'ancestor, and gaol deliveries, and sometimes for one or two and not more. In all these cases will be the court of the lord king.[4]

An examination of the origins of these three courts and of their work is in order, if John's and Henry III's role in justice is to be evaluated. The early thirteenth century was an epoch in the growth of these tribunals, for it saw the court *coram rege* become a permanent professional branch of the *curia regis*.

ORIGINS OF THE ROYAL COURTS

The origin of all three judicial branches of the royal court—itinerant justices, common pleas, and king's bench—can be traced ultimately to the *curia regis* of the Norman kings, an undefined and constantly changing group of household servants and royal vassals serving the Conqueror and his sons as advisers, administrators, and judges. On solemn occasions this body became the *magna curia regis,* as the great tenants-in-chief of the crown appeared to do honor to their lord; but ordinarily it was a much smaller group of royal servants traveling with the king while he made his eyre, sometimes augmented by local lords for a part of the journey. As the task of governing the kingdom became more complicated, the primitive *curia* broke into different branches, each with its own tasks—financial, secretarial, or judicial. Some of them continued to follow the king, but others, such as the exchequer, gave up their wandering existence and settled permanently at Westminster.

Among the common law courts which separated from the

---

[4] Bracton, II, 301, f. 105b.

central *curia,* the first in time was the itinerant judicature. The itinerant justices were not created only to serve as judges. They were to aid the Norman kings in solving the problem, common to all feudal rulers, of maintaining effective control over the local officials of the realm. One way of providing supervision was to send members of the *curia regis* into the counties from time to time to gather information by means of sworn inquests or juries. This was the means by which William the Conqueror collected the information found in Domesday Book. In an age when sharp distinctions between administrative and judicial functions did not yet exist, the king's representatives sometimes acted as judges. They might preside over the customary local courts, or they might summon juries for some special purpose. For example, in the reign of the Conqueror, Bishop Geoffrey of Coutances, acting as the king's special representative, presided several times over important trials in the counties.[5] The practice of sending itinerant justices became more frequent in the time of William Rufus, and by the reign of Henry I it seems to have been a regular feature of royal government. But very little is known about the work of these itinerant justices in the early twelfth century. Evidence of their activity comes from some "jottings" in the pipe roll of 31 Henry I (1130) and from some scattered accounts in the chronicles.[6] This slight evidence suggests that there were not yet regular circuits of justices, as there would be under Henry II.

Attempts to trace the origin of the practice of sending out judges from the royal household to hold inquests have not been too successful. Of course, the missi dominici of Charlemagne's

[5] F. M. Stenton, *Anglo-Saxon England* (*Oxford History of England,* Vol. II, 2d ed.; Oxford, 1947), pp. 640–642; for other references to early judicial commissions, see Pollock and Maitland, I, 109, n. 2.

[6] For a full discussion of the work of Henry I's itinerant justices, see William T. Reedy, "The Origins of the General Eyre in the Reign of Henry I," *Speculum,* XLI (1966), 688–724. See also Richardson and Sayles, *Governance,* pp. 175–182. Chroniclers found only the more grisly aspects of the justices' work worthy of mention; typical of the chronicle references is one to the hanging of forty-four thieves by Ralf Basset at one session in 1124 (*The Peterborough Chronicle,* ed. Cecily Clark [Oxford, 1958], p. 46).

empire come to mind at once. William Stubbs, the pioneer student of English constitutional history, suggested that the English itinerant justices may have been descended from Carolingian missi by way of Normandy.[7] Stubbs also posed the possibility that royal commissioners of this sort had heard pleas during the Anglo-Saxon period: "There is sufficient evidence that a measure of the same was taken in England as early as the days of Alfred."[8] He did not indicate, however, the nature of this evidence. Among recent students, Richardson and Sayles are quite dubious about the existence of an itinerant judicature in Anglo-Saxon England, although they do not close the door on such a possibility.[9] F. M. Stenton's *Anglo-Saxon England* contains no mention of any itinerant judicial commissions before the Conquest.

The disputed succession following the death of Henry I and the resulting civil war temporarily halted the visits of itinerant justices to the counties, and the eyre system did not again become a regular judicial instrument until the reign of Henry II. He revived the practice of his Norman predecessors in sending itinerant commissioners through the country. The early visitations by royal officials under Henry II, like those in the time of the Norman kings, had both judicial and administrative aspects. Richardson and Sayles have found some evidence for visits by itinerant justices in 1155 or 1156, shortly after Henry's accession, but they admit that the purpose of these eyres is "far from clear," and they do not believe that these visits mark the beginning of the general eyres.[10] Stubbs believed that the year 1166 marked a return to the eyres of Henry I. In that year, the great council at Clarendon produced innovations that expanded the scope of royal justice. The assize of novel disseizin brought actions concerning possession of land into the king's court, and the Assize of Clarendon provided for juries of presentment to

[7] *The Constitutional History of England* (Oxford, 1874–1878), I, 478.
[8] *Ibid.*   [9] *Governance*, p. 173.
[10] *Ibid.*, pp. 196–197; Reedy, in "Origins of the General Eyre," p. 719, finds little evidence of continuity between the eyre of Henry I and that of Henry II.

accuse those suspected of breaches of the king's peace. Stubbs noted that there was a great general eyre following the council in 1166 for the purpose of trying those accused by the juries before the itinerant justices.[11] Other students of English legal institutions, F. W. Maitland and J. E. A. Jolliffe, have placed the date ten years later, in 1176. That year, a council meeting at Northampton further expanded the jurisdiction of the royal courts. The assize of mort d'ancestor brought more possessory actions within their competence, and the Assize of Northampton added to the list of crimes to be presented by juries. According to Jolliffe, "It is in 1176 that we are first conscious that experiment is over and the time come for the parcelling of the kingdom into areas for regular judicial visitation."[12] Richardson and Sayles reject both these dates; they find that these years were a period of experimentation for Henry II, and the eyres were not yet either annual or general. They take Stubbs to task for attaching too much importance to the Assize of Clarendon, and they show that the juries of presentment resulting from it made their accusations before local officers.[13] They do recognize that there was a general eyre in 1166, but they state that implementing the Assize of Clarendon was only a small part of the justices' task.

The facts of the judicial and fiscal visitations over the eighteen years from 1166 to 1183 show plainly enough that there were not fixed circuits, and that while the order observed in one year might be loosely founded on the proceedings in the previous year, everything was provisional and subject to alteration and revision, even while an eyre was in progress.[14]

Even though the date of its origin cannot be pinpointed precisely, the general eyre—*iter ad omnia placita*—was a recognized part of the system of royal courts during the later years of Henry

---

[11] *Constitutional History*, I, 507–509.

[12] J. E. A. Jolliffe, *The Constitutional History of Medieval England from the English Settlement to 1485* (3d ed.; London, 1954), p. 212; Pollock and Maitland, I, 156, support this view.

[13] *Governance*, pp. 198–199.

[14] H. G. Richardson, "Richard fitz Neal and the *Dialogus de Scaccario*," *E.H.R.*, XLIII (1928), 161–171.

II and in the reigns of his sons Richard I and John. Evidence
that the eyres were now a permanent institution is the fact that
the itinerant justices began to keep plea rolls, which they were
required to turn over to the exchequer upon completion of their
circuits.[15] The groups of justices who went out from the *curia
regis* received lists of questions, *capitula itineris*, to ask of local
juries. The first of these lists, or articles, of the general eyre that
has survived is from 1194 in the reign of Richard I; it reveals
that the justices still had many administrative tasks in addition to
their judicial work.[16] During the reign of King John, the justices
were not sent on general eyres each year, but almost yearly some
of them made visitations of a more limited scope.[17] The last
general eyre of his reign took place in 1210, and another was not
held until 1218–1219, during the minority of his son Henry III,
when eight groups of justices visited thirty counties.[18] After this,
general eyres were commanded every few years, until the custom
came to be established that there should be one every seven
years.[19]

The king had, in addition to the courts presided over by his
itinerant justices, his central courts; and questions raised concerning their origins are even more complex. Under the Norman
kings, the *curia regis* was the highest court in the kingdom, but it
was a court "only for the great men and the great causes." [20]
There was no permanent central court with its own staff, functioning automatically without the direct supervision of the monarch. On great feast days the *magna curia regis* rendered deci-

[15] *Dial. de scac.*, p. 77.

[16] *Select Charters*, ed. William Stubbs (8th ed.; Oxford, 1905), pp.
258–263.

[17] Lady Stenton suggests that there were three general eyres, in 1202, 1208,
1210 (*Pipe Roll 13 John* [Pipe Roll Society, N.S.; London, 1953], 1211, p.
xxxiv). Of the 1202 eyre, she writes: "Although no chronicler records that a
general eyre took place in 1202 or preserves the articles on which the judges
acted, four groups of judges began work in the summer and continued it into
the autumn over a large part of England" (*Pipe Roll 4 John* [Pipe Roll
Society, N.S.; London, 1937], 1202, p. xvii). She lists the surviving eyre rolls
from the reign of John in *Lincs Assize Roll*, pp. xx–xxi.

[18] For the eyre of 1210, see *Pipe Roll 12 John*, ed. C. F. Slade (Pipe Roll
Society, N.S.; London, 1951), 1210, pp. xv–xvi. For the eyre of 1218–1219,
see Powicke, *Henry III*, p. 29 and n. 3.

[19] Pollock and Maitland, I, 156.   [20] *Ibid.*, p. 108.

sions in important cases; at other times the king's household servants acted as judges; and after its establishment, the exchequer sometimes sat as a court. Later, the system of writs and assizes initiated by Henry II caused a vast number of new legal actions to come before the *curia regis*. Machinery was needed for the judgment of these new actions, and the king tried experiment after experiment in his efforts to devise some instrument.

One of Henry's plans, put into effect in 1178, was to assign five members of the royal household—three laymen and two clerks—to handle the mass of new litigation. This tribunal would accompany the king on his travels up and down the kingdom, but would only consult him about cases too important or too difficult for them to decide themselves.[21] Stubbs, convinced of the significance of this measure in the evolution of the royal courts, traced the court of king's bench to it.[22] Maitland, England's greatest legal historian, did not accept Stubbs's view. Instead, he saw in the justices following the king the origin of the court of common pleas, the court of the bench at Westminster. According to his interpretation, this body of judges traveling with the king failed to evolve into the regular court *coram rege* because of the kings' long absences from England. Henry II spent few of his last years in England, and his son Richard was abroad for all but a few months of his ten years' reign. During these royal absences, Maitland maintained, the tribunal settled at Westminster, where the exchequer had earlier found quarters. There it sat at the exchequer, and the two bodies doubtless shared some of their personnel, although they were not identical.[23]

Maitland's version has received endorsement from a number

---

[21] Benedict of Peterborough (Howden), *Gesta Henrici Secundi*, ed. William Stubbs (Rolls Series; London, 1867), I, 207. Lady Stenton has shown that this chronicle is simply the first version of Roger of Howden's chronicle ("Roger of Howden and *Benedict*," E.H.R., LXVIII [1953], 574–582).

[22] *Constitutional History*, I, 525.

[23] Pollock and Maitland, I, 153–155. Referring to the ordinance of 1178, Maitland writes, "It is probable that we have here a measure of great permanent importance. From the following years we begin to get records which seem to put before us a tribunal which in the main is like that here described" (p. 154). See also his views in *Select Pleas of the Crown* (Selden Society, Vol. I; London, 1888), pp. xiii–xvi.

of legal historians, and it has almost become the standard account.[24] But Richardson and Sayles have attacked this interpretation of the ordinance of 1178. The latter of these two writers has written of it, "This was but one among many schemes improvised by the king's fertile inventiveness and, as it happened, it was short-lived, and we ought not to see in it the solemn foundation of a court of law simply because it chanced to be mentioned by a chronicler." [25]

Richardson and Sayles do follow Maitland in attributing the establishment of a permanent central tribunal at Westminster to the long absences of Henry II and Richard I; their view, however, is that it grew, not from the five justices appointed in 1178, but from the exchequer. They find the origin of the bench in the *curia regis ad scaccarium,* the justiciar's court held at Westminster for both financial and judicial duties.[26] They maintain that the exchequer was not solely a treasury department, but was rather a sort of general secretariat, an office for financial administration, and a court of unlimited jurisdiction—all at the same time. In short, they hold that the exchequer, when the king was outside the kingdom, performed practically all the functions of the *curia regis.* Their opinion of the work of the exchequer contrasts with long-accepted views. The traditional view of the exchequer's work can be summed up in a quotation from the great authority on medieval English administration, T. F. Tout:

It is manifest that, after the easy-going fashion of the times, the exchequer was often employed in expediting very varied business in which the king was concerned. It was, however, primarily and essen-

---

[24] G. B. Adams, *Council and Courts in Anglo-Norman England* (Yale Historical Studies, Vol. V; New Haven, 1926), pp. 217–219, 240–242; Jolliffe, *Constitutional History,* pp. 215–216; Bryce Lyon, *A Constitutional and Legal History of Medieval England* (New York, 1960), p. 282; *Royal Writs in England from the Conquest to Glanville,* ed. R. C. Van Caenegem (Selden Society, Vol. LXXVII; London, 1958), p. 30.

[25] *Court of King's Bench* IV, p. xxvii. Sayles' view has been endorsed by S. B. Chrimes, *Introduction to the Administrative History of Medieval England* (rev. ed.; Oxford, 1958), p. 49, n. 1; and A. L. Poole, *From Domesday Book to Magna Carta 1087–1216* (*Oxford History of England,* Vol. III, 2d ed.; Oxford, 1955), p. 413.

[26] *Governance,* pp. 210–211.

tially a "segregated" revenue department, and its "secretarial," nay, even its judicial aspects, were quite subordinate to its prime function.[27]

Richardson and Sayles develop some ingenious arguments to support their view. They point out that the justices of the bench usually served as barons of the exchequer too, that the two groups were housed together at Westminster, and that their titles "justices" and "barons" were interchangeable terms in the chronicles and official records of the late twelfth century.[28] Richardson buttresses his argument for the identification of the two groups with criticism of the text of the twelfth-century lawbook attributed to Glanville. In one passage of the text, Glanville enumerated the law courts of his day: *curia regis ad scaccarium et coram justitiis ubicumque fuerint.* G. E. Woodbine in his edition of Glanville placed a comma after *regis,* indicating that the *curia regis* and *ad scaccarium* were two distinct courts.[29] Richardson argues that the comma is unjustified, that the phrase *curia regis ad scaccarium* denotes a single court—the exchequer.[30] This evidence convinces him and his co-author that the court of the bench had its origin in an omnicompetent exchequer. They feel that only slowly because of the increased business did the royal officers at Westminster come to make a distinction in functions: "In the course of the twelfth century the barons or justices tended to specialise, some upon judicial and some upon financial work; but even in the reign of John there was no complete separation." [31]

The insistence of these two writers that the court of common pleas evolved from the exchequer is easy to explain; it is necessary to make the responsibility for justice rest with the justiciar rather than with the king if their thesis is to be maintained. They stress repeatedly the Angevin monarchs' long visits over-

[27] *Collected Papers* (Manchester, 1932), I, 193.   [28] *Governance,* p. 210.

[29] *Tractatus de legibus et consuetudinibus regni Angliae* (New Haven, 1932), pp. 183–184.

[30] *Memoranda Roll I John,* ed. H. G. Richardson (Pipe Roll Society; London, 1943), pp. xiii–xiv. G. D. G. Hall (p. xii), the most recent editor of Glanville, follows Richardson.

[31] Richardson and Sayles, *Governance,* p. 210.

seas, and they attribute almost all innovations in government made in Henry II's last years and in Richard's reign to the justiciar.[32] This interpretation is in direct opposition to the view of another student of the period, J. E. A. Jolliffe, who maintains that despite the increasing institutionalization of government during the twelfth and early thirteenth centuries, the king still "moves all." He emphasizes the important role that the king personally played in government.[33] While no plea rolls from Henry II's reign survive, the first ones—from the time of Richard and John—support Jolliffe's view; they reveal the monarch actively participating in the work of his courts. Perhaps the ordinance of 1178 is without any significance, known only through a chronicler's chance reference to it; but it is difficult to believe that Henry II simply allowed the justiciar to cope with the new cases as best he could at the exchequer. Furthermore, Richardson's version of the text of Glanville cannot go unchallenged. It is doubtful that Glanville was unaware of a distinction between the *curia regis* and the *scaccarium;* for his contemporaries were aware of it, as entries in the pipe rolls and passages in the *Dialogus de scaccario* indicate.[34] Glanville's *curia regis ad scaccarium* could easily refer to the *curia regis* sitting at the *domus scaccarii,* not necessarily to the court of the exchequer. In addition, the *curia regis* rolls of John's reign make it clear that the clerks of the court recognized a distinction between the "barons" of the exchequer and the "justices" of the bench.[35]

---

[32] *Ibid.,* pp. 168–169.

[33] *Angevin Kingship,* pp. 57–58, 296–297. See Richardson's reaction in his review of Jolliffe's book in *E.H.R.,* LXXI (1956), 447–453.

[34] Van Caenegem, *Royal Writs,* p. 31, cites an entry in *Pipe Roll 34 Henry II,* ed. J. H. Round (Pipe Roll Society; London, 1925), p. 155, where it is recorded that an individual owed one fine for having his plea *in curia regis* and that he owed a second fine for having another plea *in curia regis ad scaccarium.* He also cites passages from *Dial. de scac.,* pp. 32, 34, in which Richard fitz Neal makes a distinction between the king's court and the exchequer.

[35] E.g. references to *banco* in CRR, III, 274, V, 119, VI, 66, and VII, 113; and references to *barones de scaccario* in VII, 33, and VIII, 87, 309, 316. *Close Rolls* (1227–1231), p. 503, mentions both the barons of the exchequer and the justices of the bench, clearly referring to two distinct bodies.

These terms were not used interchangeably in the early thirteenth century.

No matter what may have been the origin of the court of common pleas, it was definitely recognized as a separate institution by the early thirteenth century. By the time of Henry II's sons, it had its own rolls, known as the *rotuli curie domini regis de Westmonasterio,* clearly distinguished from the exchequer records.[36] Magna Carta itself provides evidence that the barons wished to see the continued existence of a permanent court at Westminster, for chapter 17 of the first issue states that "common pleas shall not follow our court, but shall be held in some fixed place."

Yet, as Richardson and Sayles point out, there was not yet a final division of tasks between the bench and the exchequer even as late as the reign of Henry III. In his time, assizes still were heard occasionally before the barons of the exchequer,[37] and entries relating to financial matters are scattered throughout the plea rolls from John's reign. It is surprising to find among the accounts of assizes and appeals a note that the monks of St. Edmunds had brought to the court the jewels that their late abbot had bequeathed to the king.[38] The rolls sometimes contain lists of financial problems relating to the management of the royal demesne. A roll of 1201 notes two mills that were harmful to the king's mills, purprestures made on the king's land, a youth in the king's custody, and a royal manor that could be let at more profitable rates.[39] These entries are reminders that there was

[36] E.g. *CRR,* I, 57, 123, 181, 408.

[37] *Ibid.,* VIII, 87, 316, and X, 122, 142, 155.

[38] *Ibid.,* VI, 189. On page 207, it is recorded that "Geoffrey fitz Peter gives the lord king two casks of good wine of Auxerre."

[39] *Ibid.,* I, 414, Easter 1201. Similar lists of matters of financial interest to the king are found in *ibid.,* X, 68, 259; and in *Pleas of the Crown for the County of Gloucester, 1221,* ed. F. W. Maitland (London, 1884), pp. 48–49, n. 1. *CRR,* V, 53, Michaelmas 1207, contains an entry of one line: "Speak about Matilda Luvel." *Pipe Roll 9 John,* ed. A. Mary Kirkus (Pipe Roll Society, N.S.; London, 1946), Michaelmas 1207, p. 61, reveals the reason for this notation: "Matilda Luvel owes £100 and a palfrey that she not be distrained to marry." Another example is from the reign of Henry III (*CRR,* X, 260, Michaelmas 1221): "Speak with the council of the lord king

much less specialization and more overlapping of functions in the work of the royal officers in the thirteenth century. The king's judges were servants of all work, not set above and apart from other spheres of government as today.

In addition to the court of common pleas, there was a second central court, the court of king's bench, which remains to be accounted for. The Anglo-Saxon kings had summoned their wise men to aid them in doing justice, and the Norman kings had called upon their tenants-in-chief for counsel. However, the court *coram rege* of the thirteenth century was not the *magna curia regis;* it was ordinarily a court held by a few professional justices, while the great council had more the character of a deliberative body composed of the king's ministers and magnates, the prelates, earls, and barons. The question is: When did this regularly constituted court with its professional staff arise?

There is nothing to indicate that a regular court *coram rege* with its own staff, plea rolls, and procedure existed in the twelfth century.[40] Yet the king must have judged important cases concerning persons of political importance. This alone would have brought a number of actions into his court, for many persons and almost all religious houses had charters granting them the right to be tried only before the king or his justiciar. In addition, the king would have heard cases that raised difficult questions, and he received petitions for justice in cases where there was no legal remedy. The number of pleas had become great enough by 1178 for Henry II to provide for a group of five officials traveling with him to do justice; but the king's long absences from the realm prevented the growth of any permanent court sitting in his presence. Indeed, Richardson and Sayles find that Henry II's court *coram rege* was not at all significant, that it played no part in the development of English law that was taking place under him:

If we may judge by "Glanville," lawyers in the closing decades of the twelfth century gave hardly a thought to the court *coram rege:* their

---

concerning the church of St. Briavels which is in the king's gift." *CRR*, 115B, records fines offered to the king for markets.

[40] Richardson and Sayles, *Governance*, pp. 213–214.

attention was confined to the court at the exchequer and the courts of the itinerant justices. It was at Westminster that the common law of England was born and grew up.[41]

But whatever may have been the role of the court following the king under Henry II and Richard I, with John's accession to the throne it began to take on new importance. King John was no absentee monarch, for the loss of his Continental possessions in 1204 forced him to spend most of his time in England. In addition, he took a very active part in the administrative work of his kingdom, although it is difficult to know whether this was due to his abnormally suspicious nature or to his genuine interest in the details of government. In any case, his desire for close supervision did result in the creation of a new body of royal justices, as scholars have recognized. Maitland took an uncharitable view of King John's judicial activity, but he was aware that the creation of two central tribunals—one following the king and another stationary at Westminster—dates from his reign.[42] Probably John had no idea that he was setting a precedent, for he was merely reviving the custom of his ancestors in hearing pleas as he moved about the country. But his knowledge of England, his interest in legal questions, and his almost permanent residence in the kingdom meant that in his reign the king personally would become the master of the judicial system, the "fountain of justice" in practice as well as in theory. A sign that he planned a permanent court *coram rege* is the keeping of plea rolls by his justices; the first surviving one dates from John's visit to England in the spring of 1200.[43] There could be no regular court *coram rege* when the monarch was overseas, for a court must have litigants. Most of the king's subjects remaining in England would have found the expense and delays involved in

[41] *Ibid.*, p. 172.

[42] Pollock and Maitland, I, 170. See also *Court of King's Bench* I, p. xxii; Powicke, *E.H.R.*, XXXIX (1924), 267, in a review of *CRR*, Vol. I; and *Pleas before King*, I, 86.

[43] *Pleas before King*, I, 61; the text of the roll is printed on pp. 296-320, Feb.–April 1200. Lady Stenton notes that possibly a roll of proceedings before King John was begun on his visit to England in 1199, but if so, it has not survived.

following the king abroad too great.[44] Consequently, during King John's expeditions to the Continent or to Ireland, the bench at Westminster regained its position as the only central court, and pleas touching the king were postponed until his return.[45]

King John's work in establishing a dual system of royal courts was a real contribution to the development of the English judicial system.

What the King seems to have desired was what current practice provided—a flexible system with the King himself and his own court at its head, a small bench sitting at Westminster as a clearing house for pleas, and a succession of eyres dispatched through the country as the pressure of local business and the need for local taxation required.[46]

Unfortunately, this situation did not last, for the bench began to decline during the years 1207–1209, when more and more cases were removed from its jurisdiction. By the Michaelmas term of 1208, proceedings at Westminster were reduced to such an extent that the pleas for this term and for the Hilary and Easter terms of 1209 could all be recorded on a single roll.[47] That this waning resulted from a royal command is clear from the record of an assize brought before the justices of the bench in 1209. The action was postponed to be heard *coram rege* because one of the parties declared that "no plea ought to be held at Westmin-

[44] The CRR reveal only two pleas postponed to be heard before the king overseas in Normandy: RCR, II, 185, plea between William de Arden and Robert fitz Ernis concerning land in Well and Warham; CRR, I, 427–428, claim of John de Erleigh against Thomas Gernon to half the manor of Neville.

[45] Flower, *Introduction*, p. 21: "This court was the king's personal court; as it could not sit if it were physically impossible for him to be present, whether owing to his absence beyond seas or beyond the Severn in Wales, pleas in the bench which were suitable for his hearing were postponed until his return."

[46] Doris M. Stenton, "King John and the Courts of Justice," *Proc. Br. Ac.* XLIV (1958), 113–114.

[47] CRR, Vol. V, preface. The roll consists of three small membranes, one for each of the terms of Michaelmas 1208 (pp. 316–319), Hilary 1209 (pp. 321–324), and Easter 1209 (pp. 325–328). The records of the Hilary and Easter terms are made up almost entirely of postponements.

ster, and he vouches the lord king to warranty concerning this." [48]

King John is condemned by Richardson and Sayles for his command temporarily closing the court. They call his action "one of those gratuitous acts of folly of which John, for all his cleverness, was capable in a blind access of resentment." [49] Lady Stenton, who usually succeeds in finding charitable explanations for John's evil deeds, suggests that his excommunication made necessary the closing of the court at Westminster, for too few ecclesiastics were willing to serve the excommunicate monarch as judges.[50] Richardson and Sayles offer another explanation, once again tied to the justiciar. They maintain that from 1209 to 1212 the justiciar Geoffrey fitz Peter did not have the king's confidence, and that as a result John would not permit him to hold court.[51] Yet there is a simpler explanation, if one only turns to the political history of the first decade of the thirteenth century, keeping in mind at the same time John's character. Both the chronicles and the evidence in the pipe rolls for 1208–1209 paint a picture of King John as a suspicious ruler, doubtful of the loyalty of his subjects and seeking to rule them through terror. This was a time of great strain for any man, all the more for one with John's unstable temperament. He had recently suffered the loss of Normandy, and now he faced another possible defeat in his struggle with Pope Innocent III; his kingdom lay under an interdict (24 March 1208), and he personally was under the ban of excommunication (7 October 1209). Adding to his problems was his uncertainty about his vassals' loyalty in this time of danger; he feared they might seek to use his troubles with the Church as a release from their ties of fealty to him.[52] It is not surprising, then, that the king wished to have all judicial activity centered at his own court, where he could more closely supervise it. The bench, however, did not permanently cease to exist. By 1214, King John's attention had turned to preparations for his final campaign to recover his Continental possessions, and the

---

[48] *Ibid.*, V, 327.   [49] *Governance*, p. 384.
[50] "King John and the Courts," pp. 112, 118.   [51] *Governance*, p. 385.
[52] Painter, *King John*, p. 242.

royal justices once again heard pleas at Westminster.[53] Apparently the court of the bench at Westminster was active from Hilary term 1214 until Trinity term 1215, when the baronial rebellion began.[54]

With the death of King John in 1216 and the accession of Henry III, a boy of nine, there was a return to the conditions that had prevailed in the time of the absentee monarch Richard I. The court *coram rege* no longer existed, and the court of the bench at Westminster became the only central royal court. Pleas which would have come within the competence of King John's court *coram rege* were either referred to the council governing England during the king's minority or were postponed until his coming of age. The council could not judge royal charters or grants or matters directly concerning the king's interest, but it could share the royal responsibility for justice. During the minority, doubtful questions and cases with political overtones were reserved for the council; and so cases were sometimes marked *loquendum cum consilio*, just as in the time of John they had borne the note *loquendum cum rege*.[55] In 1223 the pope issued a bull declaring Henry to be of age, although it provided for the continued control of the justiciar and the council over his acts.[56] This declaration made little difference in the procedure of the court at Westminster, for three years later, in 1226, pleas were still being postponed on account of the king's minority.[57] Then, in January 1227, Henry III declared himself to be of age, and he began to issue and confirm royal charters.[58] No immediate change took place in the organization of the royal courts; there remained only one central court, the bench at Westminster. It was customary for the young king to share in the work of his

[53] *CRR*, VII, 113. The editor's note describes this roll (Trinity 1214) as a "record of proceedings before the justices of the Bench." See also Richardson and Sayles, *Governance*, pp. 385–386, esp. p. 386, n. 1.

[54] Richardson and Sayles, *Governance*, p. 386, n. 1, cites letters close and patent to the justices of the bench as late as April and July 1215.

[55] See Chapter 4, pp. 134, 138–139.   [56] Powicke, *Henry III*, pp. 43–44.

[57] *CRR*, XII, 465–466, no. 2333, Easter 1226, is the last such postponement recorded.

[58] Powicke, *Henry III*, p. 44.

courts from time to time, perhaps as part of his training in kingship. As early as 1221, cases were postponed for hearing before the king at York.[59] In the summer of 1226 and again in 1229, Henry joined his judges in taking the assizes and hearing pleas of the crown.[60] These pleas postponed for hearing in the king's presence did not raise questions of great difficulty, neither were they pleas touching the king, but the parties concerned were sometimes important figures in the kingdom.[61]

Despite these occasional references to pleas *coram rege* on the rolls of the court at Westminster, no plea rolls from a court following the king exist for the years before 1234. Most authorities maintain that there was no regularly constituted court *coram rege* until 1234; it was re-established during Henry's personal rule, 1232–1234, apparently as part of the administrative reforms made then.[62] There had been a long delay between the time Henry III came of age and the time he took actual charge of his government. For a number of years, from the death of William Marshal in 1219 until 1232, the justiciar Hubert de Burgh was more the governor of England than was the king; but in 1232 the young king took command of the country, and the powerful justiciar fell from favor. Henry then sought to bring all his officers and all branches of the government more closely under royal supervision.[63] Doubtless one aspect of this reform was the re-creation of the king's own court. The need for a court accompanying the king became greater after he began to rule person-

---

[59] *CRR*, X, 158, 161–162, Easter 1221. There are others in Trinity and Michaelmas terms 1224 (*ibid.*, XI, nos. 1784, 1928, 1971, 2286; nos. 1437, 2002, 2019).

[60] G. D. G. Hall, review of *CRR*, Vol. XIII, in *E.H.R.*, LXXVII (1962), 103.

[61] E.g. *CRR*, XIII, 64, no. 293, a day given to Hubert de Burgh and Robert de Hauville for taking their cirograph; p. 87, no. 379, plea of Peter, bishop of Winchester, against John Dacus; pp. 534–535, no. 2517, jury between the abbot of Woburn and Isabel, countess of Oxford.

[62] *Note Book*, I, 58; *Court of King's Bench* IV, pp. xxix–xxxi. Earlier, in *Court of King's Bench* I, p. xxxv, Sayles stated that the court *coram rege* might date from 1224; in Volume IV, however, he rejects that opinion.

[63] Chrimes, *Administrative History*, pp. 86–87; Powicke, *Henry III*, pp. 84–122, 329.

ally, for the justices of the bench had to consult him about more and more questions, causing delays. The solution was a return to two central law-courts, as there had been in the time of King John: one group of justices following the king and another seated at Westminster.

One question that arises concerning the rebirth of the court *coram rege* in 1234 is its relation with the king's council, since the council did take form as an institution in the reign of Henry III. During the young king's minority, the council that governed in his name had been responsible for the administration of justice, and it had sometimes considered judicial questions. No regular court developed from this council, and no special rolls recorded its judicial activities. Its occasional interventions were simply noted on the plea rolls of the court at Westminster.[64] Certainly Henry III had a group of *consiliarii*, possibly bound to him by a counselor's oath, in the years just after he attained his majority; but it is not at all clear that this group of counselors constituted a formal body that could act as a court.[65] Nevertheless, some students of the king's council have identified Henry III's court *coram rege* with the council—notably James F. Baldwin in *The King's Council in England during the Middle Ages* and G. B. Adams in his *Council and Courts in Anglo-Norman England*. Baldwin treats the question of the connection between council and courts only cursorily, but Adams devotes considerable attention to it. He holds that the court following the king was an outgrowth of the council—indeed, was identical with the council. On Bracton's view of the court *coram rege*, he observes that Bracton "nowhere shows any suspicion that this body in truth constituted a court distinct from the council. He knows of no court exercising this jurisdiction but the council." [66] It is likely that some of the king's justices were also members of the council. After all, the council's chief task was to give the king advice; then that advice would be implemented by one of the

---

[64] *Court of King's Bench* I, pp. xxxiii–xxxiv; Powicke, *Henry III*, pp. 38–40.

[65] Chrimes, *Administrative History*, 98–101.

[66] *Council and Courts*, p. 232.

regular branches of government—the exchequer, the chancery, or in the case of judicial matters, the various royal courts.[67] Certainly the monarch could reinforce the numbers of his justices with his counselors when difficult questions arose, so that the court *coram rege* sometimes seems to shade off into the council or even into a parliament.[68] Yet there is no reason to suppose that Henry's creation of a court following him resulted from a process any different from that under his father. He created a group of professional judges to accompany him on his travels and to hear cases in much the same way that Henry II and John had done.

Adams bases his argument for a different origin of Henry III's court *coram rege* on a difference in function, on the assumption that King John's court heard ordinary common pleas, while Henry III's justices exercised a superior jurisdiction. He uses the phrase "common pleas *coram rege* court" to describe the justices who met in the presence of King John.[69] By this, he indicates that it did not have the authority that Henry III's court wielded, but was simply an itinerant branch of the court of common pleas at Westminster. He even states that the term *coram rege* was used in the time of King John "in a general and untechnical sense" to refer to any royal court.[70] At the time Adams wrote, only one volume of the *curia regis* rolls for John's reign had been published. The published volumes now available show clearly that the justices themselves used the term only when referring to the court following the king; they knew the court at Westminster as *de banco* or *apud Westmonasterium*, never as *coram rege*.

If any one conclusion can be made concerning the origin of the English royal courts, it is simply that there is no single explanation. These courts were not born fully developed in the mind of some far-seeing legislator. The work of the editors of the plea rolls has made clear the complexity of the evolution of the

---

[67] Tout, *Collected Papers*, I, 192.

[68] E.g. *Note Book*, II, 292, a judgment before "the lord king at Westminster in the presence of the justiciar, the earl marshal, and other great men"; II, 564; III, 242–243, 280–283.

[69] *Council and Courts*, p. 247.   [70] *Ibid.*, pp. 228–230.

courts and has caused some old accounts to be challenged. Richardson and Sayles's account of the origin of the itinerant justices incorporates knowledge gained from the pipe rolls that was not available to Stubbs and other nineteenth-century historians. In their version of the origin of the court of common pleas, Richardson and Sayles place great reliance on the administrative records too. In spite of their polemical skill, however, they have hardly said the last word on the subject; for they try to tie the court of the bench at Westminster too closely to the exchequer, making the exchequer into an omnicompetent body exercising royal powers. They lay too much responsibility on the justiciar's shoulders and do not allow the king to bear enough. This goes against all the traditional accounts of Angevin monarchy, which has been pictured as government *per voluntatem,* government by the king's will, not the impersonal bureaucratic state that Richardson and Sayles would see. As for the court *coram rege,* its origins are neither to be found in Henry II's ordinance of 1178, as Stubbs would have, nor in Henry III's council, as G. B. Adams insists, but rather in the judges who followed King John and Henry III on their eyres.

It is certain, then, that the three tribunals of Bracton's time were the result of a long process, as the Norman and Angevin kings tried many measures to provide adequate machinery for justice. There was a large element of chance involved in the formation of the English judicial system—for example, the way in which the king's absences fostered the development of a court sitting permanently at Westminster. Far from being smooth, the system's evolution was continually interrupted, in Stephen's reign, in John's reign, and during the minority of Henry III. No one measure of Henry I created the itinerant justices, no definite legislation of Henry II created the court of common pleas, neither did a single act of Henry III create the court *coram rege.*

THE WORK OF THE COURTS

In addition to the question of the origins of the royal courts, there is another difficult question which must be answered, that of the division of tasks among the three. What distinction was there in the work of the three courts? What determined whether a suit should come *coram rege, coram justiciariis apud Westmonasterium,* or *coram justiciariis itinerantibus?* All these courts were equally *curiae regis,* and no sharp line was drawn separating their jurisdictions. All three heard similar types of pleas, both civil and criminal cases, and actions begun in one court could easily be transferred to another. Therefore, it is difficult to come to any conclusion concerning the assignment of functions to the various royal courts. An examination of the work of the courts does reveal, however, that the king and his judges recognized some distinction among the three, even though this may not have been clearly defined.

Perhaps the easiest distinction to make is that between the itinerant judicature and the two central courts. The court that the justices on eyre held was a *curia regis,* just as was the bench at Westminster or the court that followed the king; and in theory it was the equal of those two branches. For convenience, pleas were sometimes transferred from the justices *de banco* and *coram rege* to the itinerant justices. For example, in 1204 an assize of novel disseizin which came before the justices *coram rege* was postponed to a later date, "until the coming of the lord king in those parts, unless the justices should come there in the meantime." [71] Sometimes, too, the court *coram rege* performed the functions of itinerant justices, taking the assizes along the king's route. In 1236, royal letters commanded the sheriff of Lincolnshire to have all assizes of novel disseizin scheduled for the next eyre brought before the king when he traveled through Lincolnshire on his return from Newcastle upon Tyne. [72] The connection between the court of the bench and the itinerant justices was particularly close; for a general eyre, which required the services of all the king's judges in the counties, might bring a suspension of the sessions at Westminster for a term or two. If the business of the eyre was not completed during that period, the justices might transfer the cases to Westminster for conclu-

[71] *CRR,* III, 27–28, Trinity 1204; a similar case is noted in V, 268.
[72] *Close Rolls* (1234–1237), p. 277; there are similar instructions on p. 376.

sion.[73] Despite this evidence for the equality of the courts, when it came to a test, the itinerant justices were inferior to the other two branches of the king's court.[74] They received instructions to reserve all difficult questions for the king's consideration, and "Let the parties appear at Westminster" was the conclusion to many cases beyond their competence.[75] The justices kept a memoranda roll on which they recorded cases that they were unwilling to judge, either because the law was uncertain or because the litigants were persons of position.[76]

The groups of justices sent through the country from Westminster received commissions setting forth their duties, and their powers were limited by these temporary appointments.[77] When Bracton wrote his treatise in the thirteenth century, there were several types of commissions that the king could give. He wrote of the king and his itinerant justices: "He also has justices who are itinerant from county to county, sometimes to hear all pleas, sometimes for something special, for taking assizes of novel disseizin and mort d'ancestor, and gaol deliveries, and sometimes for one or two of these and not more." [78] Thus the eyres of the time of Henry III may be classed into three main groups: the general eyre, commissions to take the assizes, and commissions of gaol delivery.[79]

The highest in rank was the commission for an *iter ad omnia placita*, a general eyre. One of the prime aims of the general eyre was to safeguard all the rights and liberties of the king. It not only empowered the judges to hear all kinds of pleas, both civil and criminal, but also to make inquiries about various matters that concerned the king. For example, the justices of 1218–1219

[73] H. G. Richardson, review of *Pleas before King* in *Law Qtrly. Rev.*, LXX (1954), 570.

[74] Flower, *Introduction*, p. 53.

[75] See Henry III's instructions in 1218 to his justices in Kent (*Rot. lit. cl.*, I, 383b).

[76] The memoranda roll has survived from the Yorkshire eyre of 1218–1219 (*Rolls for Yorks*, nos. 1096–1151) and is discussed by Lady Stenton in the introduction, pp. xxvi–xxvii, xxxix.

[77] Pollock and Maitland, I, 156.   [78] Bracton, II, 301, f. 105b.

[79] For brief discussions of the nature of these commissions, see Pollock and Maitland, I, 200–201, and *Lincs Assize Roll*, pp. xxxvii–xxxviii.

were commanded to inquire about serjeanties, escheats, widows
in the king's gift, minors in the king's custody, advowsons belonging to the king, and encroachments on the king's land.[80]
Here, as in so many phases of medieval government, judicial and
administrative functions were entrusted to the same officers. The
general eyre, with its searching inquiries into all matters of
interest to the king for years past, brought dread to the inhabitants of the region visited, and it brought added revenue into the
king's exchequer through amercements both for individual criminal offenses and for local communities' faults.[81] Indeed, the first
duty of King John's justices sent on the "autumnal eyre" of 1210
was to raise money. Lady Stenton has written of that eyre,
"Entries on the London and Middlesex accounts in the present
roll [1211] do nothing to suggest that the work of the autumnal
justices was anything better than a disgraceful operation carried
out in a slovenly manner without supervision." [82] The eyre of
1210 took place under strained circumstances, however, coming
in the midst of King John's quarrel with the Church; in ordinary
times, the rendering of justice was a more important duty of the
justices. The sessions of a general eyre comprehended within
themselves all other courts. Not only did the itinerant justices
hear pleas normally coming before the county and hundred
courts of the county in which they were sitting, but any pleas
before the justices at Westminster from that county were also
adjourned for their hearing.[83]

The second form of commission authorized the justices to

[80] Powicke, *Henry III*, p. 29.

[81] W. C. Bolland, *The General Eyre* (Cambridge, 1922), p. 18: "Let me
say bluntly at once that the origin and purpose of the earlier commission out
of which the General Eyre grew, that the main purpose of the Eyre itself, was
not the administration of justice, but the gathering into the King's exchequer
as much money as possible in any way possible." At least one thirteenth-century observer held the same view: "Under the pretence of justice, they [the
itinerant justices of 1240] collected a huge sum for the use of a king who
squandered everything" (Matthew Paris, *Chronica Majora*, ed. H. R. Luard,
[Rolls Series; London, 1872–1882], IV, 51).

[82] *Pipe Roll 13 John*, 1211, p. xxv. See also Slade's study of the eyre, *Pipe
Roll 12 John*, 1210, pp. xv–xxii.

[83] Bolland, *General Eyre*, p. 32.

"take the assizes," that is to deal with only one class of litigation, the possessory actions introduced by Henry II. Sometimes they were sent to the counties with an even more specific commission, to deal solely with assizes of novel disseizin.[84] These commissions were popular with the king's subjects, for they made it possible for suitors to avoid the trouble and expense of a trip to Westminster. In chapter 18 of Magna Carta, King John promised that the possessory assizes would be taken four times a year in the counties in which they arose. Later editions of the Charter continued to contain this chapter, although they reduced the number of visitations to once a year. Notwithstanding this provision, throughout the reign of Henry III, plaintiffs, tenants, and jurors were constantly being called to Westminster from the farthest corners of the realm for possessory assizes. In the course of Henry's reign, it became customary to issue special commissions to justices to take individual assizes in the counties. Often, those commissioned were simply knights of the county; or sometimes one of the permanent justices was named and instructed to associate some knights with himself.[85]

The humblest of the commissions was assignment to the task of gaol delivery. The work must have been light; for few men were imprisoned in the thirteenth century, and those few were usually charged with homicide and were quickly hanged or pardoned.[86] In the time of Henry III, the task was most often left to three or four knights of the county. Sometimes, itinerant justices received a double commission, both for taking the assizes and for delivering the gaols. These double commissions seem to have been the rule under King John, in contrast to the practice prevailing in the reign of his son.[87] Obviously, it was unusual for

[84] Flower, *Introduction*, p. 156.

[85] The patent rolls of Henry III provide innumerable examples of appointments of knights as the justices to take a particular assize; e.g. *Pat. Rolls* (1225–1232), p. 161, where four are appointed as justices to take three assizes of novel disseizin, and four others appointed to take an assize of darrein presentment; and p. 165, where groups of four are appointed to take assizes of darrein presentment and novel disseizin.

[86] Pollock and Maitland, I, 200, and II, 645.

[87] *Lincs Assize Roll*, p. xxxviii.

questions requiring the king's attention to come before these lesser commissions. The business of the general eyre is more significant in a study of the king's relationship with his courts.

It is more difficult to distinguish between the two central courts, the court following the king and the court of the bench at Westminster. Some points about the nature of the two courts must be kept in mind. Both the justices following the king and the judges of the bench were professional royal servants, generally giving judgments without instructions from their master. The court *coram rege* was not the *commune concilium* or the *magna curia regis*. Although the judges *coram rege* formed a part of the king's train on his eyre through the country, they usually sat apart from him, and he did not often take an active part in their proceedings.[88] But he was always near, and they could easily call on him or on members of his court for advice. Both the courts were equally *curiae regis;* the two could blend into one when the king came to Westminster; and actions begun in one were easily transferred to the other. A number of times when postponements were necessary, litigants were told to appear *coram rege si fuerit in partes illas, et, si non, apud Westmonasterium.*[89]

The creators of these two courts—one stationary at Westminster and the other itinerant with the king—made no clear distinction between them. Certainly if forced to make a distinction, they would have recognized the superiority of the court that met in the king's presence. But students of the courts have sought some clearer distinction in their work. A facile explanation offered in the past, based on the later evolution of the courts, was that the court of common pleas heard civil suits and that the court following the king heard criminal cases, but no such differentiation existed in the early thirteenth century. Some students have been able to see a distinction based on modes of

---

[88] *Pleas before King,* I, p. 100; Richardson and Sayles, *Governance,* p. 189.

[89] E.g. RCR, II, 159; CRR, III, 103, 114, 119, and IV, 132. Postponements could include the itinerant justices as well. Occasionally actions were adjourned *in adventu justiciariorum, nisi dominus rex prius venerit in partes illas;* e.g. CRR, I, 27–28, and V, 268.

procedure.[90] They have pointed out that the cases heard before the bench at Westminster were chiefly the proprietary actions and possessory assizes, while the court *coram rege* had a higher jurisdiction, reviewing miscarriages of justice and unlawful procedures. Actually, the apportionment of tasks was not so logical, for the plea rolls reveal innumerable possessory assizes heard *coram rege*. Therefore, the two courts cannot be distinguished by the types of actions brought before them; they can only be distinguished by the relative importance the cases they heard had in the king's eyes.[91]

The pleas coming before the royal justices may be divided into two groups depending upon their relation to the monarch: "common pleas," that is proceedings between private individuals, and pleas that touched the king in some way. The term *communia placita* has come to be interpreted as meaning the proprietary actions and possessory assizes, but this is too narrow a definition, for appeals of felony brought by individual accusers were also common pleas.[92] That this distinction between cases was recognized by men of that day is indicated by the chapter in the Great Charter which required that common pleas be held in *aliquo loco certo*. After the reconstitution of the court *coram rege* in 1234, most pleas touching the king were heard there. The rolls of the bench after 1234 record few cases that cannot be classified as common pleas.[93]

In addition, decisions by Henry III's royal justices indicate that they made this distinction between the two courts. In 1237, Gilbert Marshal, earl of Pembroke, was vouched to warranty by an individual whose right to certain lands was being contested by the king. The earl protested that "that plea ought not to follow the lord king, since common pleas of land ought to be held in a

[90] James F. Baldwin, *The King's Council in England during the Middle Ages* (Oxford, 1913), p. 40; to some extent also C. T. Flower's view in *Introduction*, p. 25.

[91] *Court of King's Bench* I, p. xxxviii, and IV, pp. xxxi–xxxii.

[92] *Court of King's Bench* IV, pp. xxxii, xxxvi.

[93] E.g. roll 119, Hilary 22 Henry III, records one or two quo warranto proceedings, but no other pleas touching the king. Roll 120, 23 Henry III, reveals no more cases concerning the king.

certain place, and it is contrary to the charter of liberties that they follow [his court]." [94] The judges overruled his objection because this plea "specially touched the king and ought to be terminated before him." A year earlier, the earl of Chester had appealed to the article of Magna Carta governing common pleas. Four heirs of the former earl of Chester accused him of withholding their rightful inheritance. The earl raised two objections in an effort to delay the proceedings; and when they were overruled, he complained that "it did not seem to him that he ought to respond before the lord king since that plea is common, and it is manifestly against the liberties granted and against the charter of the lord king that common pleas should follow the lord king, and that any persons should be summoned before the king for common pleas and to an uncertain location." [95] His opponents protested that "because common pleas should not follow the king, it does not follow that uncommon pleas [aliqua placita singularia] should not follow the king." That is, they maintained that difficult or unusual cases should come before the court following the king. The king's justices agreed with their argument, for they postponed the plea until a later date *coram rege*. This preserved for the king his freedom to draw those cases that interested him or involved him in some indirect way into his own court, where he could watch over them more closely.

The purpose of this clause of the Charter was to restore the permanent court at Westminster and to end the expense, delays, and confusion caused by following a peripatetic court *coram rege*. Yet common pleas had come before the justices *coram rege* before the demise of the bench in 1209; and, as the cases of Gilbert Marshal and the earl of Chester illustrate, some continued to come before them during the reign of Henry III, long after Magna Carta. Litigants could bring suits in whatever royal court they chose, and there were a number of reasons why they

[94] *CRR*, 115B, m. 19d, no. 1242, Trinity 1237, pleas *coram rege*; *Note Book*, III, 233, no. 1220; discussed in Faith Thompson, *The First Century of Magna Carta* (Minneapolis, 1925), p. 44.

[95] *CRR*, 116B, m. 6, no. 1958; *Note Book*, III, 226–227, no. 1213, pleas *coram rege* 1236–1237; discussed in Thompson, *First Century*, pp. 44–45.

might prefer the court following the king. Often proceedings were transferred from one court to the other at the request of the parties; and as late as 1254 a case was removed from Westminster to the court *coram rege,* which was at Oxford at the time, *propter loci commoditatem.*[96]

It is easy to account for many of the cases coming into the court *coram rege:* requests for correction of errors of lower courts, suits involving the king's tenants-in-chief or other prominent personalities, or pleas "touching the king," where questions of royal rights, grants, or charters were raised; in short, any action where the advice of the king and his counselors might be needed. The justices at Westminster sometimes hesitated to pronounce judgment in difficult cases or to decide questions of importance to the king, and they adjourned them for hearing before the court *coram rege.* But it is less easy to explain the many common pleas which came into the king's court.

A number of scholars have tried to unravel the riddle of the court *coram rege.* G. O. Sayles writes that when the court following the king was reconstituted in 1234, it was decided that the justices at Westminster should have "exclusive jurisdiction as a court of first instance in real actions relating to the ownership or possession of land and the personal actions of debt, detinue, covenant, and account: that is to say, the pleas that touched sacred property rights and had evolved a system of procedure that precluded haste and were conveniently heard in a sedentary court." [97] Sayles has to admit, however, that this apportionment of spheres did not always hold true in practice, and he adds that "inasmuch as private parties might decide to settle disagreements in the king's bench, it was a court of common pleas as much as the common bench." [98] Perhaps the question of the jurisdiction of Henry III's court *coram rege* has been best answered by C. A. F. Meekings. He places the actions heard there in seven categories:

1. Pleas touching the king, those in which his interests as a feudal lord were involved. Cases touching on royal grants or charters made this a large category.

---

[96] CRR, 154, m. 8, cited in *Court of King's Bench* IV, p. xxxiv.
[97] *Court of King's Bench* IV, pp. xxxii–xxxiii.   [98] *Ibid.,* p. xxxiv.

2. Suits in which one of the parties had the charter-right of being impleaded only before the king.

3. Pleas transferred from one of the other courts because of some difficult or novel problem, or because of a miscarriage of justice in the lower court.

4. Pleas where the plaintiff had offered a fine to have his complaint heard *coram rege.*

5. Actions *quare contra pacem nostram, quare vi et armis,* that is, actions of trespass committed against the king's peace.

6. Suits brought by tenants-in-chief of the king, royal officers, and other prominent persons in the realm.

7. Proceedings that might be termed "state trials," either brought by or encouraged by the king against persons who had incurred his displeasure.[99]

The problem of defining the court *coram rege* can best be solved by turning to the surviving rolls themselves. An analysis of the pleas for one term of the court following King John reveals the nature of the cases that came before it, and it reveals why these cases did not come before the justices of the bench. The term chosen for examination is Easter term of 1204, the sixth year of John's reign, after his return from the war in Normandy but well before the decline of the court at Westminster had begun. Doris M. Stenton has edited the pipe roll for this same period. In editing it, she encountered numbers of fines offered to have pleas come *coram rege,* and she has compared these fines with the cases for which they were offered, found on the roll for Easter 1204.[100] A similar study must then be made of one of Henry III's *coram rege* rolls, so that the work of the two courts may be compared. The first surviving roll from the court following King Henry III is for Trinity term of his eighteenth year, the spring of 1234.[101] Since there is a roll for the court at

---

[99] C. A. F. Meekings, *List of Rolls and Writs of the Court Coram Rege Henry III* (typescript, 1957, in Literary Search Room, Public Record Office, London).

[100] *Pipe Roll 6 John* (Pipe Roll Society, N.S.; London, 1940), Michaelmas 1204, pp. xi–xx. Most of the cases are found in *CRR*, III, Easter 1204, pleas *coram rege.*

[101] *CRR*, 115B, a roll of thirty-five membranes. The first eleven membranes are from Trinity term, 18 Henry III.

Westminster surviving for the same term,[102] it is clear that this is the roll of a permanent court, not a temporary tribunal of justices from the bench sitting with the king.

The English kings never developed a hierarchical system of courts with regular procedures for appeals from lower courts to higher courts. Theoretically none of the three judicial branches of the *curia regis* ranked higher than the other. Nevertheless, in practice the court *coram rege* became the tribunal which reviewed miscarriages of justice and unlawful procedures in the county and hundred courts, in courts of private jurisdiction, and even in other royal courts (the third of Meekings' seven classes of cases).

The roll of pleas in King John's court *coram rege* for Easter term 1204 offers examples of this function—two cases in which individuals came to the king's court seeking to have the decision of a lower court reversed. Geoffrey son of Geoffrey complained that a plea of land had been brought against him in the court of the bishop of Durham by the bishop's writ, and he held that this was unjust because in the time of Henry II no freeman had been required to answer for his free tenement without a royal writ.[103] This case challenged the traditional authority of the bishop of Durham, who ruled over the county palatine of Durham as viceroy. The king's judges did not visit there, neither did his writs run there; instead, civil suits were begun by the bishop's writ and were tried in his court. The questioning of this practice gave the case enough significance for it to merit the king's attention. Eventually, the account of the proceedings in the bishop's court became so complicated that the judges' clerk was at a loss to untangle it, and he closed his account with a sad attempt at quoting a line from Horace: *Quo tenans nodo mutantem Prothea vultus.*[104] At the next term of the court, when the bishop and Geoffrey appeared for judgment, King John ordered the case postponed until he could consult his magnates.[105]

---

[102] *Ibid.*, 115A.   [103] *Ibid.*, III, 109–110.

[104] *Epistulae*, lib. i, *epistula*, I, i, 90.

[105] *CRR*, III, 131, Trinity 1204. For a fuller discussion of this case, see Chapter 5, pp. 171–172.

Also during this term a plaint was brought before the justices that was in fact an action of false judgment, although it was phrased as a private plea. William de Kivilly complained that the reeve of the hundred had wrongfully taken his cattle and horses; but the reeve replied that he had done so by order of the sheriff of Essex, as his serjeant, after a judgment. Clearly, William's complaint was against that judgment, but rather than proceed against the county court or against the sheriff, he brought an action against the serjeant who had carried out the decision.[106] Both these cases concerned complaints against proceedings in lower courts—the court of the county palatine of Durham and the county court of Essex; at other times, however, the judges in the king's presence heard charges of error against other branches of the *curia regis*—the justices on eyre and, in the reign of Henry III, even the justices at Westminster.[107]

One general rule that governed pleas coming to the court following the king was that "whatever specially touched the person of the king" should be determined before him (the first of Meekings' categories). This was the answer given by Henry III's justices to complaints against common pleas in the court *coram rege,* but the principle was not unknown to the justices of King John. The justices at Westminster and on eyre frequently postponed pleas in which royal rights, grants, or charters were at issue for hearing in the king's own court. In questions arising from royal charters, the only solution was to seek the will of the king, for neither the justices nor any private person could interpret their terms.[108] In 1203 the itinerant justices postponed a case "because in the record of that plea there is mention of a charter of the lord king which the justices do not wish to judge by themselves."[109] Similarly, the judges were hesitant to rule on questions relating to royal rights without the king. It is only to be

---

[106] *CRR,* III, 115–116, discussed in *Proc. without Writ,* p. lxxxv. No final decision is recorded in the *CRR.*

[107] See Chapter 6, pp. 190–200.

[108] Bracton, II, 109–110, f. 34, on questionable interpretations.

[109] *Lincs Assize Roll,* p. 225, no. 1265, 3 Feb. 1203. Similarly, during Henry III's minority, pleas in which royal charters were concerned were postponed until the king came of age.

expected, then, that the roll for Easter term 1204 should contain pleas touching the king. The roll records two actions brought by King John to recover churches: juries of recognition came to state whether one church was a chapel belonging to a church in the king's gift and whether the advowson of another church belonged to the king.[110] A case concerning a royal grant also came before the king's justices in that term, when the tenant replied that "he claimed nothing in that land unless by the lord king," for he had a charter of Henry II.[111]

The roll for 1204 lists a number of "common pleas," suits between private persons in which there is no indication that they concerned the king in any way. One explanation for their presence is that one of the litigants had the special privilege of being impleaded only *coram domino rege vel capitali justiciario* (Meekings' second category). The Norman and Angevin kings granted many letters and charters of protection, providing that the recipient need not plead except before the king or the justiciar. The roll for Easter term 1204 includes a number of private pleas in which one party was the head of a monastic house, and royal letters of privilege must account for their proceeding in the court *coram rege*. There can be no doubt that a letter of protection explains the presence of a plea of land brought by the abbot of Peterborough against the abbot of Crowland.[112] The suit had first come before the justices at Westminster a year earlier, but the abbot of Crowland said that he ought not to plead about any tenement belonging to his church because of the king's letters patent, granting him the privilege of pleading before the king only.[113] Although these letters granting the right to plead in the king's court explain the presence of some private suits, a number

[110] *CRR*, III, 113, church of St. Helen, Garstang, Lancs.; p. 118, church of Binstead, Hants.

[111] *Ibid.*, p. 111. Elias de la Falaise sought land from Richard de Barentin.

[112] *Ibid.*, p. 116. Other pleas involving religious houses include: p. 104, abbot of Woburn; p. 106, the Templars; pp. 111–112, prior of Nocton; p. 112, prior of Lewes against abbot of Hyde; also p. 112, prior of Kenilworth and abbot of York; p. 119, prior of St. Oswald's; and p. 120, abbot of Hyde.

[113] *Ibid.*, II, 245, Easter 1203; discussed in Flower, *Introduction*, p. 357. The letter is found in *Rot. lit. pat.*, p. 8b.

of others on the roll for Easter term 1204 must be accounted for.

Only the fact that the litigants were prominent persons in the kingdom accounts for several of the pleas on the *coram rege* roll of Easter 1204 (Meekings' sixth group of cases). For example, several suits were brought by the archbishop of Canterbury concerning the raising of river walls on the Ouse.[114] Another prominent ecclesiastic, the bishop of Chester, appeared as the defendant in a plea of advowson.[115] Still another plea coming before the king in 1204 involved two important barons in northern England, Robert de Ros and William de Albini, along with their relative, Hilary Trussebut, in an attempt to recover the manor of Market Weighton, Yorkshire.[116] Throughout the reign of King John, pleas involving prominent figures were postponed in order to be heard *coram rege*.

There was another group of persons within the kingdom in whom the king took great interest, although they were not socially or politically prominent. The Jews, a community of economic importance to the king, enjoyed special royal protection. Indeed, they and all their possessions belonged to the king, and they were allowed to remain in England only because their moneylending proved profitable to him.[117] A department of the exchequer headed by the justices of the Jews was established to watch over their affairs; and this exchequer of the Jews, like the great exchequer, handled both judicial and financial matters. The justices of the Jews had only low rank in the official hierarchy, and even though the Easter 1204 roll contains no pleas relating to Jews, several actions involving them were transferred to the court held *coram rege*.[118]

A number of the private pleas heard in the court *coram rege* in

[114] *CRR*, III, 104–105, 112–113; discussed in Flower, *Introduction*, p. 328.

[115] *CRR*, III, 112.

[116] *Ibid.*, p. 113. Hilary Trussebut was the sister-in-law of William de Albini and the aunt of Robert de Ros (Holt, *Northerners*, pp. 63–64).

[117] Pollock and Maitland, I, 468. For a recent study of the situation of the Jews in medieval England, see H. G. Richardson, *English Jewry under the Angevin Kings* (London, 1960).

[118] Examples are given in Richardson, *English Jewry*, pp. 150–151, and Flower, *Introduction*, pp. 48–51.

Easter term 1204 concerned King John's servants, whether great officers of state or lesser officials. One case on the roll marked the settlement of a debt between the seneschal of the earl of Warwick and Henry de Pont Audemar, by which the seneschal agreed to pay Henry forty pounds.[119] The case may have come before the justices following the king simply because it was more convenient, since Henry de Pont Audemar was a royal judge.[120] The king's interest in the case explains the fact that a day was given *coram rege* to Richard de Canville and Nicholas de Verdun for drawing up their cirograph, marking the compromise of a plea of dower between them.[121] King John had a double reason for interest in this case: Richard was the son of one of his trusted agents, Gerard de Canville, and the plea concerned the dower of Richard's wife, for whom Gerard had offered the king 1,000 marks.[122] For these reasons, it is not surprising that the king wished to take part in the proceedings. Important officers of the king were litigants in several other proceedings held *coram rege* in Easter term 1204. Among them were William Briwerre, a professional royal servant who served as a baron of the exchequer, sheriff of several counties, and guardian of a number of minors in royal custody, and John Marshal, nephew of the earl marshal and one of King John's trusted captains.[123]

Yet many of the litigants in pleas heard by the justices *coram rege* were neither great barons nor royal officers; the presence of their suits in this court can only be the result of their offering fines to have them heard there (Meekings' fourth group of cases). Clearly, John had embarked on a new policy of encouraging litigants to bring their actions directly into the royal courts, regardless of the threat this posed to the feudal courts of his

---

[119] *CRR*, III, 103.   [120] Foss, *Judges*, pp. 525–526.

[121] *CRR*, III, 104–117; the origin of the case can be found in *CRR*, I, 329, Hilary 1200.

[122] *Pipe Roll 2 John*, ed. Doris M. Stenton (Pipe Roll Society, N.S.; London, 1934), Michaelmas 1200, p. 87.

[123] Case of William Briwerre, *CRR*, III, 106, 114; for his career, see Painter, *King John*, pp. 10, 71–80. Case of John Marshal, *CRR*, III, 107; see also Painter, *King John*, pp. 241, 304.

barons.[124] It was only under King John that the writs praecipe and pone came into such wide use that they became writs *de cursu*. In addition, he encouraged litigants to have their suits transferred from the other branches of the *curia regis* to the court that accompanied him. King John's reasons for this are difficult to know. Certainly, financial motives played some part in the policy, for the suitors had to offer fines for the privilege of bringing a case into the court *coram rege;* but a search for added income cannot be the whole explanation, and possibly the answer is John's genuine interest in hearing pleas. Lady Stenton's study of the fines recorded on the pipe roll for John's sixth year has led her to this view. Her finding is that financial gain could not have been the king's chief consideration, for most litigants offered only one mark or even a half-mark. She summarizes her findings in this way:

That the reputation of the court *coram rege* stood high in 1204 is apparent from the large number of new fines recorded in the fine roll and the pipe roll for the privilege of having a suit heard before the King himself. The fines taken were not large and those who offered them were not always in a hurry to pay. The King seems to have been less interested in the trickle of new income which might come to the Exchequer than in the cases themselves. Indeed, many cases came into his court for which there is no evidence that any special payment was made. The lists of points, or the single points, which the judges, both *coram rege* and of the bench, refer to the King merely indicate the inclusive character of the king's interest and the close attention which he wished to give to the work of his courts.[125]

It must be noted, however, that some of the fines offered were large: four were of forty shillings, one of five marks, three of ten marks, one of twenty marks, one of £100, and one of a palfrey.[126] Unfortunately, there is a darker side to John's supervision of his

---

[124] Lady Stenton in the introduction to *Pipe Roll 6 John,* p. xxx.
[125] "King John and the Courts," pp. 109–110.
[126] *Pipe Roll 6 John,* pp. xix–xx.

courts, which Lady Stenton fails to consider. One reason for his close watch over the courts must have been the fear and suspicion that made him seek to concentrate all power in his hands.

Lady Stenton checked the fines against the pleas recorded in the *curia regis* rolls in an attempt to discover the reasons that led suitors to desire a royal audience. Not every offering for a favor recorded on the pipe roll has a corresponding entry on the plea roll, but she did succeed in finding some of the cases for which fines were offered. Individuals who had failed to receive justice in one of the inferior courts of the kingdom were willing to pay in order to have their complaints heard in the court *coram rege*, the tribunal for the review of miscarriages of justice. This explains why Geoffrey son of Geoffrey paid twenty marks to have a grand assize taken *coram rege*. He had earlier complained to the king that the plea did not lie in the bishop of Durham's court, and that it had proceeded improperly there.[127]

The court following the king naturally was less bound by customary procedures and more free to innovate in providing remedies for complaints. Consequently, a claimant might approach the king in order to gain a quick remedy in a plea of land, if one of the possessory assizes did not fill his need and he wished to avoid one of the slower proprietary actions. Certainly this explains the large fine of £100 offered by Alexander de Caldbeck to obtain a hearing before the king.[128] He offered the fine that a jury might come *coram rege* to recognize that his father had given him nine carucates of land in Caldbeck and that Reginald de Lucy had disseized him of those nine carucates before he came of age. The plea roll for Easter term 1204 reveals, however, that Alexander was not claiming the land against Reginald, who had been dead since 1199, but against his heirs, Robert de Courtenay and his wife Alice.[129] His fine to have the jury come before the king probably marked an attempt to shorten the long

---

[127] *Ibid.*, Michaelmas 1204, pp. 44–45; see above, p. 38, and Chapter 5, pp. 171–172.

[128] *Pipe Roll 6 John*, Michaelmas 1204, p. 143.

[129] *CRR*, III, 117; discussed in the introduction to *Pipe Roll 6 John*, pp. xx–xxi.

process of litigation that otherwise lay ahead in his effort to recover his inheritance.[130]

In other cases, it is less easy to learn why a litigant desired to have his plea heard by the justices following the king. For example, Agnes (or Annota) daughter of William fitz William offered a palfrey to have a writ praecipe to bring her plea against William Bardolf and his wife Elizabeth (or Isabel) before the king.[131] Elizabeth, Agnes, and a third sister, Matilda, were coheiresses of their father's honor of Hepple in Northamptonshire.[132] But Agnes and Matilda had to sue Elizabeth and her husband by writ *de rationabile parte* in order to gain their rightful shares; and when the case came before the king in Easter term 1204, Elizabeth failed to appear and offered the essoin of bed-sickness, *de malo lecti*.[133] There is nothing in the record of the case to indicate any unusual circumstances to necessitate a hearing in the court following the king. Perhaps Agnes sought a hearing there because her brother-in-law William Bardolf had some unfair advantage over her in the lower court; for another Bardolf, Hugh, was a prominent royal officer, a sheriff, and a justice at Westminster and on eyre.[134] Or perhaps Agnes had some other reason for wishing to proceed in the king's court; it is impossible to tell.

Other pleas of land that appear on the roll of pleas *coram rege* for the Easter term of 1204 came there through fines offered.[135]

[130] *Pipe Roll 6 John*, pp. xx–xxi. But his attempt failed; see Chapter 2, pp. 61–62, for the conclusion to this case.

[131] *Pipe Roll 6 John*, Michaelmas 1204, p. 44.

[132] Sanders, *Baronies*, p. 122. Elizabeth married William Bardolf before 1200; Agnes did not marry until sometime between 1205 and 1210.

[133] *CRR*, III, 105–108. A year later she and her husband appeared and sought a view of the land in question.

[134] Foss, *Judges*, pp. 54–55.

[135] *Pipe Roll 6 John*, Michaelmas 1204, p. 128. Ivo of Eastrop paid a half-mark to have a praecipe bringing a suit against Herbert of Eastrop before the king. The origin of the plea is in *CRR*, III, 94, Hilary 1204, when Herbert failed to appear. The second entry is for Easter term, p. 106, and he still did not appear. Finally, the constable of Winchester was instructed to have him present, and the sheriff was summoned to answer for his failure to produce him (*CRR*, III, 164). Warin fitz Warin paid ten marks to have a plea of land against Godfrey de Crammaville heard *coram rege* (*Pipe Roll 6*

Again the records of the proceedings fail to reveal any unusual circumstances that would account for the suitors' desire to have their cases come there. One of these pleas was an assize of mort d'ancestor for which William de Brocton and his wife paid one mark to have before the king.[136] The assize is not found in the *curia regis* rolls; in Easter term 1204, however, a date was appointed to William de Brocton, as his wife's attorney, for the making of a final concord.[137] The terms of the final concord indicate that this was not a serious suit, but a fictitious one to secure legal recognition of a transfer of lands.[138]

The possessory assizes were summary actions to settle simple questions; yet the assize of mort d'ancestor was less speedy and simple than the assize of novel disseizin, for it might raise complex questions of inheritance. Unfortunately, the record does not reveal whether there were any complications in the case that William and his wife wished to have *coram rege*. The assize of novel disseizin was the swiftest of all the possessory actions, simply answering the question of whether the defendant had recently disseized the plaintiff of his land. There was no question of the plaintiff's right to the land, merely of his possession.[139] Unless some unusual circumstances surrounded the case, it was unlikely that a plaintiff would have any reason to bring an assize of novel disseizin before the court *coram rege*.[140] One assize of novel disseizin was taken by the justices following the king in Easter term 1204. The record of the case reveals no great diffi-

---

John, Michaelmas 1204, p. 32; CRR, III, 117). The plea was postponed until the octave of Trinity, but Godfrey did not appear then (CRR, III, 125), and the case was postponed once more, until the morrow of the Assumption. The last entry referring to this case is incomplete because a corner of the roll was torn off (CRR, III, 151).

136 *Pipe Roll 6 John*, Michaelmas 1204, p. 14; discussed on p. xxi.

137 CRR, III, 119–120, William de Brocton, attorney for his wife Rose, against Richard de Sifrewast.

138 *Calendar of Feet of Fines, 7 Richard I to 44 Henry III*, ed. M. W. Hughes (Records Branch of the Buckinghamshire Archeological Society, Vol. IV for 1940), p. 28, no. 2, 17 Feb. 1205. William and Rose gave up their claim to a third of Richard's land at Chesterham in return for 100 shillings' worth of land, services, and 20 marks in cash.

139 Pollock and Maitland, II, 48–49.   140 *Pipe Roll 6 John*, p. xxi.

culty; indeed, the action proceeded quite speedily, for the defendant failed to appear, and the assize was taken by default.[141] The explanation must lie in the fact that the defendant was William de Ferrers, earl of Derby; the plaintiff may have believed that he could gain a fair hearing against such a powerful baron only in the court *coram rege*. A sign of his fears is his promise to pay the king twenty marks for having his land in peace until the action could be terminated in the *curia regis*.[142] The plea rolls contain many other cases which came before the court *coram rege* as the result of fines and which do not seem to have been at all unusual. It is possible that litigants in the counties offered small sums to bring their pleas before the court following the king when he passed through their county on his eyre in order to avoid the expense of a suit at Westminster.[143]

This survey of cases heard *coram rege* during Easter term 1204, then, shows that the court's work included both proceedings touching the king and common pleas. In general, the list that Meekings worked out for Henry III's court *coram rege* applies for John's court too. Cases from five of his seven classes are found. The only two missing are "state trials" and actions of trespass committed against the king's peace.

G. B. Adams attempted to determine the nature of cases coming before Henry III's court *coram rege* by examining the pleas in *Bracton's Note Book* for 1234–1235, but the *Note Book* only contains excerpts from the plea rolls. Adams found twenty-seven pleas excerpted there. Of this number, seventeen touched the king in some way; the other ten revealed no reason why they should have been before the king.[144] Since Adams was unable to

---

[141] *CRR*, III, 117.   [142] *Pipe Roll 6 John*, Michaelmas 1204, p. 170.

[143] *Ibid.*, introduction, p. xxi.

[144] *Council and Courts*, pp. 232–233, n. 41. The pleas examined are in *Note Book*, III, 123–152, nos. 1106–1132. The ten that showed no reason for being heard *coram rege* are: no. 1107, plea of admeasurement of dower brought by John Belet against Margery daughter of Michael de Wahulla; no. 1115, action *recordari facias* of plea in the hundred court of the bishop of Salisbury between Walkelin of Stoke, the complainant, and William of Guildhall; no. 1116, postponement of a plea of land brought by Beatrice wife of Geoffrey of Dickford against William de Travers (the action was postponed *quando justiciarii residebunt in banco vel in adventu justiciariorum cum in*

examine the unpublished rolls surviving from Henry's reign, he could not reach definite conclusions about Henry's court *coram rege*.

The greatest contrast that the roll for Trinity term 18 Henry III offers with the roll of Easter term 6 John is the presence of "state trials," proceedings brought by the king against great men who had lost his favor (Meekings' seventh class of cases). Henry III used his court *coram rege* as an instrument for the pursuit of Peter des Rivaux, Stephen Segrave, and Robert Passelewe. These royal servants had aroused his anger for their part in the death of Richard the earl marshal in the spring of 1234. The king commanded that Peter come before his court to answer charges; a number of entries relate to his many summons and failures to appear.[145] This roll also contains Stephen Segrave's summons to come and answer the king "concerning damages done to him by Stephen's counsel."[146] Then several persons brought actions against Peter, Stephen, and Robert Passelewe, probably as part of the king's program for their pursuit.[147]

There are other contrasts with the roll of King John; the large number of complaints lodged against royal officers, including three sheriffs, is striking. The sheriff of Surrey had to answer charges that he had imprisoned a man and demanded a fine of four marks without cause; the sheriff of Wiltshire was charged with taking and keeping the abbess of Romsey's livestock in

---

partes etc.); no. 1117, assize of novel disseizin brought by William Renard against John le Fay; no. 1120, proprietary action to regain a manor in Norfolk brought by Adam son of Harvey and Juliana his wife against Geoffrey son of John; no. 1125, attempt by William de Ferrers to gain custody of a minor from Elias of Esseville; no. 1126, assize of darrein presentment brought by the prior of Wallingford against Roger de Quency; no. 1128, assize of mort d'ancestor brought by Walter son of Robert against Henry Balliol and his wife Lora; no. 1129, complaint of Gregory de la Dun that Gilbert Basset did not honor an agreement concerning the keeping of hogs in his wood; and no. 1131, attempt by Ralph Jowas to obtain land from William Scissor.

[145] *CRR*, 115B, m. 1d, no. 1031; m. 7, no. 1064; m. 9d, no. 1091. For a fuller discussion of Peter's trial, see Chapter 7, pp. 207–209.

[146] *CRR*, 115B, m. 7d, no. 1059.

[147] *Ibid.*, m. 3, nos. 1038 and 1042, complaints against Peter des Rivaux; m. 3d, no. 1043, m. 6d, no. 1058, complaints against Robert Passelewe; m. 11, no. 1102, plea of land brought by the king against Stephen Segrave.

violation of a judgment of the justices at Westminster; and the sheriff of Berkshire was charged with disseizing a tenant and imprisoning his men.[148] Several men had complaints against Ralph de Willington, constable of Devizes Castle. One charged that during the king's troubles in the winter of 1233–1234, the constable had demanded horses of him, threatening imprisonment if he did not provide them.[149] A London fishmonger came to the court to complain that one of the king's buyers, Master William, had seized his boat for use *ad opus domini regis*. Unfortunately, the boat had been loaded with codfish, which had spoiled, causing the boat-owner great loss. Master William recognized the truth of the complaint, and the fishmonger was given compensation.[150] There were other charges against royal servants: a complaint by the men of a manor in the king's hand that one of the forest bailiffs had taken land from them, and a complaint that a royal reeve had closed a village market.[151]

One complaint was lodged by the king himself. William fitz Warin was summoned to explain why he had freed Hamo de Cursun, who had been imprisoned at the king's command. According to the testimony given, Hamo had been arrested at the request of the bishop of Hereford because he was a contumacious excommunicate, having remained outside the Church for more than forty days without seeking reconciliation.[152] But the letters close commanding his arrest give another reason. According to them, he was an attorney before the royal court who had sought writs wrongly in the names of his clients rather than in his own name.[153] To add to the confusion, William fitz Warin maintained that he had never imprisoned Hamo, but that he had

---

[148] *Ibid.*, m. 3, no. 1041, complaint of Roger de Bidun against the sheriff of Surrey; *ibid.*, m. 7, no. 1070 (also *Note Book* III, no. 1110), charge against the sheriff of Wiltshire; CRR, m. 10d, no. 1097, action against the sheriff of Berkshire.

[149] *Ibid.*, m. 3, no. 1037, complaint of William de Putot. Three other complaints follow.

[150] *Ibid.*, m. 6, no. 1048, complaint of Robert Joscelin.

[151] Ritherswich, formerly Peter des Rivaux's (*ibid.*, m. 11, no. 1099); and Basingstoke, Hants (*ibid.*, m. 11, no. 1100).

[152] *Ibid.*, m. 7d, no. 1060.

[153] *Close Rolls* (1231–1234), pp. 229–230, 15 June 1233.

received a writ ordering his release. The conflict between the king's charges and William's response seems to have left the judges puzzled. They postponed the case, declaring that it was *in voluntate domini regis* whether or not an inquest should be held to determine the truth of the matter.

Complaints against acts of the king himself brought by his subjects present another striking contrast with the cases on King John's *coram rege* roll. An important case is the suit by the Yorkshire baron Eustace de Stuteville for recovery of the manor of Cottingham.[154] He claimed before Henry III and his court that the manor had been taken from him *per voluntatem domini regis*. The king admitted that he had disseized Eustace *sine summonitione et sine judicio*, and the court returned possession of the manor to him. Also in Trinity term 1234, William de Huntercomb complained that he had been disseized by the king's will.[155] He testified that he held custody of the third part of a manor by charter from Henry III, but that Henry had disseized him by his will and without any compensation, even though the charter provided for an exchange at value in case the manor should be returned to its inheritors.[156] No judgment is recorded on the plea roll, but apparently the king recognized the justice of the complaint, for he did give William compensation.

Other pleas touching the king are listed on this first *coram rege* roll of Henry III, a larger number out of the total than on the Easter term roll of 6 John. A number of them are proceedings brought by the king, attempts by him to reclaim rights in land or other property. Seven of the pleas brought by the king concern manors or smaller landholdings, two of them concern forests, and one is a suit for custody of an heiress.[157] Another plea

---

[154] *CRR*, 115B, m. 1, no. 1026; also *Note Book*, III, no. 1106. See Chapter 8, pp. 250–251, for a fuller discussion.

[155] *CRR*, m. 3d, no. 1047.

[156] *Cal. Chtr. Rolls* (1226–1257), p. 139; *Cal. Pat. Rolls* (1232–1247), p. 87, Dec. 1234, a letter granting William an income of £20 a year until he should have lands with the same yearly income.

[157] *CRR*, m. 1, no. 1027; m. 7, no. 1065, and m. 9d, no. 1083, land in the king's manor of Havering, Ess.; m. 30, no. 1044, and m. 9d, no. 1085, manor of Raleigh; m. 6d, no. 1056, and m. 9, no. 1076, manor of Wattley, Notts; m.

marked a contest over jurisdiction. A man was accused of horse-theft in the court of the earl of Gloucester, but since the horse had been found in the king's forest, there was some question over whether trial should be before the earl's court or the king's court.[158] The king also brought an action of trespass against the prior of St. Swithins for building sheepfolds on royal property.[159]

Not all pleas touching the king were brought by him. Just as on the Easter term roll for 1204, a number of cases on the Trinity term roll for 1234 are common pleas. These private pleas could raise questions about royal grants and charters that needed the king's attention. One such question arose in the course of the complaint that Alexander Bacon brought against William de Ireby.[160] Alexander charged that William was withholding from him the custody of land and heirs that he had by a fine made with the king.[161] Since William de Ireby had been granted custody by Henry III of the same land and heirs,[162] this case was actually a proceeding against the king. Apparently Alexander had been disseized by the king, even though he did not state this in his account, for the writ restoring him to custody described the land and wardship as that "which he had before the lord king disseized him at the time of the conflict between the king and the bishop of Carlisle." [163] It is clear why a case such as this questioning a royal grant should have come before the court *coram rege*. Another conflict over custody of lands and of an heir indirectly involved the king. In this case, Henry III had granted custody in return for a fine, but a relative of the deceased tenant appeared in court to claim the custody and wardship.[164]

Many of the common pleas, however, do not seem to touch the

10, no. 1090, land at White Roding, Ess.; m. 11, nos. 1101, 1102, 1103, essoins, land not identified; m. 7, no. 1067, and m. 10, no. 1086, wood of Hamwood, Hants; m. 9, no. 1075, forest of Whitleywood, Northants.; m. 7d, no. 1061, custody of the daughter of Reginald Bassett.

[158] *CRR*, 115B, m. 6, no. 1050.   [159] *Ibid.*, m. 11, no. 1104.

[160] *Ibid.*, m. 3, no. 1040.   [161] Fine of £10 (*Exc. e rot. fin.*, I, 222).

[162] *Ibid.*, p. 244; *Close Rolls* (1231–1234), p. 235.

[163] *Close Rolls* (1231–1234), p. 470, 8 July 1234.

[164] *CRR*, m. 9, no. 1080, and m. 11, no. 1105, Walter de Muchegros vs. Bartholomew Peche for land and heir of Miles de Muchegros; see also *Cal. Pat. Rolls* (1232–1247), p. 230.

king in any significant way. Over a dozen of these entries record
only such routine matters as excuses for nonappearance or appointments of attorneys, so that it is impossible to learn why the
cases should have come before the king's court.[165] Other entries
supply more information, and their presence on the roll can be
explained in the same ways as were the common pleas in King
John's court *coram rege.* Three cases questioned the work of
other courts. One of them was a private plea of land, but it
touched on an earlier judgment given in an Essex hundred
court.[166] The second of the three is quite unusual. One of the
justices for gaol deliveries in Lincolnshire came into the court to
state his disagreement with his colleagues in their trial of nine-
teen prisoners accused of murder.[167] Possibly problems caused by
the abolition of the ordeal in 1216 that were still unsolved
account for the justice's dissatisfaction. The third case records a
fine of twenty shillings offered for a jury of attaint against a jury
of novel disseizin.[168]

The names of the litigants in several private pleas supply clues
which explain their presence in the court following the king.
Monastic houses still had the privilege by charter-right of having
their pleas heard before the king (Meekings' second category),
and cases touching abbots and priors came before Henry's reconstituted court *coram rege.* This fact can explain the presence of
cases concerning the prior of Pontefract and the abbot of
Kirkstead.[169] The abbot's suit was against the bishop of Carlisle,
further reason for having it come *coram rege,* and it was settled
by a compromise made in the king's presence; but the prior's

---

[165] *CRR,* 115B, m. 1, no. 1029, one who had essoined himself *de malo lecti*
seeking license to arise; m. 6, nos. 1051, 1052, m. 9d, no. 1081, and m. 10, no.
1087, essoins; m. 1, no. 1030, m. 3d, no. 1046, and m. 9, no. 1078, appointments of attorneys; m. 1, no. 1028, m. 3d, no. 1045, and m. 9, no. 1077,
replevins of land; m. 10, nos. 1092, 1093, 1095, postponements.

[166] *Ibid.,* m. 7, no. 1068, and m. 10d, no. 1098, Philip fitz Lawrence vs.
Adam of Lincoln.

[167] *Ibid.,* m. 10, no. 1089, John of Braitoft.

[168] *Ibid.,* m. 7d, no. 1062.

[169] *Ibid.,* m. 9, no. 1073, prior of Pontefract vs. Scotus, a merchant of
Senesi(?), and no. 1074, abbot of Kirkstead vs. bishop of Carlisle.

action concerned a foreign merchant, and it was postponed for hearing before the bench.

Other pleas were heard before the king because his tenants-in-chief or other great men of the realm were parties to them (the third of Meekings' categories). The first entry on the roll concerns a tenant-in-chief of the crown. It is not a description of a lawsuit at all, but notes that Henry III took the homage of Geoffrey Sturmy for lands granted to him.[170] A second entry concerning a tenant-in-chief was the suit among the three sisters of Robert de Albini over the division of his barony following his death in 1233.[171] Division of an inheritance among coheiresses was always difficult, and naturally the division of a barony would be of interest to the king. A third case centered on the custody of the lands and heir of a deceased tenant-in-chief of the king, John le Archer.[172] The parties to another suit were two extremely important figures in the kingdom; a plea of dower was brought by Eleanor, the king's sister and the widow of William Marshal junior, against her brother-in-law Geoffrey Marshal.[173] Their quarrel was ended by a final concord made *coram domino rege et suo consilio* in September 1234 at Marlborough.[174]

Towns possessing royal charters might be considered corporate tenants of the king, and royal boroughs brought their complaints to Henry III's court *coram rege*. A number of the entries on the roll for Trinity term 1234 concern merchants and municipalities. The men of Maidstone, a town of the archbishop of Canterbury, complained that the men of Rochester, a royal borough, were barring their boats on the Thames from passing Rochester bridge.[175] A market of the abbot of Keynesham was ordered closed because it competed with the market of the king's bur-

---

[170] *Ibid.*, m. 1, no. 1025; *Exc. e rot. fin.*, I, 258, records Geoffrey's payment of 100 shillings' relief.

[171] CRR, 115B, m. 9, no. 1082; Sanders, *Baronies*, p. 26.

[172] CRR, 115B, m. 10, no. 1096. This might also be classed as a plea touching the king, since he was seeking to transfer the custody from John's widow to another.

[173] *Ibid.*, m. 10, no. 1088.   [174] *Ibid.*, 115B, m. 115, no. 1154.

[175] *Ibid.*, m. 9d, no. 1079.

gesses at Bristol.[176] And a suit between two merchants of Florence, Bonachus and Bonapart, was heard.[177] There are also lists on the roll marked *loquendum* that include townsmen: the citizens of Winchester, merchants of Winchelsea, the men of the Cinq Ports, and merchants from Flanders and Germany.[178]

Other common pleas offer no easy clue to suggest the reason for their coming *coram rege*. Three are appeals for breaking the king's peace, one concerns courts of private jurisdiction, and three are pleas of land.[179] The king could command that any case he pleased should come *coram rege*, whether it concerned him directly or not. One of the parties to a suit might pay a fine to the king for such a command, a frequent practice in the time of John and one that continued under his son Henry III. For example, the roll for Trinity term 1234 records an oblation of three marks by Thomas de Drayton to have his inquiry *coram rege*.[180] A writ on the close roll for 1234 supplies the explanation for Thomas' wish to have a hearing before the king. He had been accused by a woman of murdering her husband, but he pled the exception that she brought the appeal maliciously, *de odio et atia*.[181] It is not surprising that he wanted this jury to give its verdict *coram rege*, since his life was in danger if he could not quash the appeal. Other oblations to have juries come before the justices *coram rege* are recorded on the fine rolls and pipe rolls of Henry III's reign.[182]

There are no startling differences, then, in the work of Henry

---

[176] *Ibid.*, m. 10, no. 1084.   [177] *Ibid.*, m. 7, no. 1066.

[178] *Ibid.*, m. 1, nos. 1033, 1036, and 1039.

[179] *Ibid.*, m. 6, no. 1049, appeal of burglary; m. 6d, no. 1053, clerk appealed of murder, and no. 1055, appeal of murder; m. 6d, no. 1054, plea of admeasurement of dower, and no. 1057, jurisdiction; m. 7, nos. 1069 and 1071, plea of land; m. 5d, no. 1072, final concord ending a plea of land.

[180] *Ibid.*, m. 10, no. 1094.

[181] *Close Rolls* (1231–1234), p. 522, 24 Sept. 1234. The jury declared that the widow's appeal was false.

[182] *Exc. e rot. fin.*, I, 310, for 1236, cited in *Court of King's Bench* IV, p. xxx, n. 4. *Pipe Roll 26 Henry III*, 1240–1241, records some fines to have pleas *coram rege*, e.g. pp. 102 and 335. Also, in *Note Book*, Vol. III, no. 1189, pleas *coram rege*, 1236–1237, a palfrey was offered to have a judgment before the bench removed to the king and council.

III's court *coram rege* and his father's. Lady Stenton has shown that the functions of King John's court *coram rege* were not yet firmly fixed, and Sayles has reached a similar conclusion about the court as it was reconstituted by Henry III. Meekings' list shows the variety of types of actions that still could come before the court *coram rege* under Henry III. In spite of a twenty years' break during Henry's early years, there is continuity in judicial organization. Both kings sent their justices on eyre throughout the kingdom periodically, and both seem to have regarded the courts of the itinerant justices as inferior in jurisdiction to their central courts. Both John and his son maintained two central courts, the bench sitting at Westminster and the court following the king about the country. Neither monarch seems to have envisaged the two courts as tribunals with sharply distinguished jurisdictions; and the king's interest, convenience, or financial gain were the major factors in determining where pleas were to be heard.

Yet there was coming to be a clearer distinction in the jurisdictions of Henry's court *coram rege* and his court at Westminster than in the two courts in John's time. While neither court *coram rege* concerned itself exclusively with pleas touching the king, Henry's court did devote a larger share of its work to royal matters. John's court was sometimes simply an itinerant alternative to the bench at Westminster. Fewer vital questions of royal rights, prosecution of royal servants, and challenges to royal acts came before King John's court *coram rege*.

2

The King and Procedural
Questions before His Courts

Dominus rex mandavit, per preceptum domini regis, and similar phrases occur frequently in the plea rolls of John and Henry III. The justices of the royal courts received countless instructions from their master concerning the conduct of pleas before them. Indeed, the writs that originated actions in the common law courts were royal commands to judges, sheriffs, or feudal lords to see that the purchaser received justice. Such commands quickly became writs *de cursu,* copied from a formulary and sold for a fee by chancery clerks without the necessity of a direct approach to the king. Similar to these original writs issued by the chancery were the judicial writs issued by the royal judges. Furthermore, many members of the king's household accompanying him on his travels could issue executive writs in his name. Yet the phrase "by the king's command" was not always simply a matter of form. The English kings of the twelfth and thirteenth centuries were not yet passive symbols of the nation; they were active participants in the day-to-day administration of their kingdom, and many writs doubtless record commands direct from their lips.[1] Other writs may have been drafted by royal servants and submitted to the king for his approval, but the phrases of attestation—*per Regem, teste Rege,* or *teste me ipso*—mean that

[1] V. H. Galbraith, *Studies in the Public Records* (London, 1948), pp. 124–125.

these commands had the king's personal approval even though he had taken no part in shaping them.[2]

DENIAL OF JUSTICE AT THE KING'S COMMAND

The plea rolls of the royal courts reveal numbers of cases postponed indefinitely *per preceptum domini regis;* such postponements effectively closed the courts to the persons who sought justice. These commands illustrate a certain ambivalence in the attitudes of the Angevin kings toward their courts of justice. The kings took seriously their duty to dispense justice to their subjects, expanding the scope of the royal courts; yet at the same time they regarded the courts as instruments to be used to further their own ends, particularly as a source of revenue. J. E. A. Jolliffe had in mind this attitude when he wrote, "Justice has come to be the King's trade in the hands of the great royal lawyer. What he makes, cannot he give and sell and, in the last recourse, for reasons of passion or policy withhold? If it is given by the King as *regale beneficium* to the people, may it not also be a weapon for the Crown?"[3] Since King John viewed justice in this way, it is not surprising that a number of his instructions to the royal justices order the dismissal of pleas. But in addition to direct denial of justice, his arbitrary action was indirectly responsible for a number of other postponements. Cancellations of proceedings were sometimes necessary because the king had seized the land of one of the parties to the action or, in pleas of land, because he had already determined seizin. Since the judicial clauses of Magna Carta called attention to the king's denial of justice, Henry III was less likely to open and close his courts to his subjects arbitrarily. A survey of cases reveals fewer denials of justice at his command.

[2] J. E. A. Jolliffe, *Angevin Kingship* (London, 1955), p. 150. For a thoughtful consideration of the problem of determining the extent to which royal letters represent the king's own views, see J. C. Holt, *King John* (Historical Association Pamphlet; London, 1963), pp. 8–10.

[3] *Angevin Kingship*, p. 96.

Occasionally the king knew of circumstances that would prevent an action from proceeding, and he gave this information to the justices with orders for its dismissal. Once, when King John was in court hearing pleas, he explained why a case should not be heard. Isabel de Peissi had brought an assize of novel disseizin against William de Ferrers, earl of Derby, concerning a portion of the honour of Peverel; but the king commanded that the plea be postponed indefinitely.[4] He testified that she had no right to the land except through her husband, who had held it temporarily while it was in the possession of King Henry II. He added that he had recognized the earl as heir to the honour of Peverel and had granted him the land in question as part of his inheritance. This intervention by John saved the earl of Derby the inconvenience of a lawsuit, and it is an example of John's effort early in his reign to gain the confidence of the great barons. Another time, one party to an action had died, and the king informed the justices that his widow had come to him and told him that she did not wish to proceed with the case.[5] The young Henry III ordered cases postponed indefinitely because one of the individuals involved was excommunicate and because a warrantor had been stricken with paralysis and could not speak.[6]

Cases coming into the royal courts could have political consequences. They might even affect the English king's relations with foreign princes, particularly his tangled relations with the king of France. King John might have preferred that pleas with such significant political implications not be heard. One of his commands from overseas in 1199 illustrates this. It is a writ to the justices at Westminster forbidding them to hear suits against William de Vesci or Warin de Vesci "until it shall be clear to the lord king how the king of the Scots shall bear himself toward

---

[4] *RCR*, II, 178, Easter 1200; also in *Pleas before King*, I, 314–315, no. 3188, discussed in introduction, p. 85.

[5] *CRR*, I, 375, Hilary 1201, pleas *coram rege*. Similarly, the king ordered a case postponed indefinitely because heirs in his wardship were called to warrant (*ibid.*, V, 231, Trinity 1208). The case was resumed two years later when they had come of age (*ibid.*, VI, 44, Easter 1210).

[6] *Ibid.*, XI, 178, no. 884, Michaelmas 1225; *ibid.*, XII, 37, no. 203, Hilary 1225 (also in *Note Book*, III, 81, no. 1051).

him."[7] William and Warin were tenants in the Scottish March, and John was uncertain about his relations with the Scots. He feared that if his war in France went badly, they might invade the north of England.[8] The war in France did go badly, so badly that Normandy was lost by 1204. Many pleas of land in the royal courts touched on the *terrae Normannorum*, the English tenures of those Norman knights who had abandoned their allegiance to John to do homage to Philip Augustus. Most of these knights forfeited their English holdings, but some tried to hold on to them.[9] They found the courts of England closed to them. An entry in the plea rolls of King John states the reason for a postponement: the litigant's possessions had been seized into the king's hand because he was beyond the sea with the king's enemies.[10] The council of the young Henry III decreed in 1220 that no subject of the king of France should be allowed to plead in the English courts until Englishmen gained permission to plead in his courts.[11] Later, in 1227, Henry's justices in Bedfordshire received letters close forbidding them to take an assize brought by Richard de Glanville and commanding them to inform Richard that "since he came from Normandy and entered our land of England without our leave and will, he ought to depart from our land and return to his own parts."[12] Richard de Glanville must have been one of those who had chosen to serve the king of France after the loss of Normandy.

There are other instances of the king's commands to his court

---

[7] *RCR*, II, 3.   [8] *Pleas before King*, I, 56.

[9] William Marshal was able to keep his Norman lands (Painter, *King John*, p. 148). Others were less successful. When Matilda de Courtenay brought suit in 1220, her opponents alleged that she was a subject of the French king. She replied that she was English and that she held land in both England and Normandy, just as did the earl marshal, but the justices postponed her plea (*CRR*, IX, 36–37, Trinity 1220).

[10] Geoffrey de Fercles (*CRR*, IV, 100, Easter 1206).

[11] *Ibid.*, VIII, 343, Easter 1220 (also *Note Book*, II, 99, no. 110). As late as 1233 the rule was still enforced, *Note Book*, II, 558, no. 730, Hilary 1233.

[12] *Roll of the Justices in Eyre at Bedford*, 1227, ed. G. Herbert Fowler (Beds H.R.S., Vol. III, 1916), p. 198; *Close Rolls* (1227–1231), p. 9, letter dated 4 Dec. 1227.

for postponement of pleas that cannot be explained so easily. Richard fitz Neal wrote in the *Dialogus de scaccario* of Henry II, "To some he does full justice for nothing, in consideration of their past services or out of mere goodness of heart; but to others (and it is only human nature) he will not give way either for love or for money." [13] This was true of his son John as well, for on a number of occasions he arbitrarily denied justice to individuals. An example of King John's protecting his own interest can be found from early in his reign in a case concerning the royal manor of Woodstock, an estate remembered as one of Henry II's trysting places. The Knights Templars complained that the men of the manor had disseized them of four acres of land. The men of Woodstock denied this, explaining that when Henry II had made an exchange of land with the Templars, the ownership of the four acres had been left unsettled. They said that later an inquiry had awarded the land to them. Clearly, the real defendant in this action was the king, not the men of the manor, and the justices would not proceed until they had consulted him.[14] King John first gave them permission to proceed, but later changed his mind, for an indefinite postponement of the assize is recorded later in the same year.[15]

Sometimes King John denied access to his courts, not to protect his own rights, but to show favor or disfavor to certain individuals. An early example is the case of Roger de Montbegon and Fulk Painel, both of whom had supported John in his rebellion against King Richard in 1193–1194 and both of whom could have expected the king's favor.[16] In 1199, Roger paid 500 marks to marry a rich widow in the king's custody and to gain her inheritance, and the next year he began legal action to obtain possession of his bride's heritage.[17] He brought a plea of land against William de Portu only to have the suit stopped because

---

[13] Page 120.

[14] *RCR*, II, 157, Easter 1200; also in *Pleas before King*, I, 297, no. 3117. Discussed in *Proc. without Writ*, pp. ci–cii.

[15] *CRR*, I, 319, Michaelmas 1200.

[16] On Roger see Holt, *Northerners*, pp. 22–23; on Fulk see Painter, *King John*, p. 74.

[17] Olive widow of Robert de St. John (*Rot. de obl. et fin.*, pp. 41–42).

Fulk Paniel had custody of the land in question, and he had letters from the king granting him peace concerning all his lands and wards.[18] The king's command stopped another action that Roger brought in his effort to gain the lands of William de Portt for his wife.[19] Roger de Montbegon must have felt cheated after offering a large sum for his wife's inheritance and then being unable to obtain lands that he considered a rightful part of it. John's denial of justice to Roger without consideration for his earlier loyalty or for his fine doubtlessly contributed to his break with the king. A few years later, in 1205, Roger was suspected of rebellion; still later he joined the ranks of the rebel barons, and he served on the baronial committee of twenty-five.[20]

Perhaps most disturbing are those cases in which oblations lay behind the king's prohibition of a plea. The offering of a fine or gift to the ruler in return for some favor or advantage was not regarded as bribery in the Middle Ages, and a certain amount of venality was normal in all medieval courts. But King John was faced with such financial difficulties that he had to find new methods of raising money; it is not surprising that he received fines for judicial advantage, some of which bordered on outright sale of justice. In 1206 the justices *coram rege* dismissed a jury summoned for a suit between Alexander de Caldbeck and Robert de Courtenay because Alexander's attorney had come and said that he did not wish a jury, since "it did not please the lord king that he should have it." [21] Two years earlier, Alexander had offered the king an oblation of £100 to have a jury determine whether Reginald de Lucy had disseized him of nine carucates of land in the vill of Caldbeck while he was a minor.[22] When the king received this fine Reginald had long been dead (since 1199), and Robert de Courtenay and his wife now claimed the land as his heirs. The pipe roll of 1206 still recorded Alexander's debt, but added that the jury should not be summoned because

[18] *CRR*, I, 215–216, Trinity 1200, pleas at Westminster.

[19] *Ibid.*, p. 241, Trinity 1200.   [20] Holt, *Northerners*, pp. 22–23.

[21] *CRR*, IV, 99, Easter 1206.

[22] *Pipe Roll 6 John*, ed. Doris M. Stenton (Pipe Roll Society, N.S.; London, 1940), Michaelmas 1204, p. 143. Lady Stenton discusses this case in her introduction, pp. xx–xxi.

Robert had seizin of half of Caldbeck through a fine of 300 marks and two palfreys.[23] King John's acceptance of Robert's oblation and his refusal of Alexander's jury did not irrevocably close the case, however, for he gave seizin to Robert and his wife conditionally, "that they may afterwards be impleaded concerning the whole vill of Caldbeck according to the custom and assize of the kingdom." This left Alexander free to bring a regular proprietary action to recover his whole inheritance, but meant failure for his attempt to quickly regain the nine carucates through a jury. In this instance the king is not liable to the charge of denying justice, for his action ensured that traditional process would prevail. Nevertheless, the charge of delaying and selling justice seems to apply.

There can be no doubt that King John did deny and sell justice in other cases, sometimes for fantastic sums. Less involved and more damning than the above case is one from the following year, 1207. The entry on the plea roll is brief: "The lord king commanded by his writ that the justices should not hold the plea between Henry de Longchamps and Henry de Mara and Petronilla his wife concerning the dower which Henry and Petronilla seek against Henry, because he does not wish the plea to be held." [24] The pipe roll for the same year explains why the king did not wish the plea to be held—Henry de Longchamps had offered three palfreys in order that the plea not proceed.[25] This case is not unique, for in the same year King John ordered his justices by his writ not to allow William de Carraw to be impleaded of his lands that Geoffrey de Chazey claimed against him. The entry duly notes that William's ancestors had held that land since the time of King Henry I, but it fails to note that he had paid forty ounces of gold for the king's writ.[26] Some persons who wished to gain safety from lawsuits found the price consid-

[23] *Pipe Roll 8 John*, ed. Doris M. Stenton (Pipe Roll Society, N.S.; London, 1942), Michaelmas 1206, pp. 44–45.

[24] CRR, V, 72, Michaelmas 1207, pleas *coram rege*.

[25] *Pipe Roll 9 John*, ed. A. Mary Kirkus (Pipe Roll Society, N.S.; London, 1946), Michaelmas 1207, p. 160.

[26] CRR, V, 61, Michaelmas 1207, pleas *coram rege*; *Rot. de obl. et fin.*, pp. 414–415.

erably higher. Again in 1207, King John accepted an offer of £1000 and fifteen warhorses from the baron Gerard de Furnival "for having our benevolence and in order that a suit between him and his wife Maude and Neal of Luvetot should stand over." [27]

But such cases are not limited to the period following the loss of Normandy, when John became more grasping, for an example can be cited from his early years. In 1199, Maurice de Ghent, a minor at the time, brought suit in the royal courts to gain the manor of Saltby from Nicholas de Stuteville. The two litigants were important northern barons: the young Maurice de Ghent held lands in Yorkshire and Lincolnshire, and Nicholas de Stuteville held two baronies and some lesser estates in Yorkshire. [28] Maurice offered a fine of thirty marks to have a jury of recognition, and later his guardian, William de St. Mère–Eglise, bishop of London, offered ten marks. [29] Despite the fines, in 1200 the king forbade the justices of the bench to hold the suit until he ordered otherwise. The pipe roll for the following year shows the reason: Nicholas had offered 100 marks and a palfrey to have respite from the plea. [30] King John's eager acceptance of oblations in return for quashing suits in his courts cannot have failed to make an impression on his barons. Doubtless, the treatment that Maurice de Ghent received in the king's court during his youth played some part in his decision years later to join his uncle Gilbert de Ghent in the rebellion. Gerard de Furnival also joined the ranks of the rebel northern barons. [31]

In a number of other cases that King John ordered postponed

[27] *Rot. lit. cl.,* I, 78, 19 Feb. 1207; *Pipe Roll 9 John,* Michaelmas 1207, p. 74.

[28] Holt, *Northerners,* pp. 27, 29.

[29] *Pipe Roll 1 John,* ed. Doris M. Stenton (Pipe Roll Society, N.S.; London, 1925), Michaelmas 1199, p. 252; *Pipe Roll 2 John,* ed. Doris M. Stenton (Pipe Roll Society, N.S.; London, 1934), Michaelmas 1200, p. 153.

[30] *CRR,* I, 335, Michaelmas 1200; *Pipe Roll 3 John,* ed. Doris M. Stenton (Pipe Roll Society, N.S.; London, 1936), Michaelmas 1201, p. 23. The case again came into court in Trinity term 1208 (*CRR,* IV, 15).

[31] On Maurice's participation in the barons' war, see Painter, *King John,* pp. 289, 292; on Gerard's, see Holt, *Northerners,* pp. 29, 141.

indefinitely, it is impossible to discover the circumstances surrounding them.[32] This aspect of John's administration of justice
—his opening and closing of the royal courts to serve his own
purposes—presents a sharp contrast to justice under his son
Henry III. An examination of the plea rolls for Henry's early
years fails to reveal many instances of royal commands for the
dismissal of pleas. One occurred in 1226, when Alan a vintner of
Reading sought to collect a debt for wine that Engelard de
Cigogné, former constable of Windsor Castle, had taken from
him. The king ruled that Engelard need not respond to the plea
because he had taken the wine in time of war for the provisioning of a royal castle.[33] While this ruling may be said to represent
protection of a royal servant and denial of justice to the wine
merchant, the reason for it is more easily understood than some
of John's dismissals of pleas. The unfortunate vintner had a
commodity that was deemed necessary to the war effort, and it
was expropriated. The absence of cases arbitrarily postponed by
royal command is evidence of the seriousness with which Henry
and his advisers took the king's promise made in Magna Carta
not to "deny or delay right or justice." The council of the young
king had made a real effort to restore the good old customs; [34] and
Henry III, upon attaining his majority, could hardly return at
once to the ways of his father.

Arbitrary royal action in other ways could just as effectively
deny access to the king's courts as could a writ to the justices.
The king's disseizins without judgment closed the courts to his
victims. In 1202 an assize of novel disseizin was brought against
Margaret de Ros before the justices on eyre. When they learned
that her lands had been seized by the king for debts, however,
they postponed the assize indefinitely "because it is not permitted to take an assize of land while it is in the hand of the lord
king." [35] Distraint, temporary seizure of one's lands into the

[32] E.g. CRR, II, 163; III, 176, 211, 273, 274, 341; IV, 4, 6, 68; V, 61, 200;
VI, 13, 53, 320–321.

[33] Ibid., XI, 469–470; no. 2368, Michaelmas 1226.

[34] Powicke, Henry III, pp. 38–39.

[35] Lincs Assize Roll, p. 202, no. 1143; also CRR, III, 57, Michaelmas
1203.

king's hand, was an old instrument of judicial discipline, used to compel appearance at court, but the Angevin rulers made it into a multipurpose weapon.[36] These arbitrary disseizins by King John had one very important consequence for the administration of justice in the royal courts—they produced even more delays in the already slow-moving courts as more and more lands fell into the king's hand. Postponements of cases *sine die quamdiu terra fuerit in manu regis* multiplied. Persons with claims to such lands were unable to seek restoration from the holders, since one whose lands had been seized by the king could neither plead nor be impleaded in the royal courts. They could not justly be called into court to defend their rights to land that they did not hold. Consequently, an increasing number of persons were being denied access to the courts.

This situation was not limited to John's last years, when his arbitrary actions were a scandal. One example dates from as early as the autumn of 1199. The prior of Colne sought to gain lands held by Stephen de Beauchamps through an assize of mort d'ancestor, but the action was postponed indefinitely "by prayer of Stephen because he was disseized of all his lands by precept of the lord king." [37] Similarly, in 1210, when John de Horseby sought land held by Hugh de Verli, Hugh came and stated that the land in question was seized by the king, and he did not wish to reply until the seizin should be restored to him.[38] The court agreed that he should not respond until he was once again in possession of his land. The fact that these lands were temporarily in the king's hand did at least for a time deny to the prior of Colne and to John de Horseby the opportunity of pursuing their claims in court.

Under such conditions, it is not surprising that individuals who wished to escape a court proceeding recognized the opportunities offered in pleading that their land was in the hand of the king.[39] After all, land could be in the king's hand theoretically

---

[36] Jolliffe, *Angevin Kingship*, p. 53.   [37] RCR, II, 47, Michaelmas 1199.
[38] CRR, I, 296, Michaelmas 1200.
[39] For other examples see *ibid.*, VII, 348, Trinity 1199; VII, 79–80, Hilary 1214.

and still be in the tenant's possession practically. Temporary distraint of lands was a common practice under John. Pleading that one's lands were in the king's hand was often merely an "exception," an excuse for dismissal of a plea. In the first year of John's reign an individual is found pleading that he did not wish to reply to a writ until he regained full seizin of his land, which was in the hand of the king.[40] Evidently it was some time before possession was restored to him for the case did not come to a conclusion until five years later.[41]

It was not even necessary that the land of one of the two principals be in the king's hand to cause a postponement, for in at least one case an assize was indefinitely postponed because the land of a warrantor was held by the king. When a tenant's right to his land was challenged, he "vouched to warranty" the person who had granted him the land; his grantor then replaced him as the defendant in the suit, and the remainder of the action was conducted in his name.[42] The prioress of Keldholme, the defendant in an assize of mort d'ancestor, pled that she did not know whom to call to warrant, since the land and heir of William de Stuteville, who ought to have been her warrantor, were in the hand of the king.[43] The justices told her that she need not reply to the writ as long as the land of her warrantor remained in the king's hand. Since the lands of William de Stuteville remained in the possession of the king, the assize was never taken.[44]

There are numerous other postponements in the rolls for John's reign where the only explanation offered is that the land of one party had been seized by the king. In 1202 an assize

[40] *Ibid.*, VII, 348, Trinity 1199.

[41] *Ibid.*, III, 120, Easter 1204. For a similar case see *ibid.*, III, 106, in which the tenant, Gilbert de Norfolk, pled that the assize ought not to proceed because his lands had been seized into the king's hand. But the claimant denied this, and he called the sheriff to warrant that the lands were not in the king's hand. The sheriff confirmed the claimant's denial.

[42] Glanville, pp. 70–71, lib. iii, cap. 1; Pollock and Maitland, II, 662.

[43] *CRR*, III, 91, Hilary 1204.

[44] Sanders, *Baronies*, p. 59, shows that William de Stuteville had died in 1203; his son Robert died in 1205; his uncle and heir then offered a fine to have the inheritance, but it was never paid, and the honour remained in the king's possession.

concerning a church held by Guy de Laval was postponed indefinitely because all his lands and possessions had been taken into the hand of the king.[45] Similar postponements resulted because the lands of the abbey of St. Augustine, Canterbury, of the abbot of Fécamp, of the monks of Holy Trinity, Canterbury, and of Matilda de Blankney were in the hand of the king.[46] There is no indication that, once postponed, any of these suits were ever heard.

In some cases it is possible to determine the reason for these unexplained royal disseizins that were delaying the administration of justice. Land might be in the king's possession for any number of legitimate reasons. The land might have escheated to him for default of heirs, for the felony of one of his tenants-in-chief, for the default of knight-service, or default of some other payment or service. But John held many lands in his hand for reasons not so clearly in keeping with feudal custom. In the summer of 1208 a number of cases involving monasteries were postponed indefinitely, obviously because King John had seized their lands during the Interdict.[47] Yet the king's seizure of the monasteries' lands did not long close the courts to them. At first, the royal justices' attitude toward the religious houses in the king's possession was uncertain, and the court would postpone a case if one of the parties requested it on those grounds. Later, after the summer of 1208, it was realized that the king could maintain financial control without denying the monasteries the right to pursue their pleas in the royal courts.[48] The only postponement of an action concerning a religious house because of the king's seizure between Trinity term 1208 and the end of the

[45] CRR, II, 134, Michaelmas 1202.

[46] Ibid., II, 157, Hilary 1203; III, 206, Michaelmas 1204; IV, 175, Trinity 1206; VI, 74, Michaelmas 1210.

[47] Ibid., V, 157, St. Edmunds; p. 158, Peterborough, Crowland, Sempringham; p. 161, Dereham, Lewes; p. 174, Lewes; p. 188, Tornholm; p. 199, Clerkenwell; p. 202, Osney; p. 271, St. Benet's Holme; p. 276, Turgerton, Hospital of Lincoln.

[48] C. R. Cheney, "King John's Reaction to the Interdict," Trans. Royal Hist. Soc., ser. 4, XXXI (1949), 140. Lady Stenton noted this too in her introduction to Pipe Roll 11 John (Pipe Roll Society, N.S.; London, 1948), 1209, p. xxii.

Interdict occurred in Michaelmas term 1210, when a plea involving the abbot of Waverley was postponed "because it is not known whether the abbey is in the hand of the lord king or not." [49] But this was the time of the heavy taxation of the Cistercians, when the abbot of the house fled and its monks were dispersed.[50]

In several cases parties sought postponements on the grounds that they had been disseized for debt to the king. Sometimes, however, this fact was not recorded by the court clerk. An important example is a case that was postponed because the king had seized the lands of Geoffrey de Mandeville during the summer of 1214. The entry simply declares: "The action between Mary de Talworth plaintiff and Geoffrey de Mandeville is postponed indefinitely because all the lands of Geoffrey are in the hands of the lord king." [51] His disseizin can certainly be attributed to a debt owed to the king, since in the spring of 1214 Geoffrey had pledged all his lands to King John for a fine offered for his marriage to the countess of Gloucester.[52]

Postponements of judicial proceedings which were necessary because the land of one party was in the king's hand occurred frequently enough to constitute a log jam in the flow of justice during the reign of King John. But postponements as a result of the king's arbitrary seizures of land were greatly reduced in the time of Henry III, as such actions became less frequent. Indeed, a reduction in the number of disseizins without judgment is to be expected under Henry, particularly during his minority, since his early counselors attempted to return to the custom of the realm and to turn away from the abuses of the young king's father.

---

[49] *CRR*, VII, 6.   [50] Cheney, "John's Reaction to the Interdict," p. 139.

[51] *CRR*, VII, 226, Trinity 1214.

[52] *Rot. lit. pat.*, p. 141; see Jolliffe, *Angevin Kingship*, pp. 81, 84. A similar case is that of William de Carrou. A case to which he was a party was postponed indefinitely with only the explanation that his land was in the king's hand (*CRR*, VI, 73, Michaelmas 1210). *Pipe Roll 13 John*, ed. Doris M. Stenton (Pipe Roll Society, N.S.; London, 1953), 1211, p. 63, reveals that he owed the king 4000 marks, so there can be little doubt that he was disseized for default on this large debt.

Under Henry III, then, there was a reduction in the number of cases postponed because land was held by the king. Not only was the number of such postponements reduced, but where there were postponements, there was also a change in the reason for the land's falling into the king's hand. Examples should not be expected during the time of Henry's minority, but some examples can be found during the early years of his majority. In 1227 the court postponed indefinitely a plea involving Robert, count of Dreux, because all his lands were in the hand of the king.[53] Although no reason was given for the seizure of Robert's lands, they had been seized because he was siding with Blanche of Castile in the conflict between France and England.[54] Later that same year an action was postponed *per preceptum domini regis* because the defendant maintained that the land of his warrantor, the duke of Brittany, was in the king's hands.[55] Again no reason for the seizure was offered, but possession of the lands of Peter of Dreux, duke of Brittany, did pass to the king in 1227 as a result of the agreement between Peter and the French queen in March of that year.[56] It is clear that these seizures differed greatly from the administrative and financial disseizins of John. The actions against the brothers Robert, count of Dreux, and Peter, duke of Brittany, were aimed at important figures in Henry's struggle with France. Furthermore, the forfeitures were for failure to fulfill their obligation of loyalty to their lord, and such action was easily understood by the feudal classes.

In another action from Henry's early majority, a widow sought recovery of her dower, and the tenant called to warrant a number of persons. The justices noted the fact that the land of one of the warrantors, Raymond de Sully, was in the king's hands.[57] Ray-

---

[53] *CRR*, XIII, 2, no. 10, Easter 1227.

[54] Sanders, *Baronies*, p. 10; Sidney Painter, *The Scourge of the Clergy: Peter of Dreux* (Baltimore, 1937), p. 44. *Pat. Rolls* (1225–1232), p. 129, states simply that the lands were seized *per preceptum.*

[55] *CRR*, XIII, 63, no. 285, Trinity 1227.

[56] Sanders, *Baronies*, pp. 140–141; Painter, *Scourge of the Clergy*, p. 45; *Pat. Rolls* (1225–1232), pp. 127–128.

[57] *CRR*, XIII, 523, no. 2463, Hilary 1228, plea brought by Avicia widow of William de Torrington.

mond had refused to do homage to the king or to perform the services due from his land.[58] His status did not prevent the plea from proceeding, however, as would likely have been true under King John, for the next year the case went forward.[59] Thus it is evident that disseizin was regarded by John's successor as a serious step, and not as a routine administrative measure to be used at the slightest opportunity. Consequently, postponements of pleas *sine die quamdiu terra fuerit in manu regis* were greatly reduced in number.

Just as arbitrary disseizin by the king forced the indefinite postponement of many pleas in the royal courts, so seizin by the king, that is royal grants, caused other postponements. In some pleas of land the plaintiff was met with the tenant's response that he had possession *per preceptum domini regis*. King John, like his father and brother before him, went beyond his feudal prerogatives through use of his personal power, seizing lands or granting them as a means of disciplining or rewarding royal servants.[60] The king's grants of land sometimes disregarded the rightful claims of others, but the royal courts rarely offered them a means of pressing their claims, since neither the justices of John nor those of Henry III cared to proceed with cases that contested their master's grants. One plea from Henry's early years concerning a royal charter states that the king's testimony "by charter or by word of mouth" outweighs any other proof.[61] An entry in the pipe rolls from John's reign illustrates this situation: "William bishop of London owes ten marks for having a recognition, but it should not be summoned because Nicholas de Stuteville made a

---

[58] On 7 Dec. 1229, Henry committed the land of Raymond to a custodian "until the said Raymond should do what he ought to do for the king concerning the said portion" (*Pat. Rolls* [1225–1232], p. 319). In 1230 the land was still in the king's hand (*Pipe Roll 14 Henry III*, ed. Chalfont Robinson [Pipe Roll Society, N.S.; London, 1927], p. 16). Finally, on 13 Feb. 1233, the king took the homage of Raymond de Sully (*Exc. e rot. fin.*, I, 238).

[59] *CRR*, XIII, 408–409, no. 1945, Easter 1229.

[60] Jolliffe, *Angevin Kingship*, chap. 3.

[61] *Note Book*, II, 192–193, no. 239, Hilary 1224.

fine of 100 marks for that land, and the bishop cannot have his recognition." [62] Similarly, when Geoffrey de Hope and his wife were being impleaded of their land, the justices postponed the plea indefinitely upon receipt of a writ from King John stating that "we warrant to them that land and command that they should have it in peace as long as we live." [63]

Sometimes royal protection of one's seizin was available for a price. In the first year of John's reign, Agnes wife of William de Wisteston gave the king fifty marks to have her share of her father's inheritance, which her sister's husband, Elias son of Bernard, was withholding from her. [64] She then began an action in the royal court to recover her inheritance. [65] But her plea did not go forward, for Elias gave the king sixty marks to hold his land in peace as he had held it in the time of Henry II, and the necessary writ was sent to the justices. [66] Elias was soon outbid by Agnes' husband, who offered 100 marks and a palfrey to have the plea go forward without impediment; and in 1202, three years after the origin of the case, Agnes and her opponent reached agreement. [67] The pipe roll for 1204 provides another example of a payment for protection of seizin. Peter de Brus offered the king 200 marks and two palfreys for two manors, with the stipulation that if anyone challenged his claim he was not to be disseized except by the king's command. [68]

Several of King John's instructions concerning seizin represented his efforts to repay the loyalty of his companions in the revolt he had attempted when he was count of Mortain. John had raised the standard of rebellion against King Richard in 1193–1194, while his brother was a prisoner in Germany. During his first year on the throne, he sent an order to the sheriff of

---

[62] *Pipe Roll 8 John,* Michaelmas 1206, p. 58.

[63] *CRR,* IV, 184–185, Trinity 1206; *Rot. lit. cl.,* I, 71, 24 May 1206.

[64] *Rot. de obl. et fin.,* p. 16.   [65] *RCR,* II, 44, Michaelmas 1199.

[66] *Rot. de obl. et fin.,* p. 50; *RCR,* II, 242, Easter 1200.

[67] *Pipe Roll 2 John,* Michaelmas 1200, p. 248; *CRR,* II, 112–113, Michaelmas 1202. Elias was dead by this time, and his widow and son made the final concord with Alice and William.

[68] *Pipe Roll 6 John,* p. 188.

Cambridgeshire to restore to Hugh de Mauney a manor "of which he was disseized for our service." [69] This pleasant euphemism means that Richard had dispossessed him as punishment for his participation in the revolt. Sometimes the persons who had held such lands since the rebellion of 1194 found themselves at a disadvantage when engaged in litigation with John's former allies. In 1200 the recognitors in an inquest of land declared that the tenant had gained possession when the plaintiff was disseized "for service to the lord king." [70] The court clerk left a blank space for John's decision, which was inserted later, and reads, "The lord king commands that if he was disseized on that occasion, let him have his seizin."

The plea rolls of Henry III's early years do not reveal his active intervention in cases to protect the seizin of royal favorites, but they do record several cases in which tenants defended their right by a statement that they held the land *per preceptum domini regis*. In 1217, the right to land at Marham in Norfolk was disputed, the complainant alleging that it was his by virtue of a final concord made in the court of King John, the tenant maintaining that it was his by order of Henry III. The justices decided in favor of the one who had seizin by the king's writ, but they reserved to the other the right to bring another type of action if he chose.[71]

When the prior of the Hospitalers brought an assize of novel disseizin, his opponent contended that he had the property in question by the king's command, and the sheriff produced the royal writ to support this contention. The prior replied that he did not believe the writ came from the chancery, but if it did, it was made *contra legem terrae et consuetudinem regni*.[72] The

[69] *Memoranda Roll 1 John*, ed. H. G. Richardson (Pipe Roll Society; London, 1943), p. 35.

[70] *Pleas before King*, I, 299, no. 3123, Easter, pleas *coram rege* brought by Philip de Beaumes; discussed in the introduction, p. 65. See also the case of Robert de Heriz, disseized "for service to the king," *Pleas before King*, II, 106, no. 433, assizes at Launceston, Cornwall, 18 June 1201; *Rot. de obl. et fin.*, p. 35.

[71] *Note Book*, III, 307, no. 1298, Michaelmas 1217.

[72] *CRR*, VIII, 132–133, Michaelmas 1219 (also in *Note Book*, II, 68–69, no. 176). The tenant was Adam de Bereville.

plea rolls made no further reference to this case, so there is no way of learning the outcome of the prior's accusation. Bracton, in commenting on this case, wrote that the assize of novel disseizin does not lie against one who gained possession from the king because he was not responsible for the disseizin. Obviously, the assize did not lie against the king either. Bracton also commented on the course to be followed in an assize of mort d'ancestor if the tenant offered the defense that he held at the king's will.[73] His advice was that the judges should allow the assize to proceed, but should postpone judgment until they could consult the king.

Royal action could close the king's courts to suitors in many ways. Most obvious were the commands of King John forbidding his judges to proceed with cases. These commands ceased after his death. Henry III did not actively interfere in the work of his courts to protect persons in their seizin, as had his father. But in many instances it was not the king's direct order that denied access to the courts, rather it was an indirect result of some other royal act. The justices' unwillingness to proceed with pleas involving those whose land had been seized by the king caused many delays during the reign of John, fewer in Henry's time. Their hesitancy to act in cases where seizin had been ordered by the king caused dismissal of some pleas under both kings. Probably these indirect means of denying justice affected far greater numbers than did direct royal commands to dismiss pleas. Regardless of whether pleas were dismissed by royal command or as an indirect result of some other royal action, the dismissals are evidence of the role that the king's will played in the operation of the courts.

JUSTICE DELAYED OR EXPEDITED AT THE KING'S COMMAND

Just as the king could bring proceedings in his courts to a complete halt, so could he slow or speed the course of justice, adjourning cases to later times or clearing the way for cases to be

---

[73] *Note Book*, III, 595, no. 1766, eyre in Kent 1227. Assize brought by Richard fitz Roger against Joscelin de Oye. The jurors declared in favor of Richard, and the king gave him seizin.

heard more quickly. Often the instructions postponing or hastening the hearing of pleas were royal commands in name only, for many of them were writs sold by chancery clerks without the king's knowledge. The pipe rolls of King John record payments for many more of these instructions than the king could ever have given personally. There are entries noting payments *ut loquela procedat, pro festinando judicium,* and *pro habendo respectu de placitis.* Such oblations explain many of the king's commands concerning the operation of his courts, but his orders to the justices were not all simply products of royal clerks. Such phrases as *per dominum regem, consciente domino rege,* and *per petitionem domini regis et consilii sui* indicate the personal role of John and Henry III. Added evidence of the king's activity are the cases raising questions of judicial administration that the justices noted for his attention. King John's justices *coram rege* once referred to him the problem of setting the date for hearing a plea.[74] A survey of royal instructions relating to the hearing of pleas should reveal more about the nature of the king's activity in the judicial sphere. King John was free with such royal commands, and his reasons for postponing or hastening suits are sometimes questionable. With Henry III, the reasons are less questionable.

Certainly the most frequent commands that judges of the royal courts received from their master were orders to postpone actions involving those in his service. *Per servitium regis* was one of the recognized essoins, excuses for not coming to court on the day assigned.[75] But the law governing essoins in the early thirteenth century was exceedingly complex, since it attempted to define every conceivable situation instead of declaring a few general principles. Glanville wrote that when service to the king caused a litigant's absence, the action should be postponed until his return from royal service; but he noted that those constantly engaged in the king's business should not use this as an excuse. In his effort to cover every possible circumstance, Glanville made further distinctions. If a proceeding had begun, and then a litigant offered the essoin *per servitium regis,* the justices must make certain whether he was in the king's service by royal command or by his own choice. If he had entered royal service voluntarily, they must determine whether he served within or outside the borders of the kingdom. Forty days' respite was allowed those on duty across the sea, but for those serving in England, "then it shall be at the will and pleasure of the lord king's justices to assign a shorter or longer term of delay, as may be expedient for the lord king, provided that the usual legal procedure be observed." [76]

In practice these complexities were usually avoided through writs of protection safeguarding these in the king's service from pleas. Since the time of the Conqueror and earlier, it had been the custom of the English kings to extend their special protection to their retainers, to royal favorites, and even to some religious houses.[77] The *Dialogus de scaccario* lists among the privileges of the king's servants sitting at the exchequer their immunity from all pleas during its sessions.[78] Writs of protection appear to have been granted as a matter of course to those who crossed the Channel to participate in King John's campaigns against Philip Augustus from 1201 to 1204, for the plea rolls record dozens of postponements because one of the litigants was in Normandy or in Poitou in the king's service. For example, one membrane alone of the roll of the itinerant justices at Taunton, Somerset, in the summer of 1201 records six pleas postponed "on account of service to the king overseas." [79] The roll of the justices at Westminster for Michaelmas 1203 records six writs of the king or the justiciar commanding postponements while one of the

[76] *Ibid.,* p. 16.   [77] Jolliffe, *Angevin Kingship,* pp. 87–97.

[78] Pages 45–46.

[79] *Somersetshire Pleas (Civil and Criminal) from the Rolls of the Itinerant Justices, Close of 12th Century–41 Henry III,* ed. E. H. Chadwych-Healey (Somerset Record Society, Vol. XI, 1897), pp. 4–24, assize roll 1171, m. 12d.

parties was in the king's service, besides postponements for this reason allowed by the justices themselves.[80] These writs became so general that by 1206 the clerks referred to them as *breve commune*.[81] They were sent by the king directly to the justices, or through the intermediary of the justiciar, and by the justiciar to the justices,[82] and must be distinguished from the essoins, excuses sent by the litigants themselves to explain their absence. The letters assured those serving in the king's armies in Normandy or Poitou that their tenures in England would be safe from litigation during their absence; however, some of the writs specifically excluded pleas of the crown from their protection.[83]

These writs of protection reflect John's declining fortunes in Normandy during 1202 and 1203. As John's situation became more desperate, he excused not only those who served in his feudal host from pleadings in his courts, but extended this favor to those who sent their sons, knights, or financial contributions to aid in the struggle. In 1203 the justiciar Geoffrey fitz Peter instructed the justices not to allow an individual to be impleaded of his free tenements "while his knights are beyond the sea with horses and arms in the lord king's service." [84] That same year King John forbade the justices to implead an individual because his son and heir was abroad on the king's service.[85] The year 1203 also saw the justiciar give a general order to the justices at Westminster, commanding them not to entertain pleas against anyone "while their money [*denarii*] is in the lord king's service

---

[80] *CRR*, III, 1–84. One of the justiciar's writs notes that the absent litigant is *in prisona regis Francie per servicium domini regis* (p. 32).

[81] *Ibid.*, IV, 243, Michaelmas 1206; cited in Flower, *Introduction*, p. 337.

[82] For examples of writs from the king to the justices at Westminster, see *CRR*, I, 161, 207, and IV, 225; from the king to the justiciar, *CRR*, I, 204–205, 275; from the king to the itinerant justices, *Lincs Assize Roll*, nos. 5, 18, 21, 106; from the justiciar, *CRR*, I, 275, 349.

[83] E.g. *CRR*, VIII, 175, 244, Trinity 1214. But in IV, 226, Michaelmas 1206, the justices at Westminster postponed an appeal of breaking the king's peace *sine die* because the appealed was across the sea in the king's service.

[84] *Ibid.*, II, 139, Hilary 1203. For similar entries, see *ibid.*, II, 92, 237, and *Northants. Assize Roll*, p. 53, no. 431.

[85] *CRR*, II, 172, Hilary 1203. Similarly, pp. 98, 116, 177, and *Northants. Assize Roll*, p. 71, no. 500.

beyond the sea." [86] This step had been foreshadowed by several adjournments of individual cases for this reason.[87] The Poitou campaign of 1214 brought another increase in such postponements; the roll of the justices at Westminster for Trinity term records twelve.[88]

The writs of protection not only necessitated the adjournment of proprietary actions, normally subject to long adjournments by means of essoins, but they also caused postponements of the possessory assizes, where essoins were strictly limited.[89] In at least two cases, assizes of mort d'ancestor were postponed indefinitely because the tenants had contributed money to aid the king's struggle.[90] These two assizes contrast sharply with the practice in the reign of Henry III. One of the king's commands for postponement on account of service to him found in the rolls for 1230 adds the condition, "unless that plea should be an assize of novel disseizin or darrein presentment or dower *unde nihil habet.*" [91] But the judges seem to have interpreted his command rather broadly, applying it to the assize of mort d'ancestor as well

---

[86] *CRR*, II, 157, Hilary 1203.

[87] *Northants. Assize Roll*, p. 92, no. 604, three weeks after Michaelmas 1202; *Pleas before King*, II, 265, no. 899, Michaelmas 1202; *CRR*, II, 129, Michaelmas 1202. Lady Stenton accepts these commands as evidence of John's growing desperation in Normandy (*Northants. Assize Roll*, p. xxviii); other scholars, however, have shown a remarkable reluctance to accept them at face value. H. G. Richardson in a review of Volumes LXVII and LXVIII of the Selden Society in *Law Qtrly. Rev.*, Vol. LXX (1954), suggests that the *denarii sui* in case 899 is a misreading for *dominus suus*. Flower, writing in *Introduction*, p. 345, suggests that the general order issued by Geoffrey fitz Peter (*CRR*, II, 157) is "merely a protest by the scribe against the vicarious service of the rich."

[88] *CRR*, VII, 113–258, roll 58.

[89] Glanville, p. 152, lib. xiii, cap. 7: "Because no more than two essoins are allowed in any recognition which concerns only seizin." Examples of assizes postponed on account of service to the king are: mort d'ancestor, *Pleas before King*, II, 268–269, no. 911; *Staffordshire Suits Extracted from the Plea Rolls, temp. Richard I and King John*, ed. George Wrottesley (Wm. Salt Soc., Vol. III, pt. 1, 1882), pp. 117, 121; *CRR*, I, 117; and plea of dower, *CRR*, I, 438, and IV, 234.

[90] *Pleas before King*, II, 265, no. 899, Emma de Cantilupe was tenant; and *CRR*, III, 17, Michaelmas 1203, Ralph Pirot was tenant.

[91] *CRR*, XIV, 1, no. 4, Trinity 1230, *Dominus rex mandavit.*

as to the other possessory assizes. In the same term, the royal justices gave a decision in an assize of darrein presentment putting this command into practice. The defendant essoined himself *de servitio domini regis,* but the judges ordered the assize to proceed "because when others are in the lord king's service this manner of assize along with assizes of novel disseizin and mort d'ancestor is taken and terminated." [92] The absent royal servant lost his advowson, but his amercement was placed in respite until his return to England. Later, Bracton in his treatise on English law cited this case as a precedent for the rule that the essoin *de servitio regis* does not lie in assizes of darrein presentment.[93] It would appear that here the king's command had some bearing on the judges' ruling, so that the ruler was playing a part in the formation of an important procedural rule.

A writ protecting knights serving in the king's army is one thing, but extending that protection to contributors of men or money is another. The necessity for protection in the former case can be justified by the need for men serving overseas to know that their interests at home are safe. In the latter case the only justification is that King John found himself caught in an inflationary situation where rising prices were outdistancing the static royal income, for the chief effect of these writs can only have been to increase the delays that already plagued proceedings in the royal courts. Yet it does serve to illustrate John's relationship with his courts. He and his justiciar were not bound to follow the traditional law of essoins regarding absence on the king's service, since they could extend the principle to include others. Nor were they bound to follow the admonitions of political thinkers to render justice to all "with an even-handed equity." Justice in the royal courts was not available equally to all the king's subjects; rather it was made available or withheld as suited the king's interests. At this time, King John's interest in achieving victory in his struggle to maintain his Continental territories meant more to him than his obligation to render justice equally to all his subjects.

[92] *Ibid.,* XIV, 89–90, no. 456, Trinity 1230; also in *Note Book,* II, 345–346, no. 427, assizes at Chelmsford, church of Trillaw.
[93] Bracton, IV, 78–80, f. 340.

The battle of Bouvines in 1214 put an end to the necessity for many of these delays in the work of the royal courts, since it meant that the king would remain in England most of the time. But the loss of Normandy did not mean an end to all expeditions by English kings across the sea, for they still ruled Ireland and Gascony. Henry III had not yet relinquished his claim to the lands his father had lost to the king of France, and he sailed to Brittany in the summer of 1230 with a force of several thousand men and a few hundred knights.[94] The absence of these men from England is reflected in the *curia regis* roll of Trinity term (summer) 1230, where more than a dozen of the cases recorded were postponed at the king's command because one of the parties was *in servitio domini regis ultra mare.*[95]

It was a practice of long standing to grant writs of protection not only to knights in the king's army but to all royal servants on the king's business—itinerant justices, ambassadors to foreign courts, and others. This custom continued under Henry III. Writs of protection were given to the justices on eyre forbidding them from being impleaded while engaged on the king's business. In 1219 the royal justices gave judgment in an assize of darrein presentment against James le Sauvage because he had not come when summoned. Two days later James sent a serving youth to the court, who "bore the lord king's letters attesting that James is in his service as an itinerant justice and forbidding that he should be impleaded touching any plea except by assize of novel disseizin while he was in the king's service." [96] This time the king's letters of protection were of no avail, however, for the justices refused to reopen the case once judgment had been given. Henry III continued to send royal servants to the Conti-

[94] F. M. Powicke, *The Thirteenth Century 1216–1307* (*Oxford History of England*, Vol. IV; Oxford, 1953), pp. 94–95.

[95] E.g. *CRR*, XIV, 1, no. 2, William Peverel; p. 1, no. 4, p. 22, no. 120, Gilbert Basset; p. 2, no. 9, p. 3, no. 12, William count of Aumale; p. 4, no. 26, Walter de Beauchamps; p. 4, no. 28, Walter Eskelling; p. 5, no. 32, Henry Waspail; p. 8, no. 51, Richard de Montfichet; p. 20, no. 114, Ralph Basset; p. 27, no. 145, John de Fay; p. 27, no. 146, Peter de Maulay; p. 42, no. 214, William de Lancaster; p. 52, no. 262, Falk fitz Warin and Peter fitz Herbert; p. 53, no. 266, Elias de Bolton; p. 58, no. 299, William de Stowe.

[96] *Rolls for Lincs and Worcs.*, pp. 338–339, no. 699, 11–17 Mar. 1219, pleas at Nottingham.

nent, although not in such numbers as had his father.[97] The king's envoys at the courts of European rulers also received his protection from pleas during their absences. In 1222, an assize against Master Henry de Cornhill was postponed by royal command because he was in the king's service at the papal *curia* in Rome, and in 1224 all pleas against the master of the Knights Templars were postponed because he was in Paris as the king's envoy.[98] These postponements differ from those ordered for John's officials because definite dates were given for hearing the pleas. They were not simply postponed indefinitely or until the royal servant should return from his mission.

While the king most often granted letters of protection from pleas to his knights or clerks, he sometimes placed others under his special protection. This practice dates from the time of the Conquest or even from Anglo-Saxon times, when the king extended his hand, his special protection, to his servants and friends. In the twelfth and early thirteenth centuries, this protection was still a valued sign of the king's favor.[99] The patent rolls for John's reign record great numbers of these charters and letters of protection, and the pipe rolls record many fines offered for them.[100]

[97] E.g. cases postponed for this reason: CRR, XII, 340, no. 1660; p. 402, no. 1991; *ibid.*, 163, m. 3, no. 36; Close Rolls (1227–1231), pp. 84, 171, 414, 444, 445, 554.

[98] Henry de Cornhill in Rolls for Glos., War. and Staffs, p. 605, no. 1445, pleas and assizes at Warwick; Master of Templars in CRR, XI, 456, no. 2281, Michaelmas 1224, and XIII, 62, no. 279, Trinity 1227, where he is said to be at Paris; Calendar of the Roll of the Justices on Eyre, 1227, ed. J. G. Jenkins (Buckinghamshire Archeological Society, Vol. VI, 1942), p. 15, no. 183; also William of Kilkenny, the king's messenger to Rome, CRR, 219, m. 1, no. 155.

[99] Jolliffe, Angevin Kingship, pp. 89–90.

[100] E.g. Rot. lit. pat., p. 8b, March 1202, to the abbot and monks of Crowland; p. 27b, April 1203, to Richard de Vernon while he is in the king's service; p. 39b, March 1204, to William Derman, no reason stated; p. 50, Feb. 1205, to Thomas de Wallace and Constance his wife, no reason given; p. 71b, May 1207, to Nicholas Duket, no explanation. Of these letters, only that of the abbot of Crowland seems to have been purchased (Pipe Roll 4 John, ed. Doris M. Stenton [Pipe Roll Society, N.S.; London, 1937], 1202, p. 238). A number of other religious houses purchased such letters or charters, e.g. Pipe Roll 2 John, 1202, p. 47, abbot of St. Albans; p. 109, abbot of Whitby; p.

Most religious houses received the king's protection through charters of liberties. A part of these charters was a clause granting the privilege of being impleaded only before the king or the justiciar. This privilege made necessary many postponements of actions before the itinerant justices and, less often, since the justiciar was usually present there, of actions before the bench at Westminster.[101]

These appeals to royal charters as a means of delaying a proceeding could easily become a threat to the efficient functioning of the royal courts. They were a cause of confusion for the justices during the early years of King John. In 1200 an individual brought a plea of land against the canons of Watton, but they had a charter protecting them from being impleaded for their tenements before anyone except the king.[102] The justices *coram rege* would not proceed until they had consulted the king. Just why this charter-right posed such a problem for them is not immediately clear, but the probable explanation is that the canons' charter was granted by Richard I and was not yet confirmed by John.[103] A plea before the justices at Westminster a year later centered around one of these charters. Henry de Roxby had brought a plea against the abbot of Leicester, only to be confronted by the abbot's charter.[104] Henry then obtained a writ which forbade that the action be postponed because of any charter of King Richard; the abbot responded by showing that his charter was not from Richard but from Henry II, and that he

---

147, prior and monks of Norwich; p. 207, prior of St. Swithins; p. 239, prior of Lancaster. Some were purchased by laymen, e.g. *Pipe Roll 2 John*, p. 99, William de Wrotham; *Pipe Roll 4 John*, p. 216, John de Guestling.

[101] E.g. justices on eyre: *Northants. Assize Roll*, nos. 380, 458, cases postponed because the Hospitalers have the privilege; *Lincs Assize Roll*, nos. 110, 243, 1295, 1301, Templars; no. 184, canons of Sempringham; no. 206, prior of St. Katherine, Lincs; no. 231, abbot of Thornton Curtis; nos. 328, 370, prior of Spalding; no. 437, prior of Bullington, no. 1550, Hospitalers. Justices at Westminster: CRR, I, 276, prior of Norwich; II, 37–38, abbot of Tewkesbury; II, 237, the Templars; III, 20, abbot of Savigny, Normandy.

[102] *Pleas before King*, I, 302–303, no. 3139 (also in RCR, II, 163, Easter 1200).

[103] The explanation offered by Stenton, *Pleas before King*, I, 71.

[104] CRR, I, 462, Easter 1201.

had a confirmation of it from King John. Faced with a writ and a royal charter that were contradictory, the justices could only postpone the case, so that "meanwhile the will of the lord king may be known." [105]

It does not appear that this liberty was upheld in all cases. When the abbot of Leicester was called to defend his right of presentation to a church, he proffered a charter of King Richard granting him the privilege of being tried only *coram ipso rege vel capitali justiciario ejus.* This time the gambit was unsuccessful, for he was informed that "all pleas held before the justices of the bench are understood to be held before the lord king or his chief justiciar." [106] It is uncertain whether this was a statement of the judges, a reply of the plaintiff, or the text of King John's writ initiating the action; [107] nevertheless, the plea went forward before the justices of the bench.[108]

This liberty of not being impleaded except before the king continued to raise difficulties for the justices of Henry III. In 1221 an assize of mort d'ancestor was brought before the itinerant justices at Worcester against the abbot of Bordsley, but he raised exceptions to the action. When his first objection was

[105] For a case from later in King John's reign concerned with this same problem, see *ibid.,* VII, 83. A similar problem faced the justices during John's absence on the Continent in 1214 (*ibid.,* VII, 133). The bishop of London had a letter of protection from any pleas until the king's return to England, and the justices consulted the justiciar about a plea concerning him before proceeding.

[106] *Ibid.,* I, 462, Easter 1201, pleas at Westminster.

[107] The text itself is unclear. Powicke in a review of *CRR,* Vol. I, in *E.H.R.,* XXXIX (1924), 265–266, accepts the words as the judges' statement, as does Sayles in *Court of King's Bench,* I, p. xxiii. However, Doris M. Stenton, *Pleas before King,* I, 101–102, attributes them either to the plaintiff or to the king's writ. Francis West, *The Justiciarship in England* (Cambridge, 1966), p. 117, attributes them to the king's writ.

[108] *CRR,* II, 74, Michaelmas 1201. Of course, King John was in Normandy at this time. Later in John's reign, a similar problem faced the justices at Westminster (*ibid.,* VII, 83, Hilary 1214; cited in *Court of King's Bench* I, p. xxiii, n. 4). The abbot of Chertsey produced letters patent granting him the privilege of pleading before the king or the justiciar, and he pointed out that neither of them was present. The justices postponed the case until the king or the justiciar could be consulted. Their advice is unknown, for there is no further reference in the *CRR.*

overruled, he said that he ought not to plead before the itinerant justices because Henry II had granted his house the right of pleading only before the king, and he produced a royal charter as proof. His opponent replied that the charter should not harm him because it made no mention of the liberty of pleading before Henry II's heirs. Furthermore, the abbot had not raised the question of that charter-right until the suit had already begun. The justices agreed with this argument, and they judged that the assize should proceed in spite of the abbot's exceptions.[109] Bracton referred to this suit when he discussed the right of being impleaded before the king or his justiciar in his treatise *De legibus*:

A suit is also necessarily transferred to the great court at the petition of the plaintiff or on account of the tenant's privilege, which the Templars, Hospitalers, and many others have, that they shall not respond to any plea except before the king or his chief justiciar; but if they at any time enter into a plea in spite of this privilege they cannot, repenting of it, withdraw, as in the eyre of the abbot of Reading and Martin of Pattishall in the county of Worcester in the fifth year of King Henry.[110]

John's difficulties in increasing the royal revenue are reflected in his writs of protection for those whose money was in his service. Another writ of protection from his early years reveals his preoccupation with financial matters. Susan de Planez sought to escape from following a plea in the royal courts by bringing the king's writ protecting her from pleas of land.[111] The writ

---

[109] *Rolls for Lincs and Worcs.*, pp. 482–483, no. 980, assizes and pleas at Worcester, 1221. For other examples from the reign of Henry III, see *Rolls for Yorks*, p. 69, no. 167, abbot of Meaux *Rolls for Glos., War. and Staffs*, p. 291, no. 645, prioress and nuns of Nuneaton.

[110] Bracton, IV, 60, f. 332b, cited in *Rolls for Lincs and Worcs.*, pp. 483–484 n. For a similar case, see *CRR*, XI, 499, no. 2520, Michaelmas 1224: "The plea between the prior of Ellerton plaintiff and the abbot of York concerning a division of land between them is sent back to the county by petition of the parties that it should proceed there notwithstanding the charter which the prior has that he not be impleaded elsewhere than *coram domino rege*."

[111] *CRR*, I, 363, Michaelmas 1200, pleas at Westminster; discussed in Flower, *Introduction*, p. 357.

stated that if she had offered a fine to have certain land, if she
was still in the process of paying it, and if she was keeping her
stated terms, then she should have peace from pleas. Since the
exchequer bore witness that she was keeping her terms, the
justices dismissed the proceedings brought against her. Again, in
1203, King John extended his protection to one of his debtors by
an order sent to the justiciar, Geoffrey fitz Peter, from Normandy: "We command you not to permit Robert Bertram, who
is in our debt, to be impleaded of any of his tenements until we
come to England." [112] King John sometimes sought financial gain
from his courts in more direct ways, for the pipe rolls record
offerings of money and horses *pro habendo respectu de placitis.*[113]

A more striking illustration of John's tampering with the
administration of justice for financial reasons is provided by an
assize of darrein presentment against Hamo, treasurer of York
cathedral.[114] He pled that he should not have to defend his right
of presentation without his archbishop, Geoffrey Plantagenet.
Geoffrey was an illegitimate son of Henry II, and he ruthlessly
sought power and wealth despite the handicap of his birth. He
inherited the bad temper of the other Plantagenets, and he
quarreled constantly with his half-brothers, Richard and John,
with his cathedral chapter, and with the people of York. At the
time of this assize, the quarrelsome archbishop had been feuding
with his chapter; and King John had ordered all pleas touching
the chapter postponed until the disagreement was settled, so that
the justices in obedience to royal precept postponed the assize
indefinitely. The chapter of York cathedral had paid handsomely
for the king's protection during their quarrel with Geoffrey.
They had offered him 4000 marks and four palfreys to have his
"peace, protection, and defense" and to have respite from all

---

[112] CRR, I, 252, Trinity 1203. The pipe rolls do not record Robert's debt.

[113] E.g. *Pipe Roll 4 John*, p. 115, 40 marks offered by Alexander de Ruilli;
Pipe Roll 5 John, ed. Doris M. Stenton (Pipe Roll Society, N.S.; London,
1938), p. 73, Henry de Pomeray, 10 marks or two palfreys; p. 214, Burgesses
of York offered 20 marks; *Pipe Roll 9 John*, p. 52, abbot of Westminster gave
a palfrey.

[114] CRR, II, 194, Easter 1203, pleas at Westminster.

pleas concerning their property so long as they were involved in the conflict.[115] Yet this large oblation brought the treasurer only temporary protection, for John later ordered that the assize proceed *juste secundum consuetudinem Anglie* and that it not stand over because of his prohibition, if he had prohibited it in other letters.[116]

The plea rolls for the reign of Henry III reveal a change, for there are no longer entries such as these. Only one can be found, an offering of a falcon for having an assize of mort d'ancestor placed in respite, recorded in Bracton's *Note Book*.[117] Yet one hesitates to cite this change as evidence for a lessening of royal supervision over the work of the courts, since postponements *per preceptum domini regis* or *per preceptum consilii* continue. Unfortunately, the court clerks rarely recorded the reason for the royal order. Where it can be determined that the reason was the king's letters of protection, that protection was extended for customary reasons quite different from King John's orders concerning crown debtors. Henry's letters protected such persons as those on crusade or those who had leave to abide overseas.[118] The practice of the royal courts as it is described in Glanville's treatise was to accept these reasons for absence as competent essoins— the essoin *de esse in peregrinatione* for crusaders and pilgrims and the essoin *de ultra mare* for those outside the kingdom on other business.[119]

Yet many postponements occurred in the reigns of both kings that were not due to writs of protection. The plea rolls record numbers of postponements with the phrase *per preceptum domini regis* as the only explanation.[120] It is likely that litigants who

---

[115] *Pipe Roll 5 John*, Michaelmas 1203, pp. 213–214.

[116] *CRR*, III, 57, Michaelmas 1203, pleas at Westminster.

[117] *Note Book*, II, 435–437, no. 564, Easter 1231.

[118] *Rolls for Glos., War. and Staffs*, pp. 280–282, no. 623, civil pleas at Coventry, 1221; and *CRR*, X, 240, Michaelmas 1221, protection for crusaders. According to *CRR*, XI, 441, no. 2207, Michaelmas 1224, William de Similly had leave to abide in regions across the sea.

[119] Glanville, pp. 16–17, lib. i, cap. 29; p. 14, cap. 25.

[120] E.g. *CRR*, I, 301, 329, 445; II, 184; III, 273; IV, 2, 19, 78, 91, 132; V, 61, 63, 68; VI, 262, for the reign of John. Also, the justiciar ordered postponements, e.g. *ibid.*, I, 338; III, 1, 15, 236; VII, 132.

desired a delay in their case could secure writs commanding that the litigation proceed on a later day, for some of the adjournments bear the comment *per breve domini regis*.[121] One entry recording an adjournment also includes a statement indicating that the justices were familiar with writs commanding postponements; a clerk of the court *coram rege* wrote, "And be it known that a day was not given him by writ but by precept of the king."[122] Of course, the king might instruct his justices to hear a plea on a later date for any number of reasons. Doubtless, some of these postponements were due to letters of protection, and the clerk simply failed to record that fact; or they may have been in reality transfers to another branch of the royal courts, even though recorded as postponements.[123]

Sometimes the names of the principals in an action provide possible motives for the king's instructions. Those concerned were either important royal servants or powerful barons, and the king ordered postponements so that their cases might receive special attention. The rolls of the bench during John's campaign in Normandy record numbers of commands from overseas that pleas be delayed until the king's return to England; among them are pleas involving the countess of Eu, the earl of Hereford, and the bishop of Winchester.[124] Several other cases adjourned by the king's precept involved royal servants, among them William Talbot, who gained notoriety in the chronicles as the knight who

[121] *Ibid.*, I, 329; II, 187; IV, 2, 15; II, 184, by order of the king *de ultra mare;* VII, 132, by writ of the justiciar.

[122] *Pleas before King*, I, 334, no. 3348, essoins before the king, 1201; p. 327, no. 3284, records a similar statement.

[123] E.g. *CRR*, III, 280, Easter 1205, pleas at Westminster, records the adjournment of a plea against the Templars until the Feast of St. Peter in Chains by royal command. An earlier entry, p. 273, reveals a writ ordering all pleas involving them postponed until that date to be heard before the king. It should be remembered that the Templars had the charter privilege of being impleaded only before the king or the justiciar. Similarly, under Henry III a plea was postponed by his command (*ibid.*, XIII, 57, no. 251). An earlier entry, *ibid.*, XI, 477, no. 2385, indicates that it was postponed because one of the parties was in Gascony in the king's service.

[124] *Ibid.*, I, 116, plea between Alice and William de Burgh concerning land at Benham; p. 186, plea of land between Henry de Bohun and the prior of Lanton; p. 179, appeal by Elias Marshal against the bishop's seneschal.

arrested a clerk, weighted him down with a leaden cloak, and starved him to death because he dared to complain of serving an excommunicate king.[125]

On other occasions the power of one of the litigants explains the king's postponement of the case. In the second year of his reign, King John ordered the justices of the bench to postpone a plea of advowson between Alice, countess of Warwick, and Godfrey de Lucy, bishop of Winchester.[126] His instructions were that the case be heard on the octave of St. Martin 1200 (a week after 11 November); it was not heard until Hilary term (January 1201), however, when it came to the court *coram rege*.[127] Both the countess and the bishop were prominent enough for a dispute between them to merit the king's attention; but it was likely because of the countess, wife of Waleran, earl of Warwick, that John took such interest in the case. Following the death of King Richard, the earl marshal, the justiciar, and the archbishop of Canterbury had held a meeting with the great barons to placate them and to ensure John's succession to the throne. Among the barons they met at Northampton was the earl of Warwick, who was annoyed with John because one of his favorites was withholding a portion of his wife's dower.[128] While this presentation was not a part of that question, King John may have felt a particular obligation to oversee suits involving the countess' property.[129]

Instructions to the courts to postpone proceedings did not stop with the death of King John, for the council that ruled in the

---

[125] *Ibid.*, IV, 19, Trinity 1205; for the story of his adventure with the clerk, see Painter, *King John*, pp. 270–272, who accepts the story. Richardson and Sayles, *Governance*, pp. 332–333, reject the story, terming it "pleasant monastic gossip." Other royal servants whose pleas were postponed by the king are Matthew fitz Herbert (*CRR*, I, 301), Geoffrey Luttrel (III, 273), and Robert Mauduit (VI, 320–321).

[126] *CRR*, I, 329, Michaelmas 1200.

[127] *Ibid.*, p. 402; they were given leave to agree.

[128] Painter, *King John*, pp. 12–14.

[129] Similarly, the principals in a plea adjourned by royal command in 1207 were important men: Warin fitz Gerold was a baron and a chamberlain of the exchequer, and William Malet was sheriff of Somerset (*CRR*, V, 63, pleas *coram rege*).

early years of Henry III's reign continued to command postponements. The council's instructions might be phrased as prayers or petitions, but the justices obeyed them just the same.[130] Sometimes these postponements are described in the rolls as *per preceptum domini regis*, although they date from the years before 1227.[131] Some of these postponements were necessary because of the unusual situation that found the king of England a minor. Since the king alone was competent to rule on questions of royal grants or charters, cases in which they were at issue had to be postponed until his majority.[132] However, this fails to explain many of the adjournments ordered by the council. As in the reign of King John, many postponements were requested because of the importance of the persons concerned in the case. Indeed, almost every plea that the council ordered postponed to a later date involved figures of some rank.[133] There could be no court *coram rege* while King Henry III was a minor, and so the only central court was the bench at Westminster. Under John difficult legal questions or politically significant matters could be transferred to the court held in his presence. During the minority the justices at Westminster had to postpone such cases until the council could consider the problem and advise them or, more rarely, until the council could be present to hear the case.

The absence of any court *coram rege* accounts for the council's instructions to the bench for postponements, since most of the cases concerned prominent individuals and touched on royal

[130] E.g. *ibid.*, VIII, 224–225, Hilary 1220, *per petitionem domini regis et consilii sui.*

[131] E.g. *ibid.*, XI, 12, no. 69, Hilary 1223, plea brought by the earl of Salisbury; p. 128, no. 649, Michaelmas 1223, plea between Peter fitz Herbert and the prior of St. Oswald; p. 267, no. 1323, Michaelmas 1223, plea between Joanna, widow of Geoffrey de St. Lodegar, and Earl William Marshal; XII, 115, no. 577, Trinity 1225, plea between John de Montague and William Briwerre.

[132] E.g. *ibid.*, VIII, 236, 259.

[133] E.g. *ibid.*, pp. 40, 295, archbishop of Canterbury; pp. 224–225, Robert de Vipont and the countess of Eu; p. 322, abbot of St. Augustine's, Canterbury; IX, 30, the legate Pandulf; p. 210, archbishop of York; XI, 12, no. 69, earl of Salisbury; p. 218, no. 1076, bishop of Durham and prior of Durham; p. 491, no. 2474, countess of Eu; XII, 174, no. 851, bishop of Ely and abbot of Ramsey; XIII, 137, no. 608, earl of Chester.

rights. As an illustration, in 1220 the justices postponed *per petitionem domini regis et consilii sui* a plea in which the plaintiffs were Robert de Vipont and his wife, who sought the castle and barony of Tickhill from Alice, countess of Eu and widow of Ralph de Lusignan.[134] The council may have taken part in the case because of the prominence of the countess; she was a kinswoman of the earl Warenne and of the justiciar.[135] Or it may have taken part because of Robert's position as a trusted royal servant. He had entered the royal service under Richard, serving him first as a household knight in Normandy; he continued to serve King John, becoming a sheriff and custodian of several castles and other properties, and, in fact, he had been such a firm supporter of John's during the barons' war that he was counted among the king's "evil counsellors"; he served Henry III's regency council too, for it appointed him an itinerant justice in 1218.[136] But the council could have shown interest in the case because it concerned a significant royal grant—King John had given Tickhill to Ralph de Lusignan in an attempt to win his help in Poitou. Robert, however, now claimed it as the right of his wife. The lawsuit was before the royal courts until 1222, when the judges gave a decision in favor of the countess.[137] The fact that Henry III's council intervened to postpone pleas involving royal rights indicates that close supervision of the courts in order to safeguard the interests of the monarch continued after the time of John, but here it was the king's legitimate interests that were to be protected, not such matters as collection of crown debts.

After Henry III came of age, he continued to order postponements of cases. Almost every surviving plea roll contains a few

---

[134] *Ibid.*, VIII, 224–225, Hilary 1220. The plea was postponed until two weeks after Easter, but did not proceed until Michaelmas term (*CRR*, IX, 212–213), and then no decision was reached.

[135] Kate Norgate, *The Minority of Henry III* (London, 1912), p. 137.

[136] *Rolls for York.*, pp. xxiv–xxv; Holt, *Northerners*, pp. 220–221.

[137] Sanders, *Baronies*, p. 147. For another postponement due to a grant, see *CRR*, XIII, 115, no. 577, Trinity 1225. This time the daughter of Llewelyn, prince of Wales, maintained that land was hers because of a grant from the council.

postponements at the king's command. The bench roll for Michaelmas 17–18 Henry III lists seven.[138] Sometimes the reason for the king's writ is easily seen, as in the suit in which he was one of the parties; and sometimes the reason is stated, as in the case involving the earl Warenne, who was in the king's service in Wales. But in other cases it is not so easy to discover a reason for the postponement.

Thus far only instructions ordering postponements in proceedings have been discussed, but the king could command that pleas go forward as well as that they be delayed. Proprietary actions in the royal courts with the innumerable opportunities they offered for essoins were notoriously slow-moving, and sometimes they dragged on for periods that must be measured in years rather than in weeks or months. It is hardly surprising to find oblations offered to King John in order to have pleas expedited.[139] Oblations do not necessarily indicate direct royal intervention in a case, for they could be received by the king's agents without his knowledge. Nevertheless, fines are important evidence of interference by royal officers, if not by the king himself, in the ordinary operations of the courts. Acceptance of a fine to hasten judgment meant that someone would perform a special favor and that the king's treasury would gain by the performance.

---

[138] *CRR*, 113, m. 18, no. 600, plea between the king and the prior of Holy Trinity, Canterbury; m. 19d, no. 649, abbess of St. Sulpice des Landes, Brittany, against Henry fitz Aucher (writ also in *Close Rolls* [1231–1234], p. 281); m. 25, no. 771, Roger de Wimberville against Hugh de Sanford; m. 25, no. 775, novel disseizin brought by Richard de Combe against Earl Warenne and others (also in *Close Rolls* [1231–1234], p. 331); m. 25, no. 802, appeal by men of William Longsword (also in *Close Rolls* [1231–1234], pp. 332–333); m. 30, no. 845, plea between Simon of Preston and Walter Bisit (also in *Close Rolls* [1231–1234], p. 333); m. 33d, no. 907, plea between Earl Warenne and several plaintiffs (also in *Close Rolls* [1231–1234], p. 340).

[139] E.g. *Staffordshire Suits* (Wm. Salt Soc., Vol. III, pt. 1), p. 95; *CRR*, III, 97, 343; IV, 183; VI, 13; *Pipe Roll 5 John*, p. 160; *Pipe Roll 7 John*, ed. Sidney Smith (Pipe Roll Society, N.S.; London, 1941), pp. 90, 190; *Pipe Roll 9 John*, pp. 11, 37; *Pipe Roll 11 John*, p. 49; *Pipe Roll 13 John*, pp. 62, 247; *Pipe Roll 17 John*, ed. R. A. Brown (Pipe Roll Society, N.S.; London, 1964), p. 60.

An example of the necessity for offerings to hasten judgment is a plea of advowson between the abbot of Pipewell and Hamo de Bidun.[140] In the autumn of 1207 the case was postponed until after the feast of St. Martin because King John warranted that Hamo had been with him on the day appointed for him to appear at Westminster. The next reference to the case does not come until a week after Trinity Sunday 1208, when the abbot came before the justices; but Hamo did not come, and he did not send an essoiner. The judges then noted that the plea had originally been scheduled for three weeks after Easter, but that Hamo had essoined himself, and that they had ordered him to appear in Trinity term. After his default in Trinity term, they gave him still another day for appearing, a week after the feast of St. John the Baptist (29 August).[141] Hamo appeared on that date and vouched to warranty Alice Clement, but the abbot objected that she ought not to be heard in court because she was excommunicate. Alice denied the accusation and called upon the ecclesiastical judges who had absolved her to testify that she had been restored to full communion in the Church. At this point, the royal justices could only postpone the case once more and mark it for consultation with the justiciar.[142] A year later, the plea had still not come to a conclusion, for the abbot of Pipewell offered five marks in an effort to speed judgment.[143]

But the slow movement of actions in the royal courts was not the only reason for oblations to have pleas proceed. Sometimes special circumstances arose to cause delays that only a royal command could remedy, as in the case of Walter son of Walter. He had brought a suit against the abbot of Bardney when the abbot resigned his post. Rather than begin proceedings anew against the abbot's successor, he offered King John two palfreys

---

[140] CRR, V, 83, Michaelmas 1207.   [141] Ibid., p. 380, Trinity 1208.

[142] Ibid., p. 293. Alice Clement was an apostate nun, and her questionable status had complicated other pleas before the king's justices; see Flower, Introduction, pp. 107–109.

[143] Pipe Roll 11 John, Michaelmas 1209, p. 20. There is no further reference in the CRR to indicate whether the case ever came to a conclusion or not.

to have his plea proceed in the same state in which it had been when the abbot resigned his abbacy.[144]

On other occasions, the king's intervention was purchased to save a litigant from loss of his case by default. Those who were absent from court on the day given them because of service to the king received his protection without purchase. Writs warranting royal servants' defaults were available as a matter of course from the late twelfth century on, as Glanville's *De legibus* indicates.[145] Statements that one who did not serve his day in court had the king's writ vouching that he had been absent on the king's business occur countless times in the court records of both John and Henry III.[146] As might be expected, King John did not limit his protection of defaulters to those in his service; he was willing to extend it to anyone able to purchase it.

In the autumn of 1204, Ralph de Brewer had essoined himself, and the plea that Gilbert de Ghent brought against him was postponed until the next spring. Then the justices at Westminster judged Ralph in default because he did not come before them two weeks after St. Hilary (13 January); he maintained, however, that the day given was three weeks after St. Hilary. The king then ordered the rolls of the justices searched to learn the truth of the matter, and it was found that one roll recorded the one date and a second the other.[147] King John's concern for Ralph may be explained by an oblation of sixty marks and a horse that he offered to have the king save his default, or it may be explained by the fact that Ralph's opponent was Gilbert de Ghent, for whom John had no great love.[148] Similarly, in 1203 the justices of the bench dismissed an assize utrum when the complainant failed to appear. According to custom, defaults were not allowed in summary actions such as the possessory assizes.

---

[144] *Pipe Roll 5 John*, Michaelmas 1203, p. 6. The case proceeded in Michaelmas term 1204 (*CRR*, III, 181).

[145] Glanville, pp. 5–7, lib. i, capp. 7–8.

[146] E.g. *CRR*, I, 133, 343, 369, 377; III, 178; VII, 215–216; XI, 131, no. 667; p. 135, no. 675; p. 456, no. 2281; p. 577, no. 2875; XIII, 221, no. 1019.

[147] *Ibid.*, III, 334, Easter 1205.

[148] *Pipe Roll 7 John*, Michaelmas 1205, p. 214. On John's and Gilbert's relations, see Holt, *Northerners*, pp. 26–27, 213.

But the king could dispense with this rule, and he later accepted ten marks for allowing the assize to be taken in spite of the earlier default.[149]

King John's instructions that pleas proceed were not always prompted solely by financial motives. Sometimes his commands do seem to spring from a genuine interest in the details of the administration of justice, as two cases indicate. In 1201 he was in Normandy at war with the king of France, and many of the knights of England were there in his feudal host, making adjournment of many pleas necessary. The justices at Westminster had postponed a case because one of the litigants was across the sea in the king's service, but John sent word that this was not true and he ordered the plea to proceed.[150] Again, in 1203 a plea had been postponed because the plaintiff had taken the cross; but apparently he was slow in setting out for the Holy Land, for the king sent a writ commanding the justiciar to hold that plea unless he should set forth on his pilgrimage.[151]

These cases reveal that King John instructed his justices to proceed with pleas a number of times, often in response to oblations. King Henry III and his council issued no such commands, apart from the traditional orders protecting royal servants from defaults, nor do the available financial records of Henry's early years record fines offered to hasten judgment. Although no definite statement can be made solely on the basis of the published pipe rolls and fine rolls, the fines that are listed in them would indicate that far fewer were offered for favors in the courts. Most of them are the normal oblations of one-half mark or one mark that may be regarded as court fees. There can be little doubt, then, that John encouraged the offering of fines to gain special advantage in his courts, while his successor did not do so. Of course, chapter 40 of Magna Carta was a warning to the young king and his advisers.

[149] CRR, III, 40, Michaelmas 1203; Pipe Roll 7 John, Michaelmas 1205, pp. 179–180. Assize brought by Master Matthew the Doctor. However, there is no further reference to Matthew in the CRR.

[150] CRR, II, 3, Michaelmas 1201; similarly I, 277, Michaelmas 1200.

[151] Ibid., III, 32, Michaelmas 1203.

The king could not possibly have given his attention to each process that was speeded or delayed at his command. Even though it is likely that this steady stream of commands to the justices was the work of royal clerks, the commands still indicate some royal control over the common law courts. The king may not have given individual commands concerning many cases, but he did give general instructions, which the royal clerks carried out. King John must have been responsible for the *breve commune* protecting those in his service on the Continent. These instructions indicate the king's willingness to relax the rigidity of the law, as John and Henry III gave writs of protection to their friends and servants to escape the rigid law of essoins. They indicate little interference with the courts' work that could be criticized, except John's extension of his search for revenues to the courts.

TRANSFERS OF PLEAS AT THE KING'S COMMAND

In addition to ordering cases heard at another time, the king could order them heard in another court. Theoretically, all the king's subjects had the right of appeal to him, and he could evoke any case into his court for judgment.[152] Writs equivalent to the praecipe, for the removal of suits from courts of private jurisdiction to the royal courts, and the pone, for transferring suits from county courts to Westminster, could be purchased from the chancery as early as the time of Richard I. These writs became writs *de cursu* by the time of King John.[153]

The monarch's transfers of proceedings from one branch of the *curia regis* to another are of greater interest here. All three branches—the itinerant justices, the justices of the bench at Westminster, and the justices *coram rege*—were equally the king's court, and cases could be moved freely from one court to

---

[152] Glanville, writing of the writ praecipe, spoke of cases that "ought to be, or the king is willing that it should be, tried in the king's court" (p. 5, lib. i, cap. 5).

[153] Lady Stenton in *Pipe Roll 6 John,* p. xxiii.

another. The pipe rolls record payments *pro habendo loquela coram rege, coram justitiariis de banco, coram justitiariis itinerantibus.* Many of these cases were private pleas, and neither the pipe roll entry of the fine nor the entry on the plea roll gives any reason for the transfer. Sometimes this shifting from one court to another was simply for the convenience of the persons involved. Other times, particularly in transfers from the bench at Westminster to the court following the king, the entry recording the removal adds such phrases as *per preceptum domini regis, per breve domini regis,* or *dominus rex vult.*[154]

The reasons for the king's desire to have these suits heard in his own court are clear in some cases, in others not so evident. The boundaries between the court *coram rege,* the bench, and the justices on eyre had not yet been clearly marked. Sometimes the entry states that the plea was transferred to the king's court because he wished to hear it.[155] Certainly a dispute between the citizens of London and the bishop of Winchester was a matter worthy of King John's interest, just as a question concerning the liberties of the citizens of Lincoln and the burgesses of Grimsby merited Henry III's attention. In the words of Henry's clerk who recorded the plea, it was postponed *quia negocium tangit dominum regem.*[156] This maxim that pleas touching the king should be heard before him was well known to the justices. King John's wish to see a duel was not due to "his wanton cruelty," for the criminal action that resulted in the combat had been a difficult case involving the accused's charge that the appeal had been

---

[154] E.g. *CRR,* I, 289, 293, 336, 337, 338, no reason is stated; pp. 186, 208, 268, 269–270, transferred by the king's command; *Lincs Assize Roll,* p. 217, no. 1220, postponement until it can be *coram rege* by the king's writ from across the sea.

[155] E.g. *CRR,* I, 277, case between the citizens of London and Godfrey de Lucy, bishop of Winchester; pp. 278–279, duels between Richard de Launcelles and Hugh de Stoddon and between William de Brunesland and Richard de Dunham; p. 370, assize of mort d'ancestor between Robert de Friebois and Warin de Vesci, his wife, and Richard de Frisemarais; II, 114, plea between the men of William de Warenne, earl of Surrey, and the men of Hugh de Fokinton; IV, 118, plea of land between Henry de Weston and Robert Marshal.

[156] *Ibid.,* XIV, 207, Michaelmas 1230.

made *de odio et atia,* through hate and malice.[157] King John might have wished to hear a plea concerning the earl of Salisbury even if it had not touched the important question of the maintenance of dikes in the Ouse valley,[158] and Henry III had good reason for commanding that a suit involving persons as important as Simon de Montfort and Margaret, countess of Winchester, stand over until it could come before him.[159]

But not all transfers of common pleas to the court *coram rege* are so easily explained.[160] Certainly King John encouraged the offering of fines for such transfers. Other common pleas heard before the king were those involving his officers. Royal servants often secured the privilege of having their pleas heard in the court *coram rege.* Sometimes this was granted through general letters of protection or charters of privileges, like those given to religious houses; but at other times the king issued commands that cases begun in one court be concluded before his own justices. In the summer of 1200, for example, letters close arrived from the king in Poitou protecting Godfrey de Lucy, bishop of Winchester, from being impleaded of any of his lands while the king was outside the realm.[161] The bishop of Winchester headed one of the most powerful ecclesiastical baronies in England; but Godfrey often acted as a royal judge, and he was serving as an itinerant justice in 1200.[162] The justices exceeded the king's instructions in carrying out his command, for they extended the protection to the bishop's servants and applied it to criminal

[157] Origin of the case, *ibid.,* I, 255–256; discussed in Flower, *Introduction,* pp. 314–315. A. L. Poole found in John's postponements of duels evidence of his cruelty: "This side of his character is also exhibited in his morbid delight in witnessing those bloody spectacles which in a superstitious age were regarded as manifesting the judgment of God" (*From Domesday Book to Magna Carta 1087–1216* [*Oxford History of England,* Vol. III, 2d ed.; Oxford, 1955], p. 427). But two such postponements in John's entire reign are fairly strong evidence of his blood-thirstiness.

[158] Flower, *Introduction,* p. 21.

[159] *CRR,* XIV, 426, no. 1974, Michaelmas 1232; the king's writ to the justices is recorded in *Close Rolls* (1231–1234), p. 122, with the attestation *Teste Rege.*

[160] See Chapter 1, pp. 36–55.   [161] *CRR,* I, 172.

[162] Foss, *Judges,* p. 417.

actions. Shortly after receipt of the king's letter, they postponed an appeal brought against the seneschal of Godfrey until King John's return to England.[163]

Perhaps more significant because it involves a minor royal servant is a plea concerning a church and land at Chesterton from the year 1203, during John's absence in Normandy, against a clerk in the king's service. The king's writ, dated at Rouen on 12 June 1203, commanded that the recognition brought by Samson son of William against "our beloved clerk Master Reginald of Paris" be adjourned until the king's return to England, "because we do not wish it heard except before us." [164] This instruction resulted in an awkward situation for the royal deputies in England, since Samson had offered ten marks to have the recognition. The pipe roll duly recorded his debt, although a statement added, "But it ought not to be summoned because it was forbidden by the king's writ which is in the marshal's file." [165] Samson was unwilling to wait until the king's coming to England, for he raised his oblation to fifteen marks. The entry of his fine on the pipe roll states that the jury had been dismissed "because Reginald gave the king ten marks that it should stand over, which ten marks he paid into the king's chamber in Normandy." [166] This statement is revealing: first, it shows that there was a price for protection from pleas even for royal servants; second, it indicates that King John's clerk Master Reginald was one of the clerks accompanying him in Normandy. Samson's second oblation was no more successful than the first, however, for Master Reginald informed King John that he held the land in question at the gift of King Richard and that the king should warrant it to him.[167] Apparently Reginald was correct, for the

---

[163] CRR, I, 179, Trinity 1200. Similar is a case concerning a clerk of the bishop of Norwich, postponed by the king's command because the bishop was abroad on his service (CRR, I, 401, Hilary 1201).

[164] Rot. de lib. ac de mis., p. 41; also CRR, II, 140, Hilary 1203. This case is discussed by Lady Stenton, Pipe Roll 5 John, 1203, pp. xviii–xix. The royal writs recorded in both the CRR and the Rot. de lib. ac de mis. refer to Master Reginald as "our clerk."

[165] Pipe Roll 5 John, Michaelmas 1203, pp. 5–6.   [166] Ibid., p. 6.

[167] Rot. de lib. ac de mis., p. 42.

charter rolls of King John record the grant of a church and two and a half hides of land at Chesterton to an "R. of Paris." [168]

Cases could move at the king's command in other directions, too. If it proved more convenient, the king could order pleas in the court *coram rege* moved to Westminster, as illustrated by two cases from the time of King John. He once sent a writ to the justices of the bench notifying them that the two principals in a plea of land had come before him, but "because we did not have the writ or record of that plea, we gave them a day before you in three weeks from Easter day at London." [169] Earlier the justiciar had removed to Westminster a plea involving the abbot of Walden originally scheduled to come *coram rege* "on account of other pleas which the abbot has before the lord king." [170] Transfers of proceedings from the justices at Westminster to the justices on eyre were not uncommon, for when itinerant justices were sent to a county, the practice was to adjourn the cases at Westminster pertaining to that county for hearing before them. Besides these normal transfers, the pipe rolls occasionally record oblations to have pleas sent from Westminster to the eyres, and the plea rolls reveal the king's and the justiciar's instructions for such transfers. [171] Many of these instructions must have been writs issued in the king's name and sealed with the royal seal without his knowledge; when the orders came from the king across the sea, however, it meant that the purchaser had gone to considerable trouble and expense, so that the writs were less likely to be routine writs issued for the king by members of his entourage. During King John's absence on the Continent in 1203, Geoffrey fitz Peter informed the justices of the bench that the king by his writ *de ultra mare* ordered them to put in respite an appeal of robbery so that the justices on eyre could hear it at Cambridge. [172]

Transfers from the bench to the eyres continued under Henry

[168] *Rotuli chartarum in turri Londinensi asservati,* ed. T. Duffus Hardy (Record Commission; London, 1837), p. 20a, dated 5 John.

[169] *CRR,* IV, 132, Easter 1206.   [170] *Ibid.,* III, 222, Michaelmas 1204.

[171] E.g. *Pipe Roll 1 John,* 1199, pp. 16, 127, 177; *Pipe Roll 3 John,* 1201, p. 19; *CRR,* III, 174.

[172] *CRR,* II, 280, Trinity 1203.

III. In 1228 four knights came to Westminster to choose jurors for a grand assize, and the king commanded that the jurors be given a day before the itinerant justices at Norwich.[173] Later in his reign, an action brought before the bench by the king to recover custody of a minor was adjourned for hearing before the justices *ad omnia placita*.[174] In these cases either the convenience of the litigants or of the judges must have been the determining factor. Having the case heard in the county was a convenience for the litigants, saving them the expense of traveling to Westminster or sending an attorney there. Most likely, they offered fines for this favor.

More frequent than removals of pleas from the bench to the eyres were transfers in the opposite direction. While the itinerant justices formed a branch of the *curia regis* just as did the justices of the bench at Westminster and the judges following the king, in practice they were inferior to them. They received instructions to reserve all difficult questions for the king's consideration, and they adjourned cases beyond their competence to Westminster. However, sometimes the decision to remove pleas to Westminster came not from the justices but from the king, the justiciar, or the council. The justices at Northampton in September 1202 received commands from the justiciar, in the king's absence, to adjourn four cases for hearing at Westminster.[175] A number of these transfers were necessary because one of the litigants enjoyed the privilege of being impleaded only in the king's or the justiciar's presence.[176] Other times the promi-

---

[173] *Ibid.*, XIII, 144, no. 638, Easter 1228. Later an assize of novel disseizin came *coram rege*, but was adjourned until the coming of the itinerant justices because "the writ arrived late, and no summons was made, and the jurors say that they made no view" (*Note Book*, III, 208, no. 1192, pleas of 1236–1237).

[174] *CRR*, XIV, 449, no. 2105, Michaelmas 1232.

[175] *Northants. Assize Roll*, no. 321, plea of wardship between Robert Mauduit and Thomas fitz Eustace; no. 501, suit between Henry Hubold and the abbot of Bordsley; no. 527, appeal against William de Caldecot; no. 532, grand assize between Henry Dawney of Maidford and Henry Dawney of Cornwall.

[176] E.g. cases involving the Templars were transferred for this reason (*Lincs Assize Roll*, nos. 110, 243. In other cases no explanation was offered; but since

nence of the persons concerned may have led the king to order the pleas transferred to Westminster, where he could exercise closer supervision. For example, in 1202 the justiciar commanded that a plea involving Robert Mauduit, a chamberlain of the exchequer, be removed to Westminster; and in 1221 a command in the name of Henry III ordered an assize against Fawkes de Breauté, a strong military supporter of the royal party in the rebellion, taken at Westminster.[177] Of course, any questions of special interest to the king would be heard wherever was most convenient to him. An illustration of this is a writ of Henry III ordering the justices taking the assizes at Warwick in 1222 to adjourn an assize of darrein presentment brought by the king until it could be heard at Westminster.[178] Since Henry was under age at the time, the writ was issued in his name by the council or the justiciar, if not by some lesser royal officer.

This survey of adjournments from one branch of the *curia regis* for hearing before another branch shows the flexibility of their operations, but it also indicates that they could be bent to the king's will in their operations. King John encouraged his subjects to seek to have their suits heard in the court following him, partly because of the added revenues from fines. Both John and his son commanded some pleas heard *coram rege* because of their interest in them, either because of the prominence of the persons concerned or because of the importance of the questions raised. Any plea touching the king would be heard wherever he wished it heard. The rulers had some other suits removed to different courts for reasons difficult to know, apparently for the convenience of friends or favorites in some instances, in return

---

religious houses were involved, it is likely that such a charter right was the reason, e.g. *Northants. Assize Roll*, p. 71, no. 501, abbot of Bordsley; p. 151, no. 874, abbot of Ramsey; and *Rolls for Lincs and Worcs.*, p. 2, no. 3, prior of Shelford.

[177] E.g. *Northants. Assize Roll*, pp. 38–39, no. 321; *Rolls for Glos., War. and Staffs*, p. 455, no. 1027. Later, Henry ordered postponement and transfer of an appeal of robbery against Engeram Painel because he was away in Wales on royal business (*Close Roll* [1227–1231], p. 530, 17 July 1231, *Teste Rege*).

[178] *Rolls for Glos., War. and Staffs*, p. 593, no. 1415.

for fines in others. No serious fault can be found with this practice, unless it is argued that the taking of fines meant favored treatment for the rich, but fines in return for favors were simply one of the facts of life in the Middle Ages. In general, the result was to make access to the king's courts easier for his subjects.

3

Customary Procedure
and the King's Will

One of the basic tenets held by medieval political thinkers was
the supremacy of law, and in their writings rule by law was often
contrasted with rule by arbitrary will. Of course, the views of
John of Salisbury on the prince's duty to obey the law are well
known today, but they were widely known in his own day too. A
lawyer in early thirteenth-century London, collecting the laws of
England, contrasted law and will in words he may well have
taken from John of Salisbury: *Lex est semper quod jus facit;
voluntas vero et violentia et vis non est jus.*[1] In the mid-thirteenth century, Bracton still held this opinion, writing in his
treatise, "For there is no king where will rules and not law."[2]
Indeed, the picture of King John that the chroniclers painted
was that of a tyrant; in their words, he did not rule as a true
prince in accord with the law, but rather his only law was his
despotic will.[3]

Along with these teachings of the prince's submission to the
law, there existed the notion that he ruled rightfully by his will
alone, a notion supported by theories of theocratic kingship and
legal doctrines of the Roman emperors' sovereignty. In the

---

[1] *Die Gesetze der Angelsachsen,* ed. Felix Liebermann (3 vols.; Halle,
1903–1916), I, 635–636, rule 6.

[2] Bracton, II, 33, ff. 5b and 6.

[3] E.g. Matthew Paris, *Chronica Majora,* ed. H. R. Luard (Rolls Series;
London, 1872–1882), II, 562; *Annales Monastici,* ed. H. R. Luard (Rolls
Series; London, 1864–1869), II, 282; Ralph of Coggeshall, *Chronicon Angli-
canum,* ed. J. Stevenson (Rolls Series; London, 1875), p. 170.

twelfth century, Richard fitz Neal defended the old theocratic doctrine that the king was accountable only to God in his *Dialogus de scaccario*.[4] And the prologue to Glanville's treatise cities another basis for unlimited royal power, the Roman law maxim *quod principi placet legis habet vigorem*.[5] Both John of Salisbury and Bracton were aware of these teachings, but their interpretations of them did not add to the prince's unlimited power. On the contrary, in their views, this lofty conception of kingship added new obligations and limitations.[6]

Certainly the Angevin monarchs ruled to a large extent according to their own wills, whether or not political thinkers gave them that right. They were so capable of autocratic actions exceeding the bounds of feudal tradition that *ira* or *malevolentia regis* became a familiar hazard to their subjects.[7] Given the medieval theory of monarchy and the practice of the Angevin kings, it becomes important to examine the plea rolls to determine whether their administration of justice was that of a true king or of a tyrant. From time to time they did give their justices instructions concerning the conduct of cases before them. By the time of King John, the system of assizes and writs described in Glanville's treatise had existed long enough to be regarded as the custom of the realm.[8] Did John, Henry III, and his council respect the practice of the common law courts in their instructions, or did they arbitrarily command innovations and exceptions contrary to custom?

From time to time, King John in his instructions to his justices added the command that they should proceed *secundum legem et consuetudinem Anglie* in a case that was before them. No doubt this and similar phrases were sometimes added to the

---

[4] Pages 1–3.

[5] Glanville, p. 2. See. C. H. McIlwain, *Constitutionalism: Ancient and Modern* (rev. ed.; Ithaca, N.Y., 1958), pp. 64–65.

[6] On their interpretations of Roman law doctrines of kingship, see Fritz Schulz, "Bracton on Kingship," *E.H.R.* LX (1945), 136–176. See also McIlwain, *Constitutionalism*, pp. 70–72, on Bracton's interpretation.

[7] J. E. A. Jolliffe, *Angevin Kingship* (London, 1955), chap. 4.

[8] J. E. A. Jolliffe, *A Constitutional History of Medieval England from the English Settlement to 1485* (3d ed.; London, 1954), pp. 225–226.

king's writs simply as a matter of form, a literary flourish on the part of the chancery clerks. An illustration of this is a postponement by the justices at Westminster of an action because one of the parties was on the king's service; this prompted letters from King John informing them that this was not so and commanding them to proceed *secundum consuetudinem Anglie.*[9] Yet the sample writs collected in Glanville do not contain these phrases, and it is unlikely that they always represent formulae followed by the royal clerks. Doris M. Stenton has suggested that in these commands "King John can be heard voicing his respect for the customs of the land and insisting on the observance of the law."[10] But fines offered by suitors in the royal courts to have their pleas proceed according to custom cast doubt upon this interpretation.[11] The very fact that John sometimes found it necessary to issue such instructions suggests that at other times he ordered his judges to conduct cases in ways contrary to custom. An examination of the circumstances surrounding pleas that King John ordered to proceed *secundum consuetudinem* should reveal something of his attitude toward the law of the land.

Several times King John in his instructions to the justices contrasted the custom of the realm with royal commands, and he sometimes insisted that his commands take precedence over custom. Some of his writs ordering assizes to go forward add the injunction that they proceed "justly and without delay unless it

[9] *CRR*, I, 277, Michaelmas 1200. Similarly a writ ordering a grand assize to proceed adds, "unless reason and the custom of our kingdom should impede" (II, 223, Easter 1203).

[10] Doris M. Stenton, "King John and the Courts of Justice," *Proc. Br. Ac.*, XLIV (1958), 104. She marshals in support of this statement a number of cases from the CRR. Some of them, however, do not bear out her contention. For example, she cites an order that the justiciar "without delay and according to the custom of England" should cause a final concord to be observed (*CRR*, II, 202, Easter 1203); an earlier entry shows that this command originally came from King Richard, not King John (I, 82–83, Hilary 1199).

[11] E.g. *Pipe Roll 2 John*, ed. Doris M. Stenton (Pipe Roll Society, N.S.; London, 1934), p. 99; *Pipe Roll 3 John*, ed. Doris M. Stenton (Pipe Roll Society, N.S.; London, 1936), p. 222; *Pipe Roll 5 John*, ed. Doris M. Stenton (Pipe Roll Society, N.S.; London, 1938), p. 212. For the fine offered by William de Mowbray, see below, Chapter 4, p. 160.

should be forbidden by special precept of the lord king." [12] On other occasions, the king ordered that custom take precedence over his commands. In still other cases, the king issued two conflicting commands, as an action brought by Robert fitz Walter and his wife against the abbot of St. Albans illustrates.[13] Robert's wife claimed the wood of Northaw, Hertfordshire, from the abbot as part of her inheritance. The abbot sought to have the plea dismissed by producing a royal writ protecting him from pleas until King John's return to the kingdom; he had made fine with the king for 310 marks for this and other privileges.[14] But Robert fitz Walter produced another writ directing that the case proceed according to the custom and law of England notwithstanding any writ the abbot might offer. The justices could only adjourn the case until they heard the king's will. Evidently the second writ prevailed, for the case proceeded at the next term of the bench, where it was settled by a final concord.[15] Two contradictory writs also presented a problem in the case of Hamo, treasurer of York, when the king first ordered the action adjourned and later commanded it to proceed according to custom.[16]

A similar problem arose during the minority of Henry III. In this case, permission for procedure contrary to custom came not from the king or the justiciar, but from the papal legate Pandulf, who was playing an important role in the government during the minority. The tenant in the case brought a writ of prohibition to

[12] *Pleas before King*, II, 227, no. 759, Michaelmas 1202, assize of darrein presentment between Bartholomew of Brandon Parva and his brother; cited by J. C. Holt, "The Barons and the Great Charter," *E.H.R.*, LXX (1955), 6. Also *CRR*, III, 215, Michaelmas 1204, assize of darrein presentment between Walter de Sherbourne and Alan fitz Peter.

[13] *CRR*, I, 178, Trinity 1200; p. 291, Michaelmas 1200, pleas at Westminster. Discussed in Flower, *Introduction*, p. 343, and in Charles Johnson, "Notes on Thirteenth-Century Judicial Procedure," *E.H.R.*, LXII (1947), 513.

[14] *Pipe Roll 2 John*, Michaelmas 1200, p. 47.

[15] *Ibid.*, p. 51, where the terms of the final concord are recorded.

[16] See above, pp. 84–85. An additional example is a writ of John to Geoffrey fitz Peter in which he ordered that Geoffrey do nothing against the custom of the kingdom because of any command sent earlier in regard to the case of Geoffrey de Bosco (*CRR*, III, 27–28, Michaelmas 1203).

court Christian against the plaintiff. The plaintiff declared that he had letters from the papal legate allowing him to proceed in the ecclesiastical courts in spite of the writ.[17] The justices postponed the case until it could be shown to the legate and the council. When the matter came to Pandulf's attention, he stated that he wished royal rights to be preserved, and the action went forward in the royal court as an assize utrum. J. C. Holt is not exaggerating when he says of these cases of contradictory commands, "Confusion could run little deeper." [18]

Other instructions of the king were not the result of his earlier orders contrary to custom, but were really due to a wish that customary procedure be followed. In 1201, Gilbert de Rye appealed Adam de St. Quintin of the death of his brother, and Adam sent an attorney in his place, claiming that he was his nephew.[19] The custom of England was that in criminal actions only kinsmen could appear as attorneys.[20] The king ordered the sheriff to hold an inquiry to determine whether Adam's attorney was his nephew or a near enough kinsman to defend him "by right and according to the custom of England." The jurors found no relationship between Adam and his attorney. The king was not entirely motivated in his action by a desire to see lawful procedure prevail, for Gilbert's father had offered ten marks to have the inquiry.[21]

King John took care that his courts should follow the custom of England in the limitation of minors' legal powers, for several of his writs forbade his justices to hear pleas of land touching minors until they reached an age when they could plead lawfully.[22] One of these writs was challenged by Hubert Walter,

---

[17] CRR, IX, 118–119, Trinity 1220. Another case involved the legate's order that a plea go forward in the church courts. Two ecclesiastical judges, questioned why they proceeded with a plea concerning right of advowson in spite of the king's prohibition, replied that they had letters of the legate that they could safely proceed (Note Book, Vol. III, no. 1388, Trinity 1220).

[18] Magna Carta (Cambridge, 1965), p. 88.

[19] CRR, I, 428–429, Easter 1201, pleas coram rege.

[20] Flower, Introduction, p. 404, where he discusses the case.

[21] Pipe Roll 2 John, Michaelmas 1200, pp. 184–185.

[22] CRR, I, 467, Easter 1201; II, 223, Easter 1203, order of the justiciar; and III, 64, Michaelmas 1203.

archbishop of Canterbury. The justices of the bench received the king's writ prohibiting Ralph de Clere from bringing an action against three brothers to recover some lands. John commanded that the case be postponed until he was of an age to bring an action according to custom, but "the lord archbishop, in whose custody Ralph is, says that it is not against the custom of the kingdom for the suit to proceed." [23] The archbishop had a great reputation for his knowledge of the law—he may have written the treatise usually attributed to Glanville—and he had wide experience in government, having served as Richard's justiciar and as John's chancellor.[24] Confusion was possible, for the law was uncertain about pleas touching minors. Glanville states that minors may bring the assize of mort d'ancestor, but assizes brought against minors should be postponed until they come of age.[25] Earlier, in the reign of Richard I, the justices had ruled that "minority is no ground for postponement, where the minor holds other than by right of inheritance." [26] In this case, the justices were unwilling to disregard the royal writ, and they gave Ralph and the three brothers a day before the court *coram rege*.[27]

Later, in 1205, the king ordered the justices at Westminster to

---

[23] *Ibid.*, I, 279, Michaelmas 1200. The case is discussed in Flower, *Introduction*, pp. 256–257; *Memoranda Roll 1 John* ed. H. G. Richardson (Pipe Roll Society; London, 1943), p. lxxxix; and Stenton, *Pleas before King*, I, 104.

[24] On Hubert Walter's authorship of the treatise, see Pollock and Maitland, I, 164. On his learning in the law, see *Historical Works of Gervase of Canterbury*, ed. William Stubbs (Rolls Series; London, 1879–1880), II, 406; and Roger of Howdon, *Chronica*, ed. William Stubbs (Rolls Series; London, 1868–1871), IV, 12. R. W. Southern, however, indicates that Hubert Walter was not likely to have been the author ("A Note on the Text of 'Glanville,'" *E.H.R.* LXV [1950], 81–89). Doris M. Stenton at one time accepted Ranulf de Glanville as the "most probable" author (*The Cambridge Medieval History*, Vol. V [Cambridge, 1929], chap. 17, "England: Henry II," pp. 578–579), but more recently she has suggested Geoffrey fitz Peter as the author (*Pleas before King*, I, 9). The latest editor of the treatise maintains that the author was not so significant a figure, "a royal clerk, not necessarily a judge but certainly attending the royal court" (Glanville, p. xxxiii).

[25] Glanville, p. 156, lib. xiii, capp. 12–13; Pollock and Maitland, II, 440–443.

[26] *CRR*, I, 108, Hilary 1199.

[27] The case proceeded there (*ibid.*, I, 378, Hilary 1201).

allow Roger de Butemont to represent his wife Petronilla as her attorney. Her opponent objected that since she was a minor she could not appoint an attorney, and he offered the king forty shillings to have her come before the justices to determine her age.[28] A wife who was also a minor was indeed a complication, for the law held that a minor could not have an attorney, yet it held that a wife could choose her husband to represent her.[29] Evidently King John reconsidered his original order, for a later entry records the dismissal of Petronilla's plea because she was under age.[30] Curiously, this entry refers to her, not as Roger's wife, but as his *amica,* lover or mistress.

In other instances King John's commands that a plea proceed according to custom simply meant that he was denying a request for some extraordinary proceeding. William the Falconer brought an action against Roger Bigod, earl of Norfolk, before the justices at Westminster. When the earl heard the names of the recognitors, he said that the assize ought not to be taken by them because they were all suitors (*sectarii*) of William de Albini, earl of Arundel, whose man William was.[31] His complaint that they were biased did not move King John, for he ordered the justices to take the assize *secundum legem et consuetudinem Anglie.* Both Roger Bigod and William de Albini were among the great barons of England, but in this case John obviously favored Albini. Perhaps it is worth noting that later during the barons' war the earl of Arundel would remain loyal to the king until 1216, while the earl of Norfolk joined the rebels even before Magna Carta.[32]

One of the parties in a plea of land received a similar rebuff from King John in 1212, when Robert fitz Amaury sought to gain half a knight's fee from Simon de Kyme.[33] When Simon's first line of defense failed, he brought a charter of Henry II and wished that the king would warrant it, offering him thirty marks.

[28] *Ibid.,* IV, 55, Michaelmas 1205.
[29] Pollock and Maitland, II, 408, 440.
[30] *CRR,* IV, 245, Michaelmas 1206.   [31] *Ibid.,* V, 33–34, Hilary 1207.
[32] Painter, *King John,* pp. 20–21, 287, 297.
[33] *CRR,* VI, 279–280, Easter 1212, pleas *coram rege;* discussed in Flower, *Introduction,* p. 487.

Robert then claimed to hold the land of the king, and he offered twenty marks to have the action go forward *secundum consuetudinem regni*. King John accepted the smaller oblation, and Simon had to place himself on the grand assize, a lengthy proceeding. The king may have accepted Robert's fine because he truly wished custom to prevail, but it is doubtful that Simon de Kyme could have viewed it in that light. A prominent Lincolnshire baron and an experienced royal administrator, he can only have interpreted the king's refusal to warrant his charter as an affront, perhaps connected with his heavy indebtedness to the Jews. It is not surprising that he joined other northern barons in their revolt against King John.[34]

So far all examples of royal instructions for customary procedure have come from the reign of King John. The expression *secundum consuetudinem regni* occurs much less frequently in the plea rolls of Henry III. Yet the young king did use the phrase in a writ he addressed to the justices of the bench in April 1230 just before he sailed to the Continent. He commanded them to conduct a suit between the earl of Chester and the monks of Notre Dame (or St. Marie) de Pré in Normandy over an English manor *secundum legem et consuetudinem regni*.[35] The writ itself explains the reason for the king's instructions: he wished the justices to proceed with the plea even though his warranty of the land in question had been sought and an opportunity for postponement offered. This suit had first come into court in Hilary term 1228; but judgment had been held up several times, once because the prior had brought royal charters and confirmations and had stated that the king "ought to warrant him if he dared to vouch the king to warranty as any other man."[36] Henry's command, then, is simply an attempt to end these delays.

---

[34] On Simon's career, see Holt, *Northerners*, pp. 45, 59, 168.

[35] *Close Roll* (1227–1231), p. 394, dated 30 April 1230, at Portsmouth, *Teste me ipso;* also in *CRR*, XIV, 537–538, no. 2478.

[36] Origin of the case, *CRR*, XIII, 97–98, no. 418, Hilary 1228 (also *Note Book*, II, 224, no. 272); an adjournment, *CRR*, XIII, 137, no. 608, Easter 1228; king's warranty sought, pp. 585–586, no. 2769, Hilary 1230 (also *Note Book*, II, 321–324, no. 393).

In spite of the reduced number of commands, from what is known of the attitude of the young king and his council toward justice, they can hardly have been less anxious than John that the custom of the realm should prevail. Perhaps the recurrence of this phrase in the rolls of King John is explained by his consciousness that in many of his actions he went beyond customary procedure in order to further his own ends. The king and his advisers may have felt that by presenting these practices as customary, they could "place royal actions within the letter of the law." [37] Whatever the meaning of John's instructions that his justices follow custom, they are no evidence for any deep respect for the law and custom of the realm of his part.

Since this was King John's attitude toward custom, the question arises as to how far he veered from the customary procedure of the royal courts in his instructions to his judges. Despite the sharp contrast between law and will that characterized political thought at this time, there was a realization that appeals to the royal will were sometimes necessary. The customary law of the Middle Ages in many ways was inflexible and inadequate to cope with new situations, and the courts faced many problems for which traditional law offered no guidance. The justices of the common law courts were bound to follow the custom of England, however rigid it might be, but the king as the judge ordinary of the kingdom could modify the law or make exceptions in its application. The king had a positive role in ruling on difficult questions, in redressing grievances where regular process was not available, and generally mitigating the harshness and rigidity of the law.[38]

Suitors in the royal courts recognized this role and sometimes appealed to his will. In 1242 the royal judges dismissed a suit on the grounds that a grant was contrary to the common law and

[37] Holt, "Barons and the Great Charter," p. 8. See also his *Northerners*, chap. 10, for an account of how John maintained that many of his arbitrary administrative actions were in keeping with custom.

[38] See Chapter 4, pp. 127–141, on cases about which the justices found it necessary to consult the king; Chapter 6, pp. 185–195, on the king's equitable justice when regular process proved inadequate; and Chapter 8, pp. 238–251, on proceedings against the crown, where regular procedures did not apply.

that the king had no wish to change the law of the realm. The plaintiff then petitioned the king to allow the action to proceed, "since the lord king himself is above all law." [39] The plea rolls of John and Henry III offer a number of cases in which unusual circumstances required action that normal and customary procedures could not supply. An examination of these cases will reveal to what extent the king did instruct his justices in the conduct of proceedings coming before them, and to what extent his instructions modified or contravened existing procedures in the royal courts. The king's commands dispensing with custom may be grouped into categories: first, special proceedings when none of the possessory actions was appropriate; second, orders contrary to the rules governing persons' eligibility to plead; third, commands overruling ordinary rules of law; and last, special types of juries allowed to take assizes.

The forms of action from which litigants in the royal courts could choose were limited, and they did not cover every possible situation, but the king could supply new ones if needed. In cases where normal procedures did not fit their needs, the king's subjects could ask him to "do his will." In the second year of King John's reign, Earl Patrick of Dunbar, a Scottish lord, sought to recover lands from the abbot of St. Albans and from the prior of Tynmouth. A jury came to the court *coram rege* to recognize whether Edgar, uncle of Patrick's father Earl Waltheof, who had died in 1182, had been disseized of the lands during the war between Henry II and the young King Henry.[40] The abbot and the prior objected that the jury was *contra assisam regni* because Edgar's son was living, and no one else had any right to claim those lands. If this were true, an assize of mort d'ancestor did not lie, for it must be brought by a close relative—son or daughter, brother or sister, nephew or niece—and could not be brought by a more distant kinsman, even if he were the next heir.[41] But this was not a regular assize. Earl Patrick replied to them that he sought that the recognition be made by the king's precept, and

[39] Cited in Bertie Wilkinson, *The Constitutional History of Medieval England 1216–1399* (London, 1948–1958), III, 154 and n. 11.
[40] *CRR*, I, 439, Easter 1201.   [41] Pollock and Maitland, II, 57.

the pipe roll shows that he had paid the king forty marks and four palfreys for this extraordinary proceeding.[42] The justices gave the parties a day at Westminster, but their judgment does not survive.

Also in 1201, Aubrey de Vere, earl of Oxford, had a complaint that none of the possessory assizes was tailored to fit. A jury of recognition came before the justices of the bench to determine whether his father had been seized of a certain manor held of the abbot of Westminster at the time when King Henry II disseized the abbot *per voluntatem*.[43] The jury was also to recognize whether the elder Aubrey was thereby disseized unjustly and without judgment. Certainly the justices would proceed with care in any case that suggested arbitrary action by the king's father, but there was a legal question too. The justices at Westminster were hesitant about proceeding with this action not begun by a writ *de cursu*. They considered this writ to be *extra assisam*, since it combined features of the assizes of mort d'ancestor and novel disseizin. They recognized the king's right to devise special writs to cope with unusual situations, but they felt that discussion with him was necessary before proceeding. They postponed the case and marked it for consultation with King John. What he decided is unknown, for no further reference to the case has survived.

Later in John's reign another situation that no available possessory assize could remedy arose, and again the king's will was sought. This time Ellen de Morville sought lands in Rutland and Northamptonshire from David, earl of Huntingdon, and his tenants. This was an important case, for Ellen was a member of one of the great families of the North, daughter of the hereditary constable of Scotland, and Earl David was the brother of the king of Scotland. A jury came to recognize whether Ellen's father had held the estates when war broke out between Henry II and the king of Scotland and whether he had been disseized as a result of the war.[44] Actually, his lands had been forfeited to Henry II because of his support of the young king's rebellion; then, the

[42] *Pipe Roll 3 John*, Michaelmas 1201, p. 248.

[43] *CRR*, I, 464–465; discussed in Flower, *Introduction*, p. 342.

[44] *Ibid.*, VI, 273–274, Easter 1212, pleas *coram rege*.

lands had passed to the Scottish king, who gave them to the earl of Huntingdon.[45] The earl and his tenants came and stated that they had neither placed themselves on any recognition nor did they wish to do so. Instead, they asked that the king *facere voluntatem suam*. The case had to be postponed, however, when both the earl and Ellen called to warrant the king of Scotland.[46]

According to the custom of the royal courts, certain categories of persons were not allowed to bring suits. The nonfree could not bring possessory actions; women could sue only if their husbands joined them in the suit; and excommunicates, lepers, and idiots could not bring suits at all. Occasionally the king would rule on the eligibility of a person, overruling custom. Early in John's reign he had to decide the question of a wife's right to appear in court unaccompanied by her husband. When Hawise wife of Nicholas had to defend her right to certain land, she claimed that Nicholas would not come with her because he had been corrupted by the gifts of the one seeking her land.[47] The custom of the royal courts was that both husband and wife should be present for litigation concerning the wife's land.[48] In this case, King John, moved by mercy and by counsel, and by Hawise's oblation of 40 shillings, suspended the rule and allowed her to proceed without her husband.

During Henry III's minority a question arose concerning the eligibility of an excommunicate to bring an action. When William de Forz, count of Aumale, sought to have the jury attainted which decided an assize of novel disseizin against him, Gilbert de Ghent, his opponent, denied William's right to plead in the royal courts on the ground that he had been excommunicated for participating in a tournament.[49] The prevailing opinion of the

---

[45] *Victoria History of the Counties of England* (Oxford, 1900————), *Rutland*, II, 157.

[46] *CRR*, VI, 362, Trinity 1212; no conclusion is recorded.

[47] *Pleas before King*, I, 321, no. 3237; *CRR*, I, 153, 363, 382, for the years 1200–1201.

[48] Bracton, IV, 163–164, f. 370; Pollock and Maitland, II, 408–409.

[49] *CRR*, VIII, 158, Michaelmas 1219; discussed in Flower, *Introduction*, p. 459, and in *Rolls for Lincs and Worcs.*, pp. lii–liii. Earlier, during the reign of John, the question of an excommunicate was referred to the justiciar (*CRR*, V, 293, Trinity 1208).

Middle Ages was that an excommunicate was a "spiritual leper" and that he could perform no valid legal act.[50] In this case the justices sought consultation before denying to the count of Aumale the right to follow his plea; no doubt they hesitated to apply the rule automatically because of the power of the figures involved. They turned for advice to the bishop of Winchester and to the bishop of London, both members of the governing council, and these two prelates ruled that the case should proceed, notwithstanding William's status as an excommunicate. Political expediency certainly entered into their decision to dispense with the ordinary rules of justice and allow this case to proceed despite Gilbert's protest. Gilbert de Ghent had been one of the stalwarts of the baronial party during the struggle with King John. William de Forz had managed to be an adherent both of the royalist and the baronial factions at one time or another, but he had returned to the royalist ranks by the end of 1216.[51] Furthermore, he was a very powerful young man, holding many fiefs and honours plus custody of two royal castles; and he was a source of trouble several times during the minority, even staging an abortive revolt in 1220–1221. He had not hesitated to use his influence at court in an attempt to have this assize reversed by arbitrary action of the council.[52]

A rule of law disqualified from appearing in the royal courts those whose lands were in the king's hand. Seizure of an individual's property into the king's hand ordinarily meant indefinite postponement of pleas involving him. King John overturned this rule in an assize of darrein presentment brought by Robert the Constable against Morgan, provost of the collegiate church of St. John at Beverley.[53] Morgan appears to have fled the kingdom, perhaps because of the dispute over the succession to the archbishopric of Canterbury, which was growing bitter in the summer of 1207; and the king had taken possession of his

---

[50] Bracton, IV, 328, f. 426b; *Note Book*, II, 428, no. 552; Pollock and Maitland, I, 478.

[51] Holt, *Northerners*, p. 65.   [52] Powicke, *Henry III*, pp. 39, 52–54.

[53] *CRR*, V, 87, Michaelmas 1207, pleas at Westminster, and VI, 126–137, Michaelmas 1211, pleas *coram rege*; discussed in Flower, *Introduction*, p. 183.

post. Robert approached the king and obtained his writ instructing the justices to take the assize notwithstanding the fact that the church was in the king's hand, a shocking violation of the principle that no one who was disseized should be subjected to a suit. The unfortunate Morgan must have returned and regained possession of his church, for the feet of fines record his concord with Robert in 1212.[54]

The king was able to dispense with other rules of law too. Normally, the death of one of the litigants in a suit would bring it to an end, but King John in his sixth year commanded that an assize be taken even though the one who had brought it was dead.[55] He wished that it be taken in the presence of the complainant's daughter. Probably the daughter had offered a fine for this favor to save the trouble of beginning a new action in her own name.[56]

The king's right to dispense with the ordinary rules of justice in certain situations continued to be recognized under Henry III. The law of essoins was extremely rigid, declaring that no one who essoined himself of bed-sickness could arise for a year and a day. If he recovered before a year and a day had passed, the court could give him permission to arise, but elaborate rules were laid down about the conditions.[57] These complications could be overcome by a writ from the king granting license to arise, usually a mere formality. In 1219 a writ to the itinerant justices stated frankly the reason for the king's permission: it was granted, "since his presence is necessary for the furtherance of certain business of the lord king."[58]

<hr />

[54] *Pedes finium Ebor. regnante Johanne,* ed. W. Brown (Surtees Society, Vol. XCIV, 1897), p. 171, no. ccccliv.

[55] *Three Yorkshire Assize Rolls for the Reigns of King John and King Henry III,* ed. Charles Travis Clay (Yorkshire Archeological Society, Vol. XLIV for 1910), p. 12, assize roll for 6 John.

[56] The young woman was Emma daughter of Holfrid. Unfortunately, the financial records shed no light on the case.

[57] *Rolls for Lincs and Worcs.,* pp. 301–302; Bracton, IV, 119–125, ff. 355–356.

[58] *Rolls for Lincs and Worcs.,* p. 301, no. 632. Similarly, in Trinity term 1229, Henry III granted an individual leave to arise because he was needed to warrant land in the king's custody (*CRR,* 102, m. 15).

In 1220, Henry III was called upon to set aside a more important legal rule. William Marshal the younger sought several manors in Bedfordshire and Kent from Fawkes de Breauté by writ of right, and William offered the king 1,000 marks that he might defend his right to them by his own body.[59] The rule in proprietary proceedings begun by writ of right was that a plaintiff offer battle by a champion, for it was only in an appeal of felony that it was necessary for the complainant to offer battle personally.[60] The young earl of Pembroke must have had compelling reasons for desiring this departure from custom to offer such a large oblation for it. Perhaps it was because of his knowledge that Breauté, a feudal baron of the old school, had little respect for the forms of action and only understood superior strength. The earl's kinsman, John Marshal, later brought an action against Fawkes, and the earl's account of his reply to the suit survives:

Fawkes replied that if John brought thirty royal suits he would not give him peaceful possession, and he called him and every native-born man in England a traitor, and, alleging that they were set on war, he said that he would make such war on them that the realm of England would be too small to hold them.[61]

In spite of the two men's anger, it is certain that William Marshal never faced Fawkes de Breauté in a judicial combat, for the dispute was ended by a compromise.[62]

Henry III's justices on eyre also recognized the king's power to set aside ordinary procedural rules. When an individual brought a plea of attaint against an assize that had been taken in the third year of John's reign, the justices dismissed it with the comment, "Since the justices have no special command of the lord king to take this manner of assize when it has been so long delayed, it

[59] *CRR*, VIII, 250–252, Easter 1220; also in *Note Book*, II, 89–93, no. 102.
[60] Pollock and Maitland, II, 632–633.
[61] *Royal and Other Historical Letters Illustrative of the Reign of Henry III*, ed. W. W. Shirley (Rolls Series; London, 1862–1868), I, 222, letter of William Marshal to the justiciar, 1224. The translation is Powicke's in *Henry III*, p. 63.
[62] *CRR*, IX, 205, Trinity 1220.

should be postponed indefinitely unless a special command supervenes." [63]

The jury of recognition had been closely connected with royal power since Henry II first made it widely available. It was a *regale beneficium*, a concession of the king's own prerogative procedure to his subjects; but it was also a royal monopoly, a product to be offered for sale.[64] As the jury of recognition became normal procedure, payments to have inquiries by juries changed from offerings for special favors to regular court fees. The king could modify this royal boon as he saw fit, and the financial and judicial rolls of John and Henry III record oblations to have special sorts of juries. No doubt, the king's agents received many of these fines and issued the commands sought without necessity for direct royal intervention. Yet these offerings are significant, for they reveal how ordinary procedures in the king's courts could be changed if it benefited his exchequer to do so. The jurors in the possessory assizes were ordinarily "twelve free and lawful men," while jurors in the grand assize were "twelve lawful knights." [65] The king could command, however, that the possessory assizes too be taken by knights. In 1204, King John ordered his justices *coram rege* and his justices at Westminster to have certain assizes of mort d'ancestor and novel disseizin taken by knights; in return he received oblations of a Norwegian hawk and one mark.[66]

In cases where the king's rights were concerned, the judges themselves directed that the juries be composed of knights.

---

[63] *Rolls for Glos., War. and Staffs.*, pp. 23–24, no. 77, civil pleas at Gloucester, 1221.

[64] Pollock and Maitland, I, 140–144.

[65] Glanville, pp. 148–170, lib. xiii; pp. 30–31, lib. ii, cap. 11.

[66] *CRR*, III, 129, Trinity, mort d'ancestor brought by Agatha daughter of Nicholas le Ostricier; according to *Rot. de obl. et fin.*, p. 312, she owed one mark for the assize. *CRR*, III, 224, Michaelmas, novel disseizin brought by Fraric de Burnham; *Pipe Roll 7 John*, ed. Sidney Smith (Pipe Roll Society, N.S.; London, 1941), Michaelmas 1205, p. 236, records that he owed a Norwegian hawk. King John also ordered assizes of darrein presentment taken by knights (*CRR*, I, 210; V, 209–210). For another offering to have an assize taken by knights, see *Staffordshire Suits* (Wm. Salt Soc., Vol. III, pt. 1), p. 116. The abbot of Burton offered a mark.

When the abbot of Lilleshall was charged with a purpresture on the king's land, the justices thought that the jurors were "not such men as would give anything to the king or take anything from him," and they ordered the sheriff to choose knights and upright men as recognitors.[67] Later, in an assize to determine the last presentation to the chapel at the royal castle of Hereford brought by King John, they dismissed the jurors and ordered the sheriff to replace them with knights.[68] The king did not limit himself to the number twelve in juries either. King John once ordered a jury of recognition composed of eighteen knights—six from Essex, six from Hertfordshire, and six from Cambridgeshire —to inquire into land at Heydon in Essex claimed by Thomas de Heydon against Reynold Furre.[69]

A number of fines were offered to have juries from a special field of selection, from a single hundred, from a certain area, or to exclude certain men. In the early years of King John, modest oblations for these were frequently accepted.[70] Later in John's reign, as his need for money increased, so did the amounts offered for these juries. One such example before the king's court involved a plea concerning a knight's fee in Kingsbury, which is in Warwickshire but extends to the Staffordshire boundary. The tenant offered the king ten marks to have a jury of knights from both counties, and his opponent offered the same amount to have a jury from Warwick alone. The tenant then increased his bid to twenty marks and a warhorse, and the court decided that since the land did lie on the border of the two counties it was proper for him to have jurors from both.[71]

[67] CRR, I, 287, Michaelmas 1200, pleas at Westminster.

[68] Ibid., VI, 28, Easter 1210.

[69] Ibid., I, 382, 415–416, Easter 1201, pleas coram rege. Similarly, Henry III ordered a jury of twenty-four knights in a case (XII, 303, no. 1477, Michaelmas 1225).

[70] E.g. ibid., III, 63, a mark to exclude the men of the abbot of Peterborough; p. 65, 2 marks to have a jury from a single hundred; p. 214, to have men from the vicinity of Fulbourn; pp. 231, 282, to have men from the soke of Hemsby.

[71] V, 242, Trinity 1208, pleas coram rege, John de Bracebridge against Thomas de Arden. The case is discussed in Flower, Introduction, p. 484; and John's fine is recorded in Pipe Roll 10 John, ed. Doris M. Stenton (Pipe Roll Society, N.S.; London, 1947), Michaelmas 1208, p. 164.

The rolls of Henry III indicate that he and his council were willing to grant specially selected juries too. In 1224, William de Lancaster, baron of Kendal, Westmorland, complained to the justices at Westminster that the sheriff Robert de Vipont demanded that William's men attend the county and hundred courts contrary to his liberties, which he had from King Richard and King John.[72] When the sheriff denied any unjust action, William placed himself on the country, offering to prove his accusation by a jury; but he offered a palfrey to have a recognition made by men from neighboring counties, outside Robert's power, in order to ensure a fair hearing. A question concerning a liberty was an important matter, touching as it did the king's authority over justice. The judges postponed a decision until the next term, and then the case came before the king and the council, where William's oblation was accepted. They ordered the inquiry to be made by men from the counties of Yorkshire, Lancashire, and Cumberland, excluding men from Westmorland.[73]

Certainly both King John and his successor sometimes gave their justices instructions concerning the procedure to follow in cases coming before them. This does not mean there was wholesale perversion of the custom of the courts in order to serve the king's own ends. Some membranes of the *curia regis* rolls contain no cases in which the king overturned the custom of his courts, while the other membranes generally contain only one or two each. Although there is no great evidence that John had any deep respect for custom or tradition, there is no more to support the view that he dictated procedures contrary to custom solely on the basis of personal whim. Neither the commands of John nor

---

[72] CRR, XI, 547–549, no. 2732, Michaelmas 1224. Sanders, *Baronies,* p. 57, identifies William of Lancaster as baron of Kendal; for Robert de Vipont see above, p. 89.

[73] The conclusion of the case is not recorded. In Hilary 1226 (CRR, XII, 358, no. 1758), it was postponed until three weeks after Easter "for speech with the lord king"; on that date it was adjourned until the coming of the justices to take the assizes (XII, 480, no. 2405). In another case, Henry accepted an oblation of a mark for a grand assize of eight knights from one county and eight from another (XIII, 1184, no. 833, Michaelmas 1228, Richard Trussel against Nicholas de Yealand and his wife).

those of Henry III indicate any conception that the king was not bound by the law. The king's will was not regarded as something above the law but as a vital companion of the law, something necessary to regulate the machinery of royal justice. The need for occasional royal intervention was recognized by medieval political thinkers. Even John of Salisbury, who so strongly stressed the supremacy of law, admitted the ruler's "power of dispensing with verbal strictness." [74]

The machinery of justice was not yet fully automatic in the early thirteenth century. The law of the common law courts had hard and fast rules governing only a limited number of procedures, primarily for the possessory assizes, proprietary actions, and appeals of felony. There were areas where the law was indefinite and the procedure undefined, leaving the king a certain freedom. The king could adjust the machinery from time to time in order to serve his own purposes, as when he allowed special sorts of juries in return for oblations. But his adjustments did not result in any major overhaul of the legal machine. No new forms of action resulted from these occasional royal commands. Neither did his tampering with the machinery constitute any conscious application of theories of the monarch's superiority to the law, nor did he interfere on any massive scale. He did not need to: he could always close his courts to his enemies, a more direct means of persecuting them; or he could pursue them outside the law, seizing their lands or persons without any judgment in his courts of justice; or he could secure a judgment of the exchequer, if he did not wish to proceed entirely outside the law. The *lex scaccarii* offered opportunity enough for the king to persecute those who did not enjoy his good will.

[74] *Policraticus*, ed. C. C. J. Webb (Oxford, 1909), Vol. II, lib. iv, cap. 7.

4

The King and the
Judgments of His Courts

John and Henry III supervised the administration of justice
with a steady stream of instructions on procedural questions.
More significant, however, was the monarch's advice on substantive questions, his role in the judgments of his courts. The
medieval kings worked at their task of giving justice throughout
the Middle Ages, sometimes joining their justices in hearing
cases, giving advice on points of law in some situations and
acting mercifully in others. Yet the thirteenth-century English
kings must not be pictured sitting under an oak giving justice in
the informal manner of a St. Louis at Vincennes. Neither John
nor Henry III personally pronounced judgment because custom
required that they judge through their great men or their justices, men learned in the law,[1] and because most of the judgments in the royal courts were ratifications of verdicts of juries,
which were supposedly simply statements of facts. Furthermore,
the *curia regis* had expanded so that numbers of judges were
handing down decisions in the king's name.

Even though the king rarely dispensed justice himself in his
courts, he retained responsibility for their judgments. Henry II,

[1] Bracton, II, 337, f. 119b, clearly states this principle in trials for treason or
lèse majesté; he writes that *pares debent associari, ne ipse rex per seipsum vel
justiciarios suos sine paribus actor sit et iudex*. The principle is found in
Roman law too; see Ernst H. Kantorowicz, "Kingship under the Impact of
Scientific Jurisprudence," in *Twelfth-Century Europe and the Foundation of
Modern Society*, ed. Marshall Clagett, Gaines Post, and Robert Reynolds
(Madison, Wis., 1961), pp. 92–94.

when he established his central court, directed that the judges refer important or difficult cases to him, and he gave similar instructions to his justices on eyre.[2] In the early thirteenth century, the justices still had these instructions, for the notation *loquendum cum rege* occurs from time to time on the plea rolls of both John and Henry III. Sometimes the clerk simply noted *loquendum,* but this too stood for discussion with the king.[3] Since the king did have some part in the process of judgment, he had a part in precedents that could become a permanent part of the law. Any evaluation of the monarch's role in justice must take account of those cases in which he participated. There were many ways in which he could take part. Sometimes, his intervention is readily apparent, for he may have given commands setting aside the customary legal rules. The king's power to dispense with ordinary rules in unusual situations was always recognized; it can be seen most clearly in his pardons of criminals. At other times, the justices may have postponed an action in order to consult their master. They may have hesitated to proceed because of some uncertain point of law, because of the rank or power of the litigants, or because royal rights were in question. Many pleas touched on tenures held of the king, and he had to decide questions arising from his grants or charters. In still other proceedings, the king's participation is not clearly visible, but his shadow can be seen in the background.

THE KING'S DIRECT PART IN JUDGMENTS

The law of the royal courts consisted of customary law, case law, and statute law. In spite of the importance of unwritten custom in the Middle Ages, new laws were made and the king took part in their making. These laws were not collected or codified, or even carefully recorded.[4] Sometimes the only record

[2] For the central court, see Benedict of Peterborough (Howden), *Gesta Henrici Secundi,* ed. William Stubbs (Rolls Series; London, 1867), I, 207; for the justices on eyre, see the Assizes of Northampton, sec. 7, in *Select Charters,* ed. William Stubbs (8th ed.; Oxford, 1905), p. 152.

[3] Flower, *Introduction,* p. 456.

[4] H. G. Richardson and G. O. Sayles, "The Early Statutes," *Law Qtrly. Rev.* L (1934), 203.

of them is a chance summary in a chronicle, a new form of writ on the close roll, or letters of instructions to the justices, but other times the text of the new law was recorded on the *curia regis* rolls. One of the *coram rege* rolls for 1234 records new rules to be followed by the justices in cases in which the question of bastardy arose and in cases dealing with prebendal properties.[5] This was a year and a half before the Provisions of Merton, usually termed the first "statute." Such instructions to the judges might be the result either of a great council or of commands made by the king acting alone, for there was no definite rule concerning the creation of new law. In the early thirteenth century, letters of instructions ranged from King John's command to the justices of the bench to honor only royal charters and letters confirmed by him to the instructions given by the young Henry's council to the itinerant justices concerning trials of criminals after the Fourth Lateran Council's ban on the ordeal.[6]

But these general rules and the questions they raise about the origins of legislation are not much help in learning the king's role in the work of his courts. More important is the part he played in individual cases. Sometimes the king asked for information about a case, and at other times he gave the justices information.[7] An understanding of the king's part in these cases is more useful in answering the questions: to what extent was the operation of the courts automatic and to what extent was it under the monarch's supervision? Proceedings in which the king personally took part can be grouped into four categories. First,

[5] *CRR*, 115B, m. 16–16d, Oct.–Nov. 1234 (also *Note Book*, III, 135, no. 1117). Discussed by Maitland in the introduction to *Note Book*, I, 106–108.

[6] *CRR*, I, 331, Michaelmas 1200; *Pat. Rolls* (1216–1225), p. 186.

[7] E.g. *RCR*, II, 185, Easter 1200: King John forbade the hearing of a plea until he learned more about the claim of one of the litigants. *CRR*, VI, 203–204, Hilary 1212: John was dissatisfied with the record of a final concord, and he desired certain information. *CRR*, 115B, m. 32, no. 1426, April 1235: Henry III informed his justices that he had not warranted a litigant's default and that the seizure of the litigant's lands for his default was just. *CRR*, 117, m. 10d, no. 136G, Dec. 1237: An individual sought his late brother's lands; because he had surrendered all right to the lands, Henry III denied that he was the heir.

there are those cases in which he made rulings on points of law. These are rare, but they are important, for they could give the king an opportunity to share in the shaping of the common law. Second and more common are cases that raised questions about royal charters or royal grants, so that they had to be referred to the king. The third category is closely connected to this—the king's participation in ending suits by compromise, in drawing up final concords. He would take an interest in the settlement of disputes that involved lands held of him, payments owed to him, or services performed for him. Finally, the king could take part in deciding upon punishments; he could pardon persons or he could add to their punishment by increasing their amercements.

King John, by the very fact of his accession to the throne, brought about a change in the law of inheritance. His accession instead of Arthur of Brittany's meant that a man's younger brother would be favored as his heir over his nephew, son of his older brother. Several assizes of mort d'ancestor touched on this question, and the justices proceeded cautiously. In 1201, Walter son of Simon brought an assize of mort d'ancestor before the justices taking the assizes in Cornwall.[8] He claimed that he was the rightful heir to the land of Philip his uncle, land then held by Philip's brother Hugh Sot and his sister Clarissa. Hugh came and freely admitted that Philip, his eldest brother, had held that land at the time of his death; but he pointed out that Walter's father was Simon, their middle brother. He then asked the judgment of the court whether he, Philip's younger brother, or Walter, Philip's nephew, was the nearer heir.[9] This problem must have immediately brought to the minds of the justices the *casus regis*, the question of whether John or his nephew Arthur had a better right to the kingdom of England on the death of

---

[8] *Pleas before King*, II, 144, no. 528, assizes taken at Launceston, 18 June 1201.

[9] A genealogical chart reveals the problem clearly:

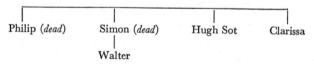

| Philip (*dead*) | Simon (*dead*) | Hugh Sot | Clarissa |

Walter

Richard. It is not surprising that they refused to give judgment and postponed the case indefinitely "because judgment is pending by the will of the king."

The same problem had arisen earlier for the justices of the bench, though not in connection with an assize of mort d'ancestor. In Easter term 1200, a jury of recognition had come into court to determine the rightful heirs to the lands of Richard de Vautort, then held by John de Vautort.[10] The jury found that Richard had two sons, Hugh, the elder, and John, the younger, and that Hugh had left a son, Simon.[11] They concluded that the sons of Simon should be the heirs to the land in question, although such a finding was at variance with the circumstances of King John's accession to the throne of England. The decision must have alarmed the royal justices. Perhaps it was to protect themselves from the king's wrath that they added to the record of the plea, "Be it known that this inquest was made by command of the lord king, not by a judgment of the court or according to the custom of the realm." Or it may have represented the justices' veiled criticism of the royal order.[12]

Even though Arthur of Brittany did not long survive to threaten John's right to the throne, another threat remained in his sister Eleanor until her death in 1241. Because of this, cases similar to the *casus regis* continued to be referred to the king in Henry III's time.[13] A case that was a quarrel between uncle and

---

[10] *RCR*, II, 189, Easter 1200.

[11] Again, a genealogical chart is helpful:

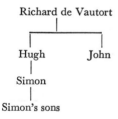

Richard de Vautort

Hugh   John

Simon

Simon's sons

[12] The first suggestion is from Lady Stenton's *Pleas before King*, I, 90–91. The second is J. C. Holt's in "The Barons and the Great Charter," *E.H.R.* LXX (1955), 8.

[13] Maitland found a case as late as 1246 in which judgment was left to the king (Pollock and Maitland, II, 285, n. 7).

niece rather than uncle and nephew came to Henry's attention in Trinity term of 1235. Matilda daughter of Henry Hose brought suit against her uncle Matthew Hose for land in several counties which she claimed as her right through her grandfather, also named Henry.[14] Matthew objected that her writ was contrary to the law and custom of England; it was neither a writ of right, nor a writ of mort d'ancestor, nor a writ *nuper obiit*, nor a writ of entry. But the court ruled that he must reply to Matilda's writ. He then argued that she could not claim the lands because her father, young Henry, had died before his father, old Henry, and had never held that land. Matthew maintained that he was the rightful heir of the old Henry because he was the astrer, the hearth-child, a younger son still at home at the time of his father's death.[15] Matilda responded with the representative principle: that Henry her father was Henry her grandfather's eldest son and heir, and that the lands descended to her as the eldest daughter and heir of her dead father.

At this point the king commanded the justices of the bench to postpone the plea until it could come *coram domino rege ubicumque tunc fuerit*. The legal question was not necessarily the only reason for Henry III's intervention. Old Henry Hose had been a tenant-in-chief of the king, and Matthew had promised the king a fine of 600 marks to have the tenements.[16] The conclusion to the controversy is not known, but a writ commanding Matthew Hose to surrender to Matilda the land she sought in one county suggests a compromise.[17]

Here the king is seen playing at least a negative role in the

---

[14] *CRR*, 120, m. 18, no. 959, octave of St. John Baptist, 18 Henry III, pleas at Westminster.

[15] Another genealogical table:

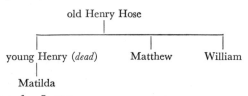

[16] *Exc. e rot. fin.*, I, 279.

[17] *Close Rolls* (1237–1242), p. 148, 13 Oct. 1238.

shaping of the law by delaying England's acceptance of the principle of representation in the law of inheritance. The delay came less through his actual judgment than through the judges', his servants', fear of casting a shadow on his title. In Glanville's time, the principle of representation was known to the judges of the royal courts but was not universally accepted. Glanville personally favored the nephew over the younger son in succession.[18] By Bracton's time the judges had the *casus regis* before them, and they tended to favor the uncle. The rule was that if the uncle first obtained seizin, the nephew had no means of obtaining a judgment, for the assize of mort d'ancestor did not lie between persons so closely related. A case in Bracton's *Note Book* bears the marginal comment, "Note that the assize of death does not lie between those heirs descending from a common stock, namely between uncles and nephews." [19] If the nephew brought some other action in an effort to gain seizin, the judges would leave the matter for the king's decision; and he could order an inquiry as he did in the case of the Vautort heirs, if he wished.[20] This state of things did not prove to be permanent, however, for the principle of representation eventually prevailed in English law.[21]

Many of the civil suits brought in the common law courts were concerned with inheritance of lands, such as those in which the principle of representation was a problem. Sometimes these could raise tricky legal questions that caused the justices to seek the king's advice. In 1205, for example, Gilbert de Ghent sought twenty librates of land from Ralph Brewer, who called to warrant Reinfrid son of Roger. Reinfrid offered in defense a number of charters, among them the confirmation of a grant by Gilbert's father, confirmed in turn by Henry II.[22] Gilbert replied that this charter should be of no value because his father had made it on

---

[18] Glanville, pp. 76–78, lib. vii, cap. 3.

[19] *Note Book*, III, 631, no. 1829. The next plea, no. 1830, has the notation that the same is true concerning a woman and her uncle.

[20] Bracton, III, 284, and IV, 46, ff. 267b, 327b; Pollock and Maitland, II, 285; T. F. T. Plucknett, *A Concise History of the Common Law* (5th ed., rev.; London, 1956), pp. 717–718.

[21] Pollock and Maitland, II, 286.　　　[22] *CRR*, IV, 42–43, Trinity 1205.

his deathbed, if he did make it, and that if King Henry had confirmed the charter of a dying man, "he had done his will and not what he ought to have done." His questioning of the charter as a deathbed grant must have been a delaying tactic, for the charter was merely a confirmation of a much earlier grant. Yet the justices of the bench marked the case *loquendum,* indicating their wish to consult King John about Gilbert's objection, perhaps because they were doubtful about its validity, perhaps because he was an important baron who must be treated delicately. Apparently the king ruled against Gilbert de Ghent.[23] If Gilbert's protest was correct, then this ruling in favor of a deathbed grant is significant because the usual practice, as seen in Glanville's treatise, was not to honor such grants. Of course, Glanville was thinking primarily of grants to religious houses wrung from dying men in fear of eternal damnation.[24] The decision may have political significance, for Gilbert was later one of the leaders in the revolt against King John. He had a number of grievances against the king, mainly centering about his claim to the earldom of Lincoln and his debts to the Jews, but the loss of this case and the £100 amercement may have added another.[25]

Another of Gilbert de Ghent's replies to the charters of Reinfrid was his declaration that a charter made by a married woman should have no value, since she was in the power of her husband and could not contradict him. The same question came before the justices of Henry III in two cases, and in both they felt the need for consultation. In the first case, a man and his wife warranted their charter confirming a grant of land they had made; but the justices consulted the council about making a final concord as well, since the land in question belonged to the wife's marriage-portion.[26] By the time of Bracton, the rule was that a

---

[23] King John's decision is not recorded in the *CRR,* but according to a plea from 1210 (*CRR,* VI, 19–21), the land Gilbert claimed was held by Reinfrid's brother, Ralph Brewer. In *Rot. lit. cl.,* I, 65b, 17 Feb. 1206, Gilbert was pardoned of an amercement of £100 levied against him as a result of his plea against Reinfrid and Ralph Brewer.

[24] Glanville, p. 70, lib. vii, cap. 1; Pollock and Maitland, II, 328.

[25] See Holt, *Northerners,* pp. 26–27.

[26] *CRR,* XI, 40–41, no. 236, Hilary 1223, council consulted. There is no indication of the outcome.

husband and wife could not dispose of the wife's lands by charter alone. Bracton maintained that only a final concord made in the king's court was a reliable means for transfer of the wife's lands.[27] The case indicates that this attitude had not yet been accepted fully in the royal courts by the early thirteenth century. The justices' doubts and resultant desire to consult the council gave it an opportunity either to hasten or retard its acceptance, thereby playing some role in the shaping of the law.

The second case from 1227 raised the question of a husband's and wife's charter, but it raised the question of contradictory royal charters too. Hubert de Burgh, the justiciar, sought recognition from a widow, Emma de Beaufeu, as her heir to certain manors. He claimed this as his right by a charter granted by Emma and her husband. Emma maintained that when she made those charters, "she was under the power of her husband, whom she could not contradict." [28] Hubert replied that she had never complained of the charter after his death. Her response was that she had no reason to complain, for she had made a charter with King John naming him as her heir.[29] She would willingly recognize Hubert as her heir if the king would return her charter. Another charter indicates an eventual compromise: Emma was granted a life interest in some of the manors and lands, while others were given to Hubert de Burgh.[30]

In 1208, King John's justices had to consult him about a woman's claim to land. Mabel, a widow, was seeking her dower from Ralph of Lenham, but he pled that he not be required to respond to her, since she had no one to warrant her dower.[31] She answered that she had a son and a daughter across the sea, although she did not know if they were alive or dead. Most likely, they had remained in Normandy after it fell to the French king in 1204. She asked the court if she should lose her dower simply because she had no one to warrant it to her. The justices could not answer her, but postponed the plea until the coming of

[27] Bracton, IV, 30–33, f. 321b; Pollock and Maitland, II, 413.
[28] CRR, XIII, 13, no. 59, Easter 1227, king consulted.
[29] Rot. de obl. et Fin., p. 320, 7 John 1205. John had seized her lands, and she paid 600 marks for their return and for freedom not to marry.
[30] Cal. Chtr. Rolls (1226–1257), p. 44, 20 June 1227; p. 49, 14 July 1227.
[31] CRR, V, 179, Easter 1208.

the itinerant justices, marking it for consultation with the king in the meantime. Evidently, King John ruled that Mabel must lose her dower, for he accepted a fine offered by Ralph of Lenham to be free of her claim.[32]

A question of inheritance again caused difficulty for Henry III's justices of the bench. In Easter term of Henry's twentieth year, Isabel daughter of Geoffrey de Fercles brought suit against Bartholomew Peche to recover the lands of her dead brother, to which she and her sister Lucy were heirs.[33] Lucy was under age and in the custody of Bartholomew, a royal servant. He tried to quash the proceeding by raising exceptions, among them the charge that Isabel was illegitimate, born seven years before her parents' marriage, and therefore no lawful heir. According to canon law, her parents' later marriage would have made her legitimate; but according to English law, she would have remained illegitimate after their marriage. Allegations of bastardy in the royal courts were topics for discussion at the great councils of this time. At a great council in the autumn of 1234 it was provided (*provisum est*) that when the exception that a person was a bastard because he was born before his parents' marriage was raised, then the plea should be sent to the bishop's court for an inquiry into the truth of the allegation.[34] But this procedure would not work because the Church courts considered such persons to be legitimate, and it was abandoned with the Statute of Merton in 1236.[35] Probably because of confusion about the definition of bastardy which had been injected into the case by Peche's exception, the case was removed from the bench to the court *coram rege*. There the decision was made that the exception of bastardy should not be permitted. Since Bartholomew

[32] *Pipe Roll 11 John*, ed. Doris M. Stenton (Pipe Roll Society, N.S.; London, 1949), Michaelmas 1209, p. 49. King John was consulted earlier, in 1204, about another plea of dower; but the entry does not record enough information to indicate the reason his advice was sought (CRR, III, 95).

[33] CRR, 116A, m. 12, no. 1793.

[34] *Ibid.*, 115B, m. 16d, no. 1178 (also *Note Book*, III, 135, no. 1117); discussed in *Note Book*, I, 106–108. A sample writ is found in *Close Rolls* (1231–1234), p. 598.

[35] *Note Book*, I, 108.

Peche could not prove Isabel's illegitimacy, Isabel gained possession of the lands she was seeking.

Another difficult question concerning land which the king's
justices could not answer alone was the problem of gages of land
to the Jews. The king profited so much from their financial
affairs that there was a special branch of the exchequer for them,
but questions concerning them occasionally came into the common law courts. In 1218 the itinerant justices wrote the regent,
William Marshal, for advice, describing the case, "that you
should know the truth of the matter, and do what pleases you
about it and what you see to be just." [36] The problem was to
determine the rightful holder of the manor of Intwood, which
had been taken into the king's hand for debts to the Jews. Its
holder, Ralph of Thiville, complained to the justices on eyre that
he had been disseized *per voluntatem et non per judicium.* The
suit was moved to Westminster, where it was shown that Ralph
had given the manor in gage to the Jewish moneylender Isaac of
Norwich.[37] Then it passed to Roger of St. Denis and his wife,
when Isaac let it to them for ten years; but later Ralph paid King
John £120 to settle his debt to Isaac and to regain seizin of the
manor. The court judged that Ralph should recover possession of
the manor, that Ralph and his wife should be freed of their
payments to Isaac, and that Isaac should be allowed to seek
compensation before the justices of the Jews. This judgment
seems to have established the principle that "a debtor had the
right to redeem his lands over the head of the creditor (who was
also the gagee) and the subtenants: on the other hand the
creditor was entitled to an equitable settlement of his claims." [38]

Sometimes the king took part in criminal proceedings. King
John must have taken an unusual interest in criminal cases, for
the plea rolls of his reign reveal a number of them bearing the
comment *loquendum cum rege.* This is surprising because rela-

[36] *Royal and Other Historical Letters Illustrative of the Reign of Henry III,*
ed. W. W. Shirley (Rolls Series; London, 1862–1868), I, 17–19, no. xiv.

[37] *CRR,* IX, 23–24, 153–154, Trinity 1220; discussed in H. G. Richardson,
English Jewry under the Angevin Kings (London, 1960), p. 144.

[38] Richardson, *English Jewry,* p. 144.

tively few of the cases coming before his central courts were criminal actions, since most of them were heard in the counties. Occasionally, lists of criminal actions to be brought to the attention of the king appear in the plea rolls from John's reign, something not encountered in the rolls of Henry III.[39] Some of these criminal actions marked for consultation with the king offer no clue about why the king should have been consulted, but in others the reason is obvious. For example, John was consulted about a clerk suspected of homicide, a case concerning the delicate problem of "criminous clerks"; about a counterfeiter, a matter touching the king's financial interests; about an idiot who confessed to a crime he had not committed, a problem that might necessitate the remedy of a royal pardon.[40] Yet there is no difficult legal question involved in these cases; they are primarily problems of judicial administration.

In other criminal proceedings, consultation with the king was sometimes necessary because of difficult legal questions raised. Early in John's reign, his justices heard a case in which an individual appealed another of murder and later withdrew his appeal, although the entire county bore witness to his guilt.[41] This case is marked *ad consilium* instead of *loquendum* in the usual fashion. The meaning of such a note is obscure; it may be that the king was absent when his counsel was needed, or he may have wished to discuss the problem raised here with his council.[42] Another thorny problem which the justices marked for consultation was a case in 1214, when a man appealed his lord of trespassing on his house and injuring him in other ways.[43]

The justices of Henry III were confronted with the problem

---

[39] *CRR*, V, 234, 269; VI, 351.

[40] *Ibid.*, V, 234, 269, Trinity 1208; VI, 351, Trinity 1212. There are other examples of such matters adjourned for consultation under Henry III; e.g. *ibid.*, VIII, 85–86, Michaelmas 1219, about a man who rescued another being held for homicide.

[41] *Pleas before King*, II, 211, no. 729, 26 April 1201, pleas *coram rege*.

[42] Lady Stenton, in *ibid.*, p. 122, offers these suggestions.

[43] *CRR*, VII, 94, Hilary 1214; pp. 165, 177, Trinity 1214. Ellis de Fernham appealed Gilbert English. Both of them were imprisoned, and they had to offer fines for release.

of accessories before the fact in a case that illustrates the violence of medieval life. A man appealed John Deulesset, his wife Emma, and three others, of robbing and maiming him.[44] He claimed that the three men had come upon him on the king's highway, gravely wounded him with hatchets, robbed him, tied his feet to the tail of a horse, and dragged him away. He added that they had done this with the counsel of John and Emma, citing as proof an incident that had taken place on the night before the crime while all were lodged in the house of John and his wife, evidently an inn. Emma had spilled a pitcher of ale, and when this angered her husband, she replied that there was one sitting in that house who ought to pay for the ale. Just what she meant by this cryptic remark is not certain, but she must have meant that there was a likely victim for robbery present. The jury found the three accused of the robbery not guilty, however, so that the case against John Deulesset and Emma was left in doubt. The judges ordered them committed to the gaol at Winchester until they could learn the king's will; unfortunately, his decision is not recorded. The English law of this age was familiar with accessories before the fact, those who counsel or abet a crime but do not actually commit it. The rule was that the accessories could not be brought to trial until the principals had been convicted.[45] Here the judges faced a novel situation: if the principals were found innocent, what should be done with those accused of being accessories? Were they guilty if they urged others to commit a crime, even though those they urged failed to commit it? The justices could only turn to the king in solving the problem.

Another aspect of criminal procedure which posed a problem for the judges was the jurisdiction of private courts, sometimes granted by royal charter. The monks of Beaulieu denied the right of the justices at Westminster to hear an appeal, maintaining that the plea belonged to their court by charter-right.[46] The

[44] *Ibid.*, XIII, 399, no. 1905, Easter 1229.
[45] Bracton, II, 361, f. 128; *Note Book*, III, 437–438, no. 1548; Pollock and Maitland, II, 509.
[46] *CRR*, IV, 287, Michaelmas 1206.

case was marked for consultation with King John. Later, in Henry III's reign, his justices encountered a problem of criminal jurisdiction too. They found that in the liberty of Copeland, Northumberland, it was customary for men to be outlawed in the court of the lord of the liberty. Following his outlawry in that court, he would be outlawed by the county court.[47] Outlawry in the court of a liberty was contrary to the customary practice of the mid-thirteenth century, for according to Bracton only the county courts and the London husting could outlaw a man. Not even the royal courts could do that.[48] The king's answer to the justices on this question was not recorded.

That the king personally played some part in the judgments of his courts is clear from these cases. Further evidence is supplied by the cases raising relatively minor questions that the judges noted for his attention. King John's justices at Westminster once consulted him about the date for hearing a plea.[49] The young Henry III's justices consulted his council about the order in which they should take up two problems raised in a single plea.[50] Later they consulted him for a ruling on whether the period of King Richard's captivity in Germany was "time of war" or not.[51] Other questions referred to the king concerned jurors who failed to appear and sheriffs who failed to carry out the justices' instructions.[52]

A much larger group of actions in which the king took part are those touching on royal rights. The English monarch was not only the governor of his realm but also the possessor of it, a great feudal lord with many vassals, large landholdings, and other properties. Because of his position as a great landholder, many private pleas touched him in some way. A litigant might present

---

[47] *Note Book*, III, 171, no. 1154, pleas *coram rege* 1235–1236.

[48] Bracton, II, 353–354, f. 125b.

[49] *CRR*, VI, 3, 89, 108, Hilary and Michaelmas 1210.

[50] *Ibid.*, VIII, 325–326, Easter 1220.

[51] *Ibid.*, 113, m. 7, no. 349, Michaelmas 17–18 Henry III. The ruling was that it was not to be considered "time of war."

[52] E.g. jurors: *ibid.*, V, 173, Easter 1208, and 264, Trinity 1208; IX, 29, Trinity 1220. Sheriffs: X, 61, Easter 1221; XI, 240, no. 1191, Michaelmas 1223. Knights viewing an essoiner: VI, 19, Hilary 1210.

a royal charter or cite a royal grant in support of his suit. Or there might be some dispute over the obligation for the services due to him from the land. In these suits, the king might be better informed than the justices, so that he could take part in their judgment.

Many pleas involved properties once held by the king or his predecessors and granted away by charter. Because of this, questions of interpretation of royal charters frequently faced the royal judges, and they had to consult the king in answering them. A plea from the time of Henry III centering around a royal charter concludes with the statement, "The testimony of the lord king by charter or by word of mouth [*viva voce*] exceeds all other proof." [53] Neither the justices nor any private individual could dispute the king's charters, so that in cases of questionable interpretation or conflicting terms the only solution was to seek his will. In 1203 the itinerant justices postponed a case "because in the record of that plea there is mention of a charter of the lord king which the justices do not wish to judge by themselves." [54]

Questions involving royal charters that arose during Henry III's minority had to be postponed until his majority. The justices postponed a plea in 1220 because "the council of the lord king dares not make a judgment on the lord king's charters." [55] Later, during the Buckinghamshire eyre of 1227, a tenant defended his right to a manor by presenting a charter of Henry II. The itinerant justices adjourned the case to Westminster because they were "unwilling to judge the intention of King Henry II without the king's assent." [56] In the spring of 1235, the

[53] *Note Book*, II, 182–183, no. 239, Hilary 1224. See Bracton, I, 109–110, f. 34, on questionable interpretations of charters, and pp. 170–175 on conflicting royal grants.

[54] *Lincs Assize Roll*, p. 225, no. 1265, 3 Feb. 1203; similarly, CRR, IV, 231, Michaelmas 1206, pleas at Westminster. In 1207, the justices consulted the king about a charter he had made when he was count of Mortain (CRR, V, 60–61).

[55] CRR, VIII, 236, Hilary 1220.

[56] *Calendar of the Roll of the Justices on Eyre, 1227*, ed. J. G. Jenkins (Buckinghamshire Archeological Society, Vol. VI, 1942), p. 32, no. 360, case of the earl of Gloucester seeking the manor of Risborough from William de Similly. This postponement must have discouraged the earl, for no record of a

plea roll records one case revolving around royal charters in which *dominus rex ore proprio pronunciavit judicium.* The bishop of Bath was disputing with Henry III over their respective rights in a certain wood. When the bishop presented his charters, the king admitted that he had not remembered them, and he gave judgment in the bishop's favor.[57]

These cases make clear that when one party to an action presented a royal charter in proof of his right, this was powerful support for his claim. Bracton's comment on a case in which the tenant presented charters of Richard I and John in evidence is this: "Note that neither a plea nor a duel nor a grand assize proceeds contrary to evidence presented by the king through his charters." [58] But attempts to gain the king's support did not always succeed. In 1238 the men of the priory of St. Swithin's complained that the prior and monks were demanding new services of them, more than those they had owed to the king's predecessors. Apparently, the men claimed to be inhabitants of the ancient demesne of the crown, for the services of tenants of the ancient demesne remained unchanged even though the king was no longer their lord.[59] The men's complaint failed to gain them relief, since Henry III refused to involve himself in their case.[60]

Many lands passed through the king's hands. Escheats, forfeitures, and wardships brought estates into his possession; permanent grants and temporary custodies turned them over to others. A person's suit seeking land from another might be met with the response that the tenant held "by the king's will." This drew the king into the suit as a third party, and the justices had to

---

later suit survives, and William was still in possession of the manor in 1242; see *Victoria History of the Counties of England* (Oxford, 1900——), Buckinghamshire, II, 38.

[57] *CRR,* 115B, m. 25d, no. 1305. The bishop of Bath claimed the wood of Cheddar, Somerset, maintaining that the king had only rights of vert and venison there. See Chapter 8, pp. 245–246.

[58] *Note Book,* II, 181, no. 226, Hilary 1224.

[59] Pollock and Maitland, I, 385: "Thus, once ancient demesne, always ancient demesne."

[60] *CRR,* 117, m. 12, no. 149B (also *Note Book,* Vol. III, no. 1237).

postpone such cases for consultation with him. Several cases from the time of Henry III illustrate this.[61] In these cases, the king could in effect pronounce judgment. For example, one of the cases postponed was a suit brought by a widow seeking her dower from the abbot of Maldon.[62] The abbot sought to escape from the suit by saying that he held the land at fee farm of King Henry III. The roll records the king's decision: "Because the lord king does not desire any injury but wishes justice to be shown to all, he concedes that the lady should have her dower." He added that the abbot should come to the exchequer for an adjustment of his rents.

Other problems arose in connection with royal grants of land, and the justices turned to the king for advice about them. One case brought into question the grant of a manor by King John to William Bret.[63] The circumstances surrounding the grant are interesting, for William's father had lost the manor on account of his support of John, while he was count of Mortain, during his revolt against Richard in 1193–1194. John, following his accession to the throne, sought to restore to the heir of his old ally the lands King Richard had confiscated; but the heir found someone else in possession of the estate granted him, and he had to bring an action to secure his grant. The possessor of the land maintained that while the manor was in the hand of King Richard, he had purchased a writ to have an inquiry into his rights. According to him, the jurors had confirmed his right to the land by reason of a debt owed to his uncle. William Bret, however, had given a fine to King John "to have such seizin of that land as Robert Bret his father had on the day on which he was disseized of that land and of his other lands." The justices were unwilling to decide a case which would necessarily mean contradicting the will of one king, either Richard or John. They postponed the case until they could learn the will of King John,

[61] CRR, XII, 234, no. 1145; XIV, 139, no. 697; ibid., 115B, m. 27d, no. 1378; 116A, m. 1, no. 1549; and Note Book, III, 595, no. 1766, where Bracton comments that in such cases, "the truth should be sought by means of jurors, but the king's will should be awaited."

[62] CRR, 115B, m. 27d, no. 1378, 5 Feb. 1235.

[63] Ibid., I, 207–208, 245, Trinity 1200, pleas at Westminster.

and he commanded that the plea be heard before him.[64] Both claimants were summoned to appear on that date, but William's opponent neither came nor essoined himself, perhaps knowing what the outcome would be. William Bret appeared and gained seizin of the manor by default.[65] The course of this action illustrates how the royal will operated in cases in which King John had a personal interest, as well as the problem the justices faced in dealing with royal grants.

Contradictory royal grants continued to be cause for consultation under Henry III. Once, in 1221, the justices on eyre had to consider an action in which a grant was alleged to have been made by the council governing England during the minority. Giles de Erdington brought an assize of mort d'ancestor regarding a manor held by the daughter of Llewelyn, prince of Wales.[66] She claimed that she received the manor from one who had been granted it by the council, but Giles denied this. The justices could only postpone it "for speech with the lord king and his council," passing on what information they had gained about the case from the sheriff. His testimony supported Giles' contention that the council had not granted that land, for inquiry showed that Giles' father had been in possession at the beginning of the barons' war. It is likely that the individual who gave it to Llewelyn's daughter had simply taken advantage of the confusion of the baronial revolt to occupy it. The action dragged on through a seemingly endless series of postponements until at last she lost the case by default.[67]

Again in 1221, Henry III's council had to advise the itinerant

[64] *Ibid.*, p. 338, Michaelmas 1200.

[65] *Ibid.*, pp. 264–266, Michaelmas 1200, pleas *coram rege*. For a similar case see *Pleas before King*, I, 297–298, no. 3118, civil pleas at Shrewsbury, 1221; or *RCR*, II, 157–158. The king was consulted about the men at Lancaster, who had paid a fine for their liberties, but were being prevented from exercising them. See also *Pleas before King*, I, 299, no. 3123, Easter 1200, pleas *coram rege*; discussed by Lady Stenton on p. 91.

[66] *Rolls for Glos., War. and Staffs*, pp. 464–465, no. 1049; discussed by Lady Stenton on pp. l–li.

[67] *CRR*, X, 280, Trinity 1222; XI, 428, no. 2134, Michaelmas 1224; XII, 85–86, no. 444, Trinity 1225; p. 203, no. 1008, Michaelmas 1225; p. 445, no. 2202, Easter 1226.

justices about contradictory grants made by King John. Ivo and Hugh Pantulf brought an assize of novel disseizin against William de Gamages to recover land they had held at bail of King John before the baronial rebellion. The land had passed into the king's possession as part of the escheat of the Normans, when its holder remained in France after 1204. Then, in 1216, John took the land from the Pantulfs and granted it to William de Gamages "as his right and inheritance," since his brother had held it before the loss of Normandy. The young king's council commanded the justices to postpone the case until the rolls of John's reign could be searched, and then they ruled that William de Gamages should remain in seizin.[68] The Pantulfs were not amerced for bringing an assize wrongfully, probably because they were a great Shropshire family and because they had lost the land in the baronial war.

Other cases touching the king about which the justices often wished to consult him concerned his title to lands, privileges, or services. The justices would hardly wish to do anything that might diminish royal rights. On the contrary, their unwillingness to proceed in such actions without consulting the king reveals them as careful defenders of royal rights. Furthermore, the king was sometimes the most reliable source of information about questions of rights; he might know whether or not an individual held of him and by what services he held. Consequently, pleas involving the king's possessions, or what might possibly be his possessions, were frequently referred to him by the royal judges. Among such pleas is one in which Henry d'Oilly claimed that a piece of land was part of his Oxfordshire barony, while his opponent maintained that it pertained to a royal serjeanty.[69] The justices would not allow a grand assize to proceed until they first heard the will of the king. King John was willing to have the assize proceed, but it was never taken, for Henry's departure to

---

[68] *Rolls for Glos., War. and Staffs*, pp. 449–451, no. 1018; discussed by Lady Stenton on pp. xlix–xl.

[69] *CRR*, I, 176, Trinity 1200, pleas *coram rege*; discussed in Flower, *Introduction*, p. 455. Henry d'Oilly was baron of Hook Norton, Oxon. (Sanders, *Baronies*, p. 54).

join the king's forces in Normandy made an indefinite adjournment necessary.[70] Another plea involving royal rights from the
early years of King John arose over the terms of a final concord
made in the king's court. There was controversy between the two
parties concerning responsibility for the forinsec service due
from the land they had exchanged.[71] Since a dispute over forinsec service was in effect a question of the responsibility for the
military service due to the king from the land, the justices at
Westminster wished to speak to him about the case.[72]

Similar questions of royal rights arose under Henry III, and
his justices would not proceed without his advice. On one occasion they had to consult him about a case in which two men
claimed to hold the same land of the king by different services:
one by the service of one-fifth part of one knight, the other by
the service of killing wolves in the royal forest.[73] If the king was
of any help to his justices in this case, he was exceedingly well
informed about his rights. On another occasion Henry's justices
were faced with a question, not of his rights, but of those of the
queen-mother Isabel of Angouleme, and they sought his advice.
They wrote asking to know his pleasure concerning an assize of
mort d'ancestor which had been brought against the queen-
mother.[74] The king's reply to the justices' letter is not known, but
later he did make an exchange of land with the person who had
brought the assize, giving him twelve librates of land in exchange for the land he claimed of the queen.[75]

On other occasions, there was only a remote possibility of royal
rights being jeopardized, yet the justices still consulted the king
before proceeding. Often their questions dealt with lands held at

---

[70] *CRR*, I, 429, Easter 1201. For a similar plea see *RCR*, II, 157, Easter
1200. In 1206 there was a question of the advowson on a royal manor, and
the justices would not give judgment until they had consulted the king (*CRR*,
IV, 178–179, Trinity 1206).

[71] *CRR*, I, 448, Easter 1201; II, 12, Michaelmas 1201.

[72] Pollock and Maitland, I, 238–239.

[73] *CRR*, XII, 171, no. 837, Michaelmas 1225 (also in *Note Book*, III, 518,
no. 1870).

[74] Shirley, *Royal Letters*, I, 10–11, no. ix, Easter 1217 or 1218.

[75] *Rot. lit. cl.* I, 298b, 20 Feb. 1217.

some time by one of the king's predecessors and later granted away.[76] Similarly, the suggestion that royal rights were at stake led to consultation with the king about an assize of darrein presentment held before Henry III's justices *coram rege*. When William de Ferrers, earl of Derby, sought advowson of two churches, it came to light that the manors on which they were located had once been held by King Richard, but that King John had later granted them to the earl. There was some doubt over whether the right of presentation to the two churches had been included in the grant of the manors. The justices sent the record of this action to the king, "without whom they did not wish to proceed in judgment," but he commanded that they render judgment. They then ruled in favor of the earl of Derby, declaring, "It is considered that the lord king can seek nothing against that fine and charter." [77] Even though the decision went against the king, it probably did not displease him. At the time he was concerned by the discontent of his magnates; they had expressed dissatisfaction at a meeting of the great council in January 1237, and he had tried to conciliate them by adding three new members to his council, among them Earl William de Ferrers.[78] The old earl of Derby was one of the great barons of the realm, and he had faithfully served King Richard and King John as well as Henry III. He had been one of the strongest supporters of the royalist cause in the north of England during the civil war, 1215–1217. This prudence on the part of the king's justices in cases in which his rights were in question strengthens the impression that their first loyalty was to the monarch and only secondly to any abstract conception of the law. These cases also indicate that the king did not always dispense justice to all impartially and impersonally; on the contrary, sometimes he could be a respecter of persons, tempering his judgments with political prudence.

[76] *CRR*, I, 463, Easter 1201.

[77] *Note Book*, III, 249–250, no. 1236, pleas *coram rege* 1237–1238. For a similar case in which land formerly held by King John was at issue before the justices of Henry III, see *CRR*, XII, 234, no. 1145, Michaelmas 1225.

[78] Powicke, *Henry III*, pp. 152–154.

Many actions in the king's courts never reached the stage of judgment at all, but were settled by a compromise, a final concord. Compromise settlements reached out of court frequently ended suits before the royal justices, particularly the proprietary actions, which were subject to delays and postponements; but the parties had to gain the court's license for an agreement, the *licentia concordandi*. The final concord was used to end disputes in Anglo-Saxon and Norman times, and as lawsuits increased in the last years of the twelfth century, its use increased. The pipe rolls after 1181 show an increase in the number of offerings made for leave to agree.[79] A final concord was valued as a means of ending litigation because the "foot" of the fine was kept at the treasury as evidence that could not be lost, destroyed, or forged.

Granting permission for ending a suit by final concord was generally a routine matter for the royal justices. But a number of the disputes ended by final concords concerned the king in some way, and he sometimes took part in making the compromise. In some cases he did little more than give his assent, as King John did in the second year of his reign in a plea between William de Lanvaley, hereditary constable of Colchester Castle, and the baron Hugh de Beauchamps. The justices at Westminster gave them a day during the next term for taking their cirograph, so that meanwhile they could seek the king's assent.[80] This action,

[79] Doris M. Stenton, *English Justice between the Norman Conquest and the Great Charter 1066–1215* (Philadelphia, 1964), pp. 8, 51.

[80] CRR, I, 227, Trinity 1200; this did not end the litigation between them, however, for pleas continued (I, 340, 401; II, 4–5, 187; III, 14). Nor did this series of pleas end the litigation, for in 1240 a compromise was recorded between Beauchamps and Hawise de Burgh, granddaughter of William de Lanvaley (*A Calendar of the Feet of Fines for Bedfordshire . . . of the Reigns of Richard I, John, and Henry III*, ed. G. Herbert Fowler [Beds H.R.S., Vol. VI, 1919], p. 206, no. 458). On Lanvaley, see Painter, *King John*, pp. 59, 332, and Sanders, *Baronies*, p. 92; on Beauchamps, see Sanders, *Baronies*, p. 40. The same year, the king gave his consent to a final concord between the count of Guines, Flanders, and Simon de Abrincis (*CRR*, I, 265, Michaelmas 1200, pleas *coram rege*). Several postponements of the case followed (I, 400; II, 40, 64). None of these entries reveals the nature of the dispute, but *Pipe Roll 3 John*, ed. Doris M. Stenton (Pipe Roll Society, N.S.; London, 1936), Michaelmas 1201, p. 290, records an offering by Simon of 100 marks and a palfrey against the count concerning the manor of Newton.

an attempt to deprive Beauchamps of his barony of Eaton and Sandy, naturally gained the king's attention. He would watch closely the terms of any concord affecting such an important tenure.

The king's permission was necessary for any final concord that touched services owed to him. In John's reign, Albreda Marmion and Ralph de Pembridge reached agreement concerning the right to a manor and responsibility for the knight-service due from it. Since Albreda held the manor directly of the king and owed knight-service to him, she could not make an agreement without his leave, and the making of the final concord was postponed until she obtained his license to agree.[81]

King John played a role in the making of final concords throughout his reign. In 1201 he informed his justices *coram rege* that John Marshal and the master of the Templars had agreed to accept his arbitration of a plea of land.[82] In 1203 he directed the justices to act as arbitrators in a case. Several persons had brought an assize of novel disseizin against John of Branchester, archdeacon of Worcester, one of the king's favorite clerks. King John sent a writ to his judges informing them that the archdeacon was in his service and commanding them to "inquire diligently by those of whom the truth can best be ascertained, and, the truth being known, make peace between the parties." [83] Much later, in the thirteenth year of his reign, John again took part in the compromising of a plea of land. A final concord made at the Tower of London in the presence of the king and a number of the magnates ended a suit brought by Gilbert son of Roger and his wife against Robert Bainard.[84] As part of the

---

[81] *CRR*, VI, 2–3, 14, Michaelmas 1213, pleas at Westminster.

[82] *Ibid.*, I, 374, Hilary 1201. The final concord is recorded in I, 439–440, Easter 1201, pleas *coram rege*. Similarly, the itinerant justices in 1201 postponed a plea for the justiciar's arbitration (*Pleas before King*, II, 188, no. 645, pleas and assizes at Taunton).

[83] *CRR*, II, 209–210, 238, Easter 1203, pleas at Westminster; cited in Flower, *Introduction*, p. 15. On the career of John of Branchester, see Painter, *King John*, pp. 79–80.

[84] *CRR*, VI, 150–151, Michaelmas 1211; discussed in Flower, *Introduction*, p. 173.

agreement, the king, the justiciar, the earls of Pembroke and of Winchester, and several barons promised that they would do their best to see that when William de Percy, lord of the land involved, came of age, he would take the homage of Gilbert; the final concord would have been invalid without the assent of the lord of the land. King John's interest in the case is explained by the fact that William Briwerre, one of his most influential advisers, was William de Percy's guardian.[85]

King Henry III in his early years took a hand in the making of a final concord that touched him through his right of wardship. The daughters of Richard de Lucy, Mabel and Alice, were royal wards; and King John had granted their custody to Thomas de Moulton, who had married Richard's widow, their mother.[86] In 1224 the king summoned William de Forz, count of Aumale, to explain why he withheld from royal custody half the barony of Egremont, which should have passed to the Lucy daughters.[87] The inheritance had been complicated by a lack of male heirs which had necessitated a series of partitions among sisters. Since the Lucy girls and the count of Aumale were descendents of the sisters who had shared in the divisions, the case was important both because prominent figures were concerned and because a royal right, wardship of heiresses, was at stake. The count of Aumale had gained great favor under John, but he had a reputation for unreliability and bad faith due to his changing sides several times during the civil war. His reputation for unreliability was strengthened during the minority when his attempt to retain Castle Bytham and other lands led him to rebellion in 1221.[88] The bringing of the suit for Egremont at this time is evidence of the cost of his rebellion in influence with the royal government. Thomas de Moulton, the girls' guardian, had been one of John's sheriffs; but he had gained the king's ill-will due to financial difficulties and had suffered loss of his office, and even imprisonment. Although he was one of the more prominent

[85] Holt, *Northerners*, p. 21.   [86] *Ibid.*, p. 97; Sanders, *Baronies*, p. 24.
[87] *CRR*, XII, 247, no. 1223, Michaelmas 1224.
[88] Holt, *Northerners*, p. 65.

rebels, he returned to the service of Henry III, attaining the position of a respected justice in the royal courts by the time of his death in 1240.[89]

Thomas acted as attorney for the king, and he stated the claims of the Lucy heiresses. He said that due to default of male heirs the lordship of Egremont had been divided among three sisters: Alice, who died without heirs; Cecily, maternal grandmother of William de Forz; and Mabel, mother of Richard de Lucy.[90] William's attorney pled an exception; he maintained that the writ was improper because it stated incorrectly that the daughters of Richard de Lucy were in the king's hand, since actually they were married. Thomas replied that, though married, they were under age and the king's wards; he did not add that they happened to be married to his sons.[91] The count's attorney then pled another exception, maintaining that by the right the king did not have custody of the land because it was not held by military service but by cornage, a rent paid in oxen. The court rejected both these exceptions, ruled that the daughters should recover their seizin and the king his custody, and found William de Forz in mercy. The case had come to a conclusion, but another division of the land had to be made, for the count retained a right to half the estates. This made a new action necessary, this time between the count and Thomas, the

[89] On Thomas, see Painter, *King John*, pp. 120, 294, and Holt, *Northerners*, pp. 54, 57–59, 182–183.

[90] A genealogical chart makes clear the basis for the dispute (based on Sanders, *Baronies*, pp. 115, 134–135, 142):

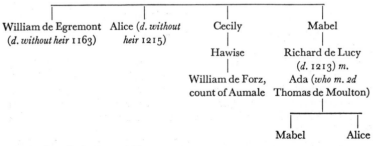

William de Egremont   Alice (*d. without*   Cecily   Mabel
(*d. without heir* 1163)   *heir* 1215) | |
                                        Hawise   Richard de Lucy
                                          | (*d.* 1213) *m.*
                                 William de Forz,   Ada (*who m.* 2d
                                 count of Aumale   Thomas de Moulton)
                                                         |
                                                  Mabel   Alice

[91] Sanders, *Baronies*, p. 24, n. 2.

girls' guardian, but their plea was compromised amicably in the presence of the king.[92]

Henry III was called upon to sanction other compromises that concerned him. One of them changed a landholder's status from tenant-in-chief of the king to subtenant, but the king's feudal privileges were carefully protected. It was recorded that the concord was made "saving the lord king's right" and "if it should please the lord king, without whom the concord cannot stand." [93] In this case, like many others, the justices waited upon the king's will in matters that touched his rights.

The king could withhold as well as give his leave to conclude suits by compromise. In the late summer of 1239, he commanded his justices to refuse to allow Hubert de Burgh and the abbot of Croxton to make a final concord, ending their plea of land.[94] No doubt, the reason for the king's refusal was the renewal of his old quarrel with the former justiciar, which was reaching its height at just this time. Hubert de Burgh had been the most powerful man in the kingdom in the years just after Henry came of age, but in 1232 the king had turned on him, driven him from the government, seized his lands, and harried him into hiding. Some of the great men had come to Hubert's defense, provoking the government crisis of 1232–1234. The king later repented of his persecution of Hubert, and the two were reconciled; but Henry revived the quarrel in 1239, once his enemy was old and defenseless.[95]

Leave to agree out of court was an accepted means of terminating pleas of land, and the plea rolls are full of final concords concerning property; but final concords ending appeals of felony

---

[92] *CRR*, XII, 177–179, no. 866, Michaelmas 1225; pp. 324–325; no. 1576, Michaelmas 1225.

[93] *Note Book*, II, 331–332, no. 403, Easter 1230, pleas at Westminster, compromise between Alice, countess of Eu, and Emma de Beaufeu. A compromise made in 1227 ensured that the new tenant would continue to make payments to the king (*CRR*, XIII, 49, no. 216). The king gave his consent and notified the exchequer that the new tenant would be responsible for the payments.

[94] *CRR*, 120, m. 18d, no. 966, octave of St. John Baptist 1239, pleas of the bench.

[95] Powicke, *Henry III*, pp. 141 and 765–766, app. C.

are rare. According to Glanville's treatise, appealor and appealed could be granted license to agree by the king or his justices, and such agreements are occasionally enrolled.[96] King John seems to have reserved the right to grant leave to himself. In 1207, Richard de Unfraville brought an appeal against Eustace de Vesci, alleging that he unjustly deforced him of the custody of a minor. The king then amerced James of Potterne, a royal justice, 100 marks because he had given them leave to agree *sine licentia regis*.[97] The plea rolls for the second half of John's reign record a number of licenses to agree in criminal cases granted *per regem*. The large oblations sometimes offered for the king's permission indicate that John's increasing financial difficulties were influencing his administration of justice. The appealed in a criminal action of 1213 offered twenty marks for license to agree, and the justices postponed the case for consultation with the king; King John did not give his permission for the agreement until the fine was increased from twenty to forty marks.[98] In another case, the oblation was much larger, but the accusation was more serious, for three men were appealed of seizing, beating, and imprisoning the king's serjeant while he was on official business.[99] The three accused gave the king 300 marks and three good palfreys to be allowed to make peace with their victim.[100]

Henry III too allowed the appealor and appealed to settle out of court, but he lacked his father's interest in profiting from the

[96] Glanville, p. 172, lib. xiv, cap. 1.

[97] *CRR*, V, pp. 58–59, Michaelmas 1207, pleas at Westminster. He later pardoned the amercement (*Pipe Roll 9 John*, ed. A. Mary Kirkus [Pipe Roll Society, N.S.; London, 1946], Michaelmas 1207, p. 207). However, the *CRR* account of the case does not seem to indicate that the judges gave them permission to agree; for Eustace was found in mercy, and the pipe roll, p. 74, records his amercement as 300 marks. *Rot. lit. cl.*, I, 114, 20 April 1208, records James' pardon. On his career, see Foss, *Judges*, pp. 529–530.

[98] *CRR*, VII, 24, Michaelmas 1213; *Rot. de. obl. et fin.*, p. 514, 25 Dec. 1213.

[99] *CRR*, VI, 236, Hilary 1212.

[100] *Ibid.*, pp. 280, 285, Easter 1212, pleas *coram rege*. Another purchase of permission to agree in an appeal was made the same term (p. 265): Robert Wood appealed Walter de Grancourt, and Walter offered three good palfreys for leave to agree (*Pipe Roll 14 John*, ed. Patricia M. Barnes [Pipe Roll Society, N.S.; London, 1955], Michaelmas p. 182).

grant of permission. A plea roll entry in 1223 records the names of a number of persons appealed of breaking the king's peace, and concludes, "And be it known that all have the lord king's license to agree, so that all are in mercy; and the lord king pardons them of their amercement." [101] Later the king's writ to the justices at Westminster informed them that he had granted license to agree in an appeal of robbery.[102]

The inflexibility of the law in medieval England has already been noted, and this rigidity meant that the criminal law was often needlessly harsh. Here the king's capacity to dispense with traditional rules served a useful function, that of tempering justice with mercy. Sometimes the king could mitigate the harshness of the penalties demanded by custom, although in the case of King John this was not always due solely to a quality of mercy. Once when he was hearing pleas at Northampton a husband and wife were brought into court charged with homicide, but he allowed them to escape punishment by taking the habit of religion. His decision was the result of a bargain struck by William de Braose, who had offered the king 100 marks on their behalf.[103] In January 1214, John granted letters patent to Roger de Presthope pardoning him of the death of John de Patton.[104] Once again, it is doubtful that thoughts of mercy alone moved the king, for it was the time when he was preparing his great military expedition to recover his Continental possessions, and Roger promised to contribute two horses in return for his letters of protection.[105]

[101] *CRR*, XI, 41, no. 238, Hilary 1223.

[102] *Ibid.*, 113, m. 3, no. 251, Michaelmas 17–18 Henry III.

[103] *Pipe Roll 5 John*, ed. Doris M. Stenton (Pipe Roll Society, N.S.; London, 1938), Michaelmas 1203, p. 58, discussed on p. xix. Later, under Henry III, the wife was not cloistered but was in court suing for her dower, and the record of her plea adds detail to the story (*Rolls for Glos., War. and Staffs*, pp. 627–628, no. 1298, pleas and assizes at Gloucester).

[104] *Rot. lit. cl.*, I, 162, Jan. 1214, *Teste me ipso*. The letters proved valuable in 1221, when Roger was presented before itinerant justices at Shrewsbury for that death (*Rolls for Glos., War. and Staffs*, p. 549, no. 1279).

[105] *Rot. de obl. et fin.*, p. 520.

Despite the opportunities for abuse, the king's pardons served a needed function, for English law provided no other remedy in cases of justifiable or involuntary homicide. The royal justices could not acquit or pardon an individual found guilty of homicide by misadventure or in self-defense; they could only bid him hope for the king's pardon.[106] The plea rolls provide a number of examples of the need for royal pardons in such cases. In 1212, Roger de Stainton was arrested because he had thrown a rock that accidentally struck and killed a girl; the justices showed the case to King John, and he, *motus misericordia,* pardoned Roger the death.[107]

John's son and successor, once he had come of age, also gave merciful judgments in cases of accidental deaths. In 1225 the itinerant justices consulted him about a girl who had accidentally struck a boy's head with a stone while she was playing with it. The boy seemed to have suffered no harm, but he fell sick and died less than a month later. She feared a charge of homicide and fled to sanctuary in a church, but the jury of presentment stated that the boy died from illness, not from the blow on the head. The justices then ordered that she be held in custody until the king could be consulted.[108] In Michaelmas term 1237, Henry III was moved to merciful action by a case that the archbishop of York called to his attention. When a woman took refuge in a church of his province following the death of her daughter, he petitioned the king on her behalf, saying that the girl had died by mischance and not by felony.[109] Henry III pardoned her

[106] Pollock and Maitland, II, 479; Bracton, II, 378, f. 134.

[107] *CRR,* VI, 351, Trinity.

[108] *Somersetshire Pleas (Civil and Criminal) from the Rolls of the Itinerant Justices, Close of 12th Century–41 Henry III,* ed. E. H. Chadwych-Healey (Somerset Record Society, Vol. XI, 1897), p. 60, no. 282; also in *Select Pleas of the Crown,* ed. F. W. Maitland (Selden Society, Vol. I; London, 1888), p. 119, no. 188. The king's decision is not recorded. For a similar case, see *Rolls for Yorks,* p. 415, no. 1134. A seven-year-old boy wounded another child with a knife so that she died. The justices on eyre adjourned the case to Westminster, where the boy was pardoned "for the king's sake."

[109] *CRR,* 117, m. 6d, no. 1101, Michaelmas 1237; cited in Flower, *Introduction,* pp. 497–498.

when it was found that her daughter's death was accidental, caused when she held the child's head between her legs while giving her a beating for stealing a neighbor's apples.

Not only were royal pardons necessary if death was caused by misadventure, but they were also necessary if one took another's life in self-defense. About the same time, Henry III ordered Ralph de Foun's outlawry for the death of Robert son of Matilda postponed until an inquiry was made into the facts of the case.[110] Jurors were to recognize whether Ralph was accused maliciously, *de odio et atia*, or, if the accusation was justly made, whether he killed Robert in felony or in self-defense. The jurors came and stated that Ralph was a forester of William de Ferrers, earl of Derby, and that Robert was a habitual poacher in the earl's forest. When the forester discovered Robert in the forest, the poacher attacked and wounded him, so that Ralph in defending himself killed him. Because of this, King Henry pardoned him of the death *de gratia sua et non per judicium*. The case indicates that homicide in self-defense was punishable and that pardon in such an event was not a matter of course in the law of the thirteenth century.[111] That the law's inadequacy was recognized is shown by the number of royal pardons recorded on the patent rolls of Henry III—a dozen or more a year.[112]

But along with a more merciful attitude in cases of death through accident or in self-defense, old Germanic notions on the right of private vengeance lingered. Not even the king's pardon could protect the slayer from the revenge of his victim's kinsmen.[113] Some writs granting pardon for death by mischance recognized this by adding the phrase, "On condition that he stand trial if anyone will proceed against him." [114] A striking example of this comes from the pleas of the crown heard before the king's justices at Northampton in 1202, when a jury of

---

[110] *Note Book*, III, 229–230, no. 1216, pleas *coram rege* 1236–1237.

[111] *Note Book*, III, 230, Maitland's note.

[112] E.g. *Cal. Pat. Rolls* (1232–1247), 18 Henry III, pp. 31–79, records ten pardons for deaths and three for larceny; 20 Henry III, pp. 130–165, records eleven for deaths, three for arson, and one for larceny.

[113] Pollock and Maitland, I, 513; II, 482–483; Bracton, II, 373, f. 132b.

[114] *Rot. lit. pat.*, I, 4; *Cal. Pat. Rolls* (1232–1247), pp. 19, 57.

presentment stated that Hugh the priest's son had been appealed twice for the same murder. The county court was asked to explain how this came about, and they complied, giving a long description of Hugh's troubles reaching back to the time of King Richard.[115] He had been outlawed for the death of Richard Rumbaud on the appeal of his victim's family and had fled, but after a long time he returned bearing the justiciar's writ to the sheriff of Northamptonshire:

Know that the lord king has pardoned Hugh, son of the priest of Grafton, of the flight and outlawry adjudged against him for the death of a certain murdered man, and in his letters has required of us that we help restore peace between him and the kinsmen of the slain. And therefore we command that you help Hugh to make that peace, and make known to us by your sealed letters what you do about this, since we are bound to make it known to the lord king.

This letter was read in the county court, and Hugh was told that he must find pledges for keeping the peace. Meanwhile, the kinsmen of Richard Rumbaud heard of his return, and they appeared at the next session of the county court prepared to appeal him once more. Hugh, however, unable to find pledges and fearful of the wrath of his victim's kin, did not appear again at the county court. Since he failed to appear at three successive courts, he was outlawed a second time; in the words of the clerk, "he should bear the wolf's head as he had before."

The king's pardon could not do one other thing; it could not restore the recipient's lands once they had escheated for felony. The law concerning escheats was that if a tenant was outlawed or convicted of felony, his land escheated to his lord, after the king had exercised his ancient right to year, day, and waste.[116] It was only natural that persons who received letters of pardon from the king should seek to regain their lands. Such a case came before the royal court in 1234, when John of Dorsington, who had received Henry III's pardon for homicide, brought suit to

<hr />

[115] *Northants. Assize Roll*, pp. 14–15, no. 66, 15 Sept. 1202, discussed in introduction, p. xxv.
[116] Pollock and Maitland, I, 351.

regain his lands.[117] The holder of the land maintained, however, that John had held his land of him and that after a year and a day in the king's hands, it had reverted to him; and he sought judgment "whether the lord king can pardon more than belongs to him?" In an earlier case in which a pardoned outlaw sought recovery of his lands, the tenant made a similar defense. He said that the king's pardon restored only what was the king's to give, "namely his peace and the protection of his dwelling place." [118] The decision of the court in these cases is not recorded, but Bracton in his treatise on the laws of England, composed about two decades later, agreed with the tenants. He wrote that a royal pardon does not restore escheated lands, for the king cannot give what is another's.[119]

Many, if not most, pleas in the royal courts ended with at least one of the parties being found "in the king's mercy." This could mean financial ruin under the Angevin monarchs, for they were quite arbitrary in assessing amercements.[120] The amercements of his courts provided King John with an easy way of extorting money or of pursuing personal enemies; yet only a few times were amercements made *per regem*.[121] In 1202 the justices on eyre in Lincolnshire found Gilbert de Ghent and Falcmar of Barton guilty of novel disseizin, and they amerced Falcmar 100 shillings; however, they adjourned the assessment of Gilbert's amercement to London.[122] Whether this was because of his baronial status or because of instructions from the king is unknown.

---

[117] *Note Book,* II, 648–649, no. 840, Hilary 1234, pleas at Westminster.

[118] CRR, XIV, 303, no. 1427, Easter 1231, plea brought by Fulk fitz Warin.

[119] *Note Book,* II, 649, Maitland's note; Bracton, II, 373, f. 132b.

[120] Holt, *Northerners,* p. 181; A. L. Poole, *Obligations of Society in the Twelfth and Thirteenth Centuries* (Oxford, 1946), p. 91.

[121] *Pipe Roll 2 John,* ed. Doris M. Stenton (Pipe Roll Society, N.S.; London, 1934), 1200, p. 18; *Pipe Roll 8 John,* ed. Doris M. Stenton (Pipe Roll Society, N.S.; London, 1942), 1206, pp. 8, 32, 64, 85, 98, 209. Amercement *precepto Regis, Pipe Roll 12 John,* ed. C. F. Slade (Pipe Roll Society, N.S.; London, 1951), 1210, p. 117. Amercements referred to the king, CRR, IV, 132; V, 227, 247.

[122] *Lincs Assize Roll,* p. 27, no. 173. The pipe roll does not record any amercement.

Again, in 1206, when Alan fitz Roland was found in mercy for novel disseizin, the justices of the bench noted that he was to be amerced before the king, perhaps because he was a tenant of King John's honour of Wallingford, perhaps because he was a strong and troublesome noble.[123] Whatever the reason for these amercements by the king, they seem to have been contrary to custom. According to Glanville's treatise, amercements of free men were to be assessed "by the oath of lawful men of the neighborhood," [124] but it cannot be determined from the plea rolls if juries did actually decide amercements in John's time.[125] Glanville is silent on the amercement of earls and barons, but the ideal that they must have sought was amercement by their peers, not by the king or his officers. In actual practice, they were amerced at the exchequer; one of the *curia regis* rolls states that "Henry is the lord king's baron; he is to be amerced at the exchequer." [126]

King John's financial dealings with his barons amounted to arbitrary exactions whenever he found it possible, and this extended to the amercements imposed in his courts, although he did not often personally assess amercements. But heavy amercements did not fall only upon the baronage. Any litigant coming before the royal justices was liable to be amerced to the limit of his ability to pay. Chapters 20, 21, and 22 of the Great Charter represent an attempt to end the practice, prevalent in John's last years, of basing amercements on capacity to pay rather than on the nature of the offense.[127] Chapter 20 restated the custom that amercements of ordinary people should be imposed by juries of

[123] *CRR*, IV, 132, Easter 1206; discussed in Flower, *Introduction*, p. 29. *Pipe Roll 9 John*, Michaelmas 1207, p. 189, records an amercement of 100 shillings against Alan for disseizin.

[124] Glanville, p. 114, lib. ix, cap. 11; Pollock and Maitland, I, 411, and II, 514.

[125] J. C. Holt, *Magna Carta* (Cambridge, 1965), p. 231, n. 2, discusses this problem and concludes, "But since amercements were so numerous and were usually uniformly assessed at ½ or one mark, it seems likely that juries were used only when the debtor protested against the amercement."

[126] *CRR*, II, 67, Henry de Bollei.

[127] See *Pipe Roll 12 John*, p. xxii, for an account of this practice during the eyre of 1210.

men from their neighborhood, and chapter 21 provided that barons should not be amerced except by their peers. This baronial privilege soon came to be of doubtful value because of the interpretation given by the king's judges. Bracton in his comment on this provision of Magna Carta defined the barons of the exchequer and the justices *coram rege* as a court of peers.[128] Neither of these groups of royal servants was likely to be overly sympathetic to the barons; their amercements would be simply confirmations of the king's wishes.

Nevertheless, the council of the young Henry III did attempt to implement this provision of Magna Carta, for it instructed the justices on eyre in Kent to amerce all who fell into the king's mercy before them *exceptis comitibus et baronibus qui coram concilio nostro amerciandi sunt.*[129] Certainly the barons would have recognized the members of the council as their peers. In one instance the young Henry seemed to return to the arbitrary ways of his father; this was in the case of the count of Aumale's withholding custody of the lands of the Lucy heiresses from the king. The justices of the bench ruled that the count was in mercy, and they concluded, "And when it should please the lord king to speak of damages, let him do his will." The king later assessed the damages at the rather large sum of 600 marks.[130] In another case, Henry delayed assessing an amercement until he could take counsel with William de Warenne, earl of Surrey.[131] The old earl Warenne had been a loyal friend of King John's, and the amercement concerned his son-in-law Hugh de Albini, the young earl of Arundel. He had fallen into the king's mercy when he failed to prove his right to hear pleas *de vetito namii* in some of his territories, which the king was contesting. Many

[128] Bracton, II, 330, f. 116f; discussed in L. W. Vernon Harcourt, "The Amercement of Barons by Their Peers," *E.H.R.*, XXII (1907), 732, and Holt, *Magna Carta*, p. 232.

[129] *Rot. lit. cl.*, I, 383b.

[130] *CRR*, XI, 247, no. 1223; p. 544, no. 2710, Michaelmas 1224. Other amercements referred to Henry III are in *CRR*, IX, 544, no. 2710, and *Rolls for Lincs and Worcs.*, p. 608, no. 1264.

[131] *CRR*, 117, m. 2d, no. 27, Michaelmas 1237, pleas *coram rege*.

years later, in the reign of Edward I, amercements for serious offenses were still sometimes made *ad voluntatem regis*.[132]

The king could pardon amercements as well as impose them. Needless to say, the plea rolls of King John's reign offer no evidence of his excusing those in his mercy. The plea rolls record only a few pardons of amercements, and they were pardons of persons too poor to pay. For example, a roll of the itinerant justices in Yorkshire in 1204 consisting of eight membranes records three pardons on account of poverty.[133] In contrast, the plea rolls for the early years of Henry III record numbers of pardons of amercements by the king and his council; and the eyre rolls show that during the minority the itinerant justices also canceled many amercements, usually on account of the poverty of those amerced.[134] The instructions they received from the council must have differed greatly from those of the justices sent on eyre by King John in 1210, when their chief purpose seems to have been to raise as much money as possible.[135] The council was making a genuine effort to fulfil the promise made in chapter 20 of the Great Charter that amercements should not exceed an individual's ability to pay.[136] Curiously, the phrase, "He is pardoned for the king's sake," sometimes occurs; perhaps, as Lady Stenton suggests, observation of this chapter was re-

---

[132] Harcourt, "Amercement of Barons," pp. 734, 736.

[133] *Three Yorkshire Assize Rolls for the Reigns of King John and King Henry III,* ed. Charles Travis Clay (Yorkshire Archeological Society, Vol. XLIV for 1910), pp. 9, 14, 16. Also CRR, II, 16, 295; III, 11, 280; VI, 220, 286, 330, 371, 382. Most of these pardons date from 1212.

[134] E.g. amercements pardoned by the king, CRR, IX, 198; XI, 41, no. 238; p. 527, no. 2633; XII, 61, no. 342; p. 464, no. 2322; XIV, 147, no. 728; by the council, VIII, 196; XI, 50, no. 288; by the treasurer, VIII, 34; by the justiciar, VIII, 331; by the itinerant justices, *Rolls for Lincs and Worcs.,* nos. 217, 283, 430, 886, 933, 1022, 1030, 1142. Even the amercements imposed on entire villages for allowing criminals to escape were pardoned because of poverty, nos. 1349–1351. See also *Rolls for Yorks,* nos. 37, 46, 59, 61, 72, 100, 172, 209, 274, 355, 367, 579, 669, 944.

[135] *Pipe Roll 13 John,* ed. Doris M. Stenton (Pipe Roll Society, N.S.; London, 1953), 1211, pp. xxxiv–xxxv.

[136] *Rolls for Lincs and Worcs.,* p. lxvi; *Rolls for Yorks,* p. li; Flower, *Introduction,* p. 497.

garded as a means of aiding the soul of King John.[137] The justices taking the assizes at Shrewsbury in 1221 pardoned the amercement of a chaplain "for God's sake and for thirty masses for the soul of King John." [138]

There can be no doubt that both King John and his son had a vital part to play in the judgments of their courts, even though they did not pronounce judgment themselves. Many times the royal judges sought their master's advice about pleas, and many times he shared in settling suits, helping draw up final concords. Most of the cases in which the king participated concerned royal lands or rights in some way. His word was final in any dispute centering on lands held of him or services owed to him. No one could question a royal charter. This points up the fact that the justices were first of all the king's servants, who were unwilling to do anything that would reduce his rights.

They recognized his position as the source of all justice in the kingdom too, for they did occasionally consult him on difficult points of law. These cases are rare, and they do not reveal any great royal influence in determining the future course of the law. The king could impose his will on the courts in opposition to established law and tradition, but his commands rarely constituted precedents for future judgments. When legal points were referred to the ruler, they were usually combinations of legal and political or legal and financial questions. His decisions in these pleas show him sometimes moved by political considerations. Both John and Henry III recognized that the common law courts could be made to serve as instruments of royal policy, yet neither of them dared to push this too far. There is no evidence that they deliberately turned their backs on the law to hand down judgments that could be considered unlawful. The assessment of amercements did give King John a financial weapon against his enemies, a weapon that the barons tried to blunt in Magna Carta. Perhaps this is less true of Henry III, but he and his justices were still careful to guard royal interests.

Yet the king's will had a necessary place in the work of his

---

[137] Lady Stenton in *Rolls for Yorks*, p. li.
[138] *Rolls for Glos., War. and Staffs*, p. 465, no. 1050.

courts, for he was the ultimate arbiter of all questions, the "judge ordinary of the realm." He alone could soften the harshness of the letter of the law. His will might sometimes deflect the course of justice, but other times it might serve as a vital companion of the law, adding a quality of mercy to its harsh justice.

THE KING'S INDIRECT PART IN JUDGMENTS

The plea rolls do not picture John or Henry III personally handing down judgments in the common law courts, yet they did take part in the work of justice. Sometimes the king's role in a decision is clear, for he may have assessed an amercement or issued a pardon. Other times his part is not so clearly visible, although his shadow can be seen in the background. He would hardly dare openly to turn his back on law and custom, but he sometimes had opportunities to change the course of justice enough that the decision must be labeled "political." Some of the *curia regis* rolls, chiefly those from John's reign, contain lawsuits in which the king's figure can be detected dimly in the background, shaping judgment to serve his political ends.

Some suits seem to have been inspired by John as indirect ways of weakening his opponents among the great barons. In others, judgments were given that suited his schemes against these opponents. The defendants in these actions later appeared among the rebels. The lesson in this was not lost on Henry III and his council, for they made less effort to use the courts indirectly as instruments for the implementation of political policies.

It has been seen that the royal justices consulted the king about difficult cases. Sometimes, the only explanation for their desire to consult him is his special interest in the persons involved in the case. In 1210, two merchants from Cologne accused of rape and robbery attracted King John's notice. They complained to his court that the sheriffs of London had seized them, imprisoned them with common criminals, and held them until they paid three marks. According to the record of the case, they complained that all this had been done to them in spite of letters patent from the Emperor Otto granting them his protection.[139] The court clerk must have misunderstood the German merchants, for the emperor's letters of protection would have had no value in England. Actually, King John had granted letters of protection to citizens of Cologne in England.[140] The justices' desire to consult the king must be explained by the political significance of the persons involved. Emperor Otto IV was John's nephew and his ally against the king of France. King John's alliance with Otto was an essential part of his scheme to build a great coalition in order to recover Normandy, and so it was important that he and the emperor remain on good terms.[141] Therefore, any action involving the emperor's subjects in England should have been called to the king's attention.

Another case in which the political importance of the parties involved appears to explain the justices' consultation with King John concerned knight-service. For whom a knight should perform his service was the question confronting the justices *coram rege* in a case in 1207. Richard Malebisse complained that Hugh de Boton had done homage to William de Percy for land in Wheldrake after he had earlier done homage to Richard for the same land, and he charged that by his action Hugh had disseized him of services due him.[142] Hugh placed himself on the grand assize to determine whether he ought to hold of Richard Malebisse or of William de Percy. It is possible that the justices felt it necessary to consult the king because of the legal complexity of the case. Usually the grand assize was simply a means of determining whether tenant or complainant had the better right to land, but here no one was questioning Hugh's right to hold the

---

[139] CRR, VI, 54, Michaelmas 1210; the case is discussed in Flower, *Introduction*, pp. 308–309.

[140] Thomas Rymer, ed., *Foedera, conventiones, litterae et . . . acta publica* (London, 1727), I, 133.

[141] A. L. Poole, *From Domesday Book to Magna Carta 1087–1216* (*Oxford History of England*, Vol. III, 2d ed.; Oxford, 1955), pp. 449–455, for John's diplomatic maneuvers.

[142] CRR, V, 53, 78–79, Michaelmas 1207; discussed in Flower, *Introduction*, pp. 216–217. Richard paid 25 marks to secure Hugh's presence in court (*Pipe Roll 9 John*, Michaelmas 1207, p. 71).

knight's fee, rather the question was of whom he held it. Yet there are other possible explanations for the justices' desire to consult the king. This action involved a royal right, the knight-service due from the land, and it would be in the king's interest to have the question of responsibility for that knight-service settled. More likely, the justices wished the king's advice because leading figures in the case—Richard Malebisse and the guardian of William de Percy, William Briwerre—were important royal servants. Richard had joined John in his rebellion against his brother in 1193–1194, and he had been keeper of the royal forests in Yorkshire until 1204, but he was currently under royal surveillance for his misdeeds while keeper of the forests. William Briwerre had been one of the administrators of Richard I, and he continued to be a loyal royal servant under John, as is shown by his appointment to be sheriff and custodian of a number of wardships.[143] The decision of the court was that Hugh de Boton should perform his service to Richard Malebisse; the situation became more complicated, however, when Hugh declared that he would never do service for Richard, perhaps because of his difficulties with the king.[144] The court then ruled that Richard should seize Hugh's knight's fee and hold it until his death, saving to Hugh's wife and her heirs their rights.

Sometimes cases reveal no trace of direct royal supervision, but the judges' treatment of them leaves the impression that King John was watching closely, in some indirect way making his influence felt. The parties to these proceedings were great barons, and the judgments handed down could have had a bearing on the balance of baronial power in the kingdom. The pleas could have been brought only with the king's consent, and possibly only by his command.

One of these pleas is a lawsuit between William de Stuteville and William de Mowbray for the Mowbray barony. According to the chronicler Roger of Howdon, this suit was ended by a final

---

[143] For their careers, see Holt, *Northerners*, pp. 75, 161–163 (on Malebisse), and 218, 234–235 (on Briwerre).

[144] *Ibid.*, p. 161. Richard Malebisse had stolen trees from the royal forest both for his own use and for sale.

concord made *voluntate regis*.[145] The basis for the suit lay in contention between the grandfather of William de Mowbray and Robert de Stuteville for the title to the barony of Cottingham, Yorkshire, in the time of Henry II. They had reached a compromise, so that Robert gained ten knight's fees to be held of Mowbray.[146] In his first year as king, John issued a charter to Robert's son, William, promising him justice in an action to recover the entire Mowbray barony in return for a fine of 3,000 marks.[147] William de Mowbray then offered the king 2,000 marks to have the plea proceed *juste et secundum consuetudinem Anglie*.[148] The case came before King John's court *coram rege* in 1201 at Louth in Lincolnshire, where a final concord was reached. William de Mowbray gave to William de Stuteville a manor in Warwickshire and nine knight's fees in addition to the ten given earlier to Robert de Stuteville.[149] In effect, Mowbray's promise of 2,000 marks gained him nothing, for he still lost a portion of his lands. According to the chronicler, it was considered lawful to reopen a dispute that had been settled years earlier in Henry II's reign because the settlement had never been confirmed by the king.[150] Certainly royal confirmation of agreements involving knight-service to the king was customary, but Mowbray must have regarded this as a flimsy excuse devised to mulct him, and he was in no hurry to pay his fine. It is doubtful that William de Stuteville would have dared to bring this suit if he had not known that he had the king's support. Mowbray's resentment over his treatment at the hands of John must have contributed to his leadership later in the baronial cause. As Sidney Painter wrote in a discussion of the case, "William de

---

[145] *Chronica*, ed. William Stubbs (Rolls Series; London, 1868–1871), IV, 117–118. The case is discussed in Painter, *King John*, pp. 29–30, and Holt, *Northerners*, p. 172.

[146] Sanders, *Baronies*, p. 37, n. 3.

[147] Painter, *King John*, p. 29; *Cartae Antiquae Rolls 1–10*, ed. Lionel Landon (Pipe Roll Society, N.S.; London, 1939), p. 60, charter no. 102, 22 April 1200.

[148] *Rot. de obl. et fin.*, p. 102.

[149] *CRR*, I, 380, Hilary 1201; Howdon, *Chronica*, IV, 117–118.

[150] Howdon, *Chronica*, IV, 118.

Mowbray's hatred of John seems to have been well founded early in the reign." [151]

Another suit that arouses the suspicion that King John was the instigator is one brought against the constable of Richmond, Roald fitz Alan, in 1208.[152] The constable and the king were not on good terms: Roald had resisted paying the thirteenth, and John had seized Richmond castle.[153] Since John had seized the lands in question as part of his escheat of the Normans, and since he had then granted them to Roald in return for a large fine, the suit cannot have had much basis. It is possible that it was part of John's program for pressuring Roald. The memory of this case may have been one of the grievances that led Roald into the rebels' camp in 1215.

Other cases show how those in the king's favor could have advantages in the courts. One of these is the suit brought by William de Braose against Henry de Nonant for the barony of Totnes in 1200–1205. In those years, William de Braose was a powerful Welsh marcher lord and a strong supporter of the king; it was not until several years later that John became so angered at him and took such dreadful revenge. A fine that William offered arouses suspicions concerning his suit; he offered £100 to have it come *coram rege*, and he promised to pay 700 marks instead of the £100, if he won his case.[154] William's claim to the barony was not strong, traced from the marriage of his grandfather to a daughter of the lord of Totnes in the time of the Norman kings. Weakening his claim even more was King William II's grant of the estates to Henry de Nonant's grandfather and the long possession of his family.[155] Nevertheless, the suit was settled by a final concord that divided the barony between the two men.[156] Clearly, Henry de Nonant was not powerful

---

[151] Painter, *King John,* p. 30.

[152] *CRR,* V, 147–48, Hilary 1208, pleas *coram rege;* for a fuller discussion, see Chapter 8, pp. 255–256.

[153] Holt, *Northerners,* pp. 46, 179, 207.   [154] *Rot. de obl. et fin.,* p. 46.

[155] For the history of Totnes, see Painter, *King John,* pp. 41–42; and Sanders, *Baronies,* pp. 89–90.

[156] *Fines, sive pedes finium,* 1195–1214, ed. Joseph Hunter (Record Commission; London, 1844), II, 65–66.

enough to defend his right against the suit of one who had the king's support.

Another case lends itself to the interpretation that King John's influence lay behind the decision of the court, especially since the loser was Eustace de Vesci, later a conspirator against the king and one of the leaders of the discontented barons. In 1211 he brought suit in the royal court against Geoffrey de Hickling for the service due from one knight's fee.[157] Geoffrey said that his ancestors had been the men of Eustace's ancestors, and that Eustace's father had been his guardian following the death of his own father. Then Eustace's father had transferred the custody to Robert de Valoines, who took Geoffrey's homage, and whose son later took his homage. Since the Valoines family had gained his service only through wardship, Geoffrey was uncertain to whom he owed service. He was willing to render it to whomever the court should declare, either to Eustace or to Thomas de Valoines, grandson of Robert. Eustace asked the court to have a jury of knights to recognize whether or not Geoffrey had done homage to Thomas' ancestor while he was in his custody; the justices denied his request, however, and ruled in favor of Thomas de Valoines, since his father had died in seizin of the homage and service. This decision may have been in accord with the letter of the law, for Thomas' ancestors had last been in possession of the service. But it left open the question of right, since a minor could easily be influenced by his guardian to do him homage. Eustace de Vesci must have attributed the decision to the king's ill-will.[158] To add insult to injury, the entry on the plea roll bears a note that Eustace should be summoned to answer for a debt to the Jews. Little more than a year after this suit, Eustace was implicated in a plot against King John, and he fled the kingdom to take refuge with his father-in-law, the king of Scotland.[159]

In 1212 two other suits in the royal court can be found in which the judgments are suspect even though within the letter of the law, for they coincided so closely with the king's wishes.

[157] CRR, VI, 135–136, Michaelmas 1211; cited in Flower, *Introduction*, p. 408.
[158] Painter, *King John*, p. 258.   [159] *Ibid.*, p. 267.

The suits probably owed their origins to conspiracies of King John against powerful barons whom he did not wish to confront directly. In the first of the suits, Earl William Longsword of Salisbury sought the barony of Trowbridge, the most important fief of Henry de Bohun, earl of Hereford. At the same time, Henry was called into court in a plea of service to the king concerning the service he performed for his barony of Trowbridge and to whom he owed it.[160] Bohun had refused to pay the full amount of scutage demanded by the king. There must have been some connection between these two actions, both coming at the same time. Perhaps the purpose was to prove that the earl of Hereford should hold the barony of the earl of Salisbury, for Bohun and the king were enemies, while William Longsword was the king's half-brother and was loyal to him. Bohun did not come to the court, but offered the essoin *de malo lecti*, bed-sickness. The judges accepted his essoin in the suit with William Longsword, and they assigned him another day; but in the plea of service, they ruled that the essoin could not be allowed and that his lands should be forfeit to the king. Technically, this decision was correct: no essoin could be offered in a plea of service and failure to appear brought forfeiture of lands, although they could be replevied later.[161] This ruling, in accordance with custom or not, must have pleased the king, for it enabled him to seize the lands of Henry de Bohun and to turn them over to his half-brother. Later, Bohun sought to recover his lands by replevin, but without success, and he did not regain them until years later. As part of King John's agreement with the barons in 1215, he promised to restore the lands he had seized *injuste et sine judicio*. Among the writs he issued commanding restitution of such lands was one concerning the honour of Trowbridge,[162] but in the confusion of the rebellion the command was never carried out. Years after the rebellion, Henry de Bohun's

---

[160] CRR, VI, 270, 320, 344, Trinity 1212; discussed in Painter, *King John*, pp. 210, 262–263, and in Holt, *Magna Carta*, pp. 121–122.

[161] Glanville, pp. 33–34, lib. ii, cap. 16; *Pipe Roll 14 John*, p. xxvi.

[162] *Rot. lit. cl.*, I, 215, 19 June 1215; cited in J. E. A. Jolliffe, *Angevin Kingship* (London, 1955), p. 328, n. 1.

son, Humphrey, brought suit to recover the lands from the countess of Salisbury, and they reached a compromise that ended the dispute.[163]

On the same day that the suit against Bohun was opened, Geoffrey de Say brought suit against Geoffrey fitz Peter, the justiciar, for the barony of Pleshy, the old Mandeville barony.[164] The case is confusing, but it does seem to illustrate the king's use of his courts to secure his will. At the time the case was begun, John and his justiciar were not on good terms, and the king may have encouraged Geoffrey de Say's suit as a way of harassing Geoffrey fitz Peter.[165] It was not until two years later, in Hilary term of 1214, that the case was concluded; and by that time both the principals had died, so that it had to be re-opened against the justiciar's son, Geoffrey de Mandeville. The king commanded his new justiciar to handle the case in the way that seemed best to him.[166] The royal judges dismissed the suit against Geoffrey de Mandeville on a technicality; because his opponent's writ named more lands than he actually held, they ruled that he need not reply to it.[167] This dismissal was in accord with the letter of the law, and at the same time it served King John's purposes. The justiciar's son was an important baron, but he was deeply in debt to the king, and he was tending toward the rebel party, which was forming by 1214. Perhaps King John was trying to win his favor, seeking to prevent his joining those barons plotting rebellion; he must have soon given up his attempt, however, for about the same time he seized Geoffrey's lands for his debts and accepted 15,000 marks from the young

---

[163] *CRR*, XII, 528–529, no. 2646, Easter 1226. The final concord, dated 1229, is listed in *A Calendar of Feet of Fines Relating to the County of Wiltshire, Remaining in the Public Record Office, from Their Commencement in the Reign of Richard I to the End of Henry III*, ed. Edward A. Fry (Wiltshire Archeological and Natural History Society, 1930), p. 21.

[164] *CRR*, VI, 270, Easter 1212.

[165] Holt, *Magna Carta*, pp. 122–124; Painter, *King John*, pp. 262, 278; Richardson and Sayles, *Governance*, p. 385. Lady Stenton, in *English Justice*, p. 104, n. 66, disagrees about the ill will between the king and the justiciar.

[166] *Rot. lit. cl.*, I, 168b.   [167] *CRR*, VII, 110–111.

Geoffrey de Say for them.[168] There is no record of any further proceedings in the common law courts concerning the Mandeville barony. Probably the king proposed to carry out his bargain with Geoffrey de Say through the operations of the exchequer. But John's "combination of bribery and coercion" failed to win either of the two young barons, for they both became rebels in 1215.[169] Regardless of the exact nature of the king's manipulations in these cases, they do show the close connection between the royal courts and royal policy, and they do show clearly why some barons believed that John had tampered with justice in order to persecute them.

The *curia regis* rolls of Henry III's reign do not record cases such as these. He was hesitant to attempt to tamper with the course of justice in the way that his father had. Occasionally, the judges consulted King Henry because of the political prominence of the parties to an action. Once, during his minority, the itinerant justices consulted his council about a criminal proceeding because the accused happened to be an important local Welsh lord, Howel son of Adam.[170] Later in Henry's reign, the decision to proceed against the powerful baron Fawkes de Breauté in an attempt to end his defiance of the royal court made consultation necessary. The justices referred to the king some of the special assizes of novel disseizin brought against him, and they also referred to Henry actions involving those who had supported Fawkes in his rebellion at Bedford Castle.[171]

It is difficult to account for this absence of cases revealing indirect royal pressure in the time of Henry III. It cannot be that

[168] *Rot. lit. cl.*, I, 168b. The suggestion that John was seeking to win Mandeville's favor is Painter's in *King John*, p. 263.

[169] Holt, *Magna Carta*, p. 124.

[170] *Rolls for Glos., War. and Staffs*, pp. 567–568, no. 1346; discussed in introduction, pp. xlviii–xlix. He held the manor of Lawton, Salop, of the king by serjeanty (*Rot. lit. cl.*, I, 441b).

[171] *CRR*, XI, 386, no. 1928, and 387, no. 1973, assizes brought before a special judicial commission at Dunstaple, June 1224. *Ibid.*, XI, 356, no. 1784, case involving Walter de Godarville, who had been at Bedford Castle with Fawkes (*Rot. lit. cl.*, I, 616). *CRR*, XI, 456, no. 2286, William le Gras was also against the king at Bedford Castle (*Pat. Rolls* [1216–1225], p. 454).

he was less concerned than his father with protecting royal interests. Neither can it be that his relations with his barons were so friendly that he found it unnecessary to seek to take action against them. Both rulers had their differences with the great men of England. One answer may be Henry's awareness that many of the rebels who fought his father in the war of 1215–1217 believed that they had suffered injustices in his courts. Another answer may lie in differences in the characters of the two men: Henry seems to have been less cunning than his father. Rather than confound his enemies in the devious ways so often followed by his father, he found himself confronting them directly in head-on collisions, as can be seen in the great state trials of his reign and in the periodic outbursts of baronial resistance.

5

The Great Men of the Realm Give Counsel

The royal justices sometimes consulted the king before giving judgment in doubtful cases, but traditional medieval conceptions of government required that the king himself take counsel when giving justice. The notion that the great men of the realm should advise the king is a heritage both from feudal principles and from earlier Germanic traditions. There was little difficulty in putting this theory into practice during the Norman period, when the jurisdiction of the king's court was limited to cases between his feudal tenants-in-chief. The theory remained in the time of the Angevin kings, but it was more difficult to make it a reality. Glanville praised Henry II because he sought the counsel of men "most learned in the laws and customs of the realm whom he knows to excel all others in sobriety, wisdom and eloquence."[1] After Henry's legal reforms the number of pleas heard in the royal courts became so great that not even the monarch himself could give his attention to them all, much less consult his magnates. The earls, barons, and bishops came to play a reduced role in the administration of justice, a task that was increasingly left to professional judges.

No doubt the king took counsel informally before deciding questions referred to him by his justices. Indeed, the plea roll records that one of King John's decisions—allowing a wife to appear in court without her husband—was reached *per consi-*

---

[1] Glanville, prologue, p. 2.

lium.[2] In such instances, advice was likely to come from the king's familiar counselors, who accompanied him on his travels about the country; if the king found that he needed the advice of the great men of the realm, however, he could afforce his court by calling on his barons and prelates for counsel. This practice of calling on the king's counselors to augment the court in cases of great importance was known to Bracton in the mid-thirteenth century. In his study of English law he wrote, "But if such a thing never happened before, and the judgment is obscure and difficult, the judgment should be referred to the great court [*magna curia*], that it may be determined by the advice of that court."[3] No distinction was made between the court composed of the king's professional justices and the court including other royal officers and the barons and bishops; both were essentially a single tribunal, the *curia regis.* Some scholars find in this judicial work of the king's council the beginnings of parliament, for they believe that the essential function of a parliament was the dispensing of justice.[4] Yet the *magna curia regis* in the twelfth and early thirteenth centuries was more often a deliberative body for debate on matters of war and peace, taxation, and custom than it was a trial court.[5] Nevertheless, there are a few cases from the reign of John and more from the reign of Henry III in which the great men of the kingdom were consulted. The

[2] *CRR,* I, 382, Hilary 1201; see above, p. 113.

[3] Bracton, II, 21, f. 1b, cited in Sayles, *Court of King's Bench* I, p. xxvi. Sayles assumes that *magna curia* is a reference to Henry III's council. H. G. Richardson, however, argues that Bracton used the term as a synonym for the court of the bench and that he was referring to difficult questions coming before the justices on eyre ("The Commons and Medieval Politics," *Trans. Royal Hist. Soc.,* ser. 4, XXVIII [1946], 22, n. 2). This interpretation leaves open the question of where unusual problems confronting the other courts would be heard.

[4] Among the supporters of this thesis are F. W. Maitland in his introduction to *Memoranda de Parliamento* (Rolls Series; London, 1893), reprinted in *Selected Historical Essays of F. W. Maitland,* ed. Helen M. Cam (Cambridge, 1957), pp. 52–96; C. H. McIlwain, *The High Court of Parliament and Its Supremacy* (New Haven, 1910); and H. G. Richardson and G. O. Sayles. For a summary of the opinions of the latter two, see Sayles, *The Medieval Foundations of England* (2d rev. ed.; London, 1950), chap. 27.

[5] W. S. Holdsworth, *A History of English Law* (London, 1903–1923), I, 28.

increase in these cases under Henry does seem to point toward the growth of another court, the high court of parliament.

Such cases are exceedingly rare during the reign of King John —only three instances in the plea rolls during all his reign. The first case occurred in the second year of John's reign when the earl of Chester and William de Bethune came before the justices *coram rege* to claim land that was in the king's hand.[6] The judges postponed the action until the morrow of Low Sunday (2 April 1201), "because the lord king wishes them to do by the counsel of his barons what he ought to do to each." Probably John planned to hold a council at Westminster on that date, for there was a prospect of war with France, and the king needed to summon his feudal host for foreign service.[7] John's desire to have the advice of his barons about this case can be explained by the importance of the persons involved. Ranulf, earl of Chester, was one of England's most powerful barons, and John's relations with him at this time were not happy. Indeed, it is likely that the king regarded the earl as his worst enemy among the English baronage.[8] William de Bethune, advocate of the abbey of St. Vaast, was an important vassal of the count of Flanders, and he held the honour of Rothersthorpe in England.[9] The lands of the advocate of Bethune had been seized into the king's hand, and he had offered a fine to recover them. It is likely that his contest with the earl of Chester represented a part of his attempt to recover his English possessions.[10] Unfortunately, no further information about this case is recorded in the plea rolls other than the brief entry recording its postponement, so that its conclusion cannot be determined; however, a royal letter of 1203 assigns the advocate's lands to the custody of his brother Baldwin.[11]

---

[6] *CRR*, I, 392, Hilary 1201.

[7] *Pleas before King*, I, introduction, pp. 117–118.

[8] Painter, *King John*, p. 29: "Thus from his accession to the end of 1204 John had refused all favors to Ranulf of Chester and had even deprived him of part of his rightful inheritance."

[9] *Ibid.*, p. 24; Sanders, *Baronies*, p. 141.

[10] *Pipe Roll 2 John*, ed. Doris M. Stenton (Pipe Roll Society, N.S.; London, 1934), Michaelmas 1200, p. 61.

[11] *Rot. de lib. ac de mis.*, p. 4, 13 June 1203.

The second example from the reign of John is a case in which both William Marshal and William de Reviers, earl of Devon, with his wife the countess of Meulan, sought possession of the manor of Sturminster in Dorset.[12] The decision was a difficult one because of the prominence of the contending parties; the earl marshal was a great lord and one of King John's stalwarts, having aided him in gaining his crown, but John's relations with the earl of Devon are not so clear. In 1200 the king had tried wooing him, but by 1204 he seems to have grown suspicious of him.[13] An added difficulty in this case was the countess' avowal that she had been disseized of the estate *per preceptum domini regis*. This already difficult problem became even more complicated when the earl of Devon and his wife failed to appear before the justices on the fourth day. William Marshal then sought immediate seizin of the land in question; the king was cautious, however, and sought the advice of his counselors. They were unwilling to give an opinion and suggested that the action be postponed until the morrow of the Assumption (16 August 1204), when "the lord archbishop and other great and wise men of the land" would be present. This is an unusual example of the king's familiar counselors declaring themselves unqualified to give advice, so that the matter was postponed for consideration by the *magna curia regis*. Such a course may have offered a diplomatic means for the king to avoid a decision that must offend one of two important figures. The court records reveal no further reference to this case, but on the date assigned for the hearing of the plea a great council was held at Worcester with a number of magnates attending.[14] What decision the assembled great men of the kingdom reached regarding the complaint of the countess of Meulan is unknown. Evidently she was unsuccessful in her pleading, for shortly afterward King John issued

---

[12] *CRR*, III, 124, 147, Trinity 1204, pleas *coram rege;* discussed in Flower, *Introduction*, pp. 16–17.

[13] Painter, *King John*, pp. 30–31, on the king's relations with the earl of Devon; pp. 36–37, on William Marshal.

[14] H. G. Richardson, "The Origins of Parliament," *Trans. Royal Hist. Soc.*, ser. 4, XI (1928), 153–154.

letters close and patent granting the manor of Sturminster to William Marshal.[15]

The third case about which King John consulted his magnates also involved an important individual, Philip de Poitiers, bishop of Durham. The bishop of Durham ruled over the county of Durham as viceroy. He and his court were responsible for governing the county without interference from royal officials. The proceeding centered about the important question of royal rights within the county palatine of Durham and the question of contempt of a royal command. In 1204, Geoffrey the son of Geoffrey complained that a plea of land had been brought against him in the court of the bishop of Durham by the bishop's writ. He maintained that this was unjust because in the time of Henry II no freeman had been impleaded concerning his free tenement in the bishop's court without a royal writ,[16] although traditionally civil suits in the county of Durham were brought by the bishop's writ and were tried in the bishop's court. Here was a test of the doctrine found in Glanville's treatise that no man need answer for his free tenement without the king's writ.[17] Eventually Geoffrey placed himself on the grand assize and brought a writ of peace forbidding the bishop of Durham to hold that plea.[18] The bishop's court refused to obey the royal command and proceeded with the case.

When the bishop's attorney came before the royal justices, he denied any wrong. He offered as evidence a charter of King John granting to Bishop Philip certain liberties, including the right to hear pleas brought by his own writ and not by the king's. Geoffrey asked that a jury of lawful men who were not of the bishop's liberty recognize whether or not Philip's predecessors

---

[15] *Rot. lit. pat.*, p. 45, and *Rot. lit. cl.*, I, p. 7b, 9 Sept. 1204.

[16] *CRR*, III, 108–110, Easter 1204, pleas *coram rege;* discussed in G. T. Lapsley, *The County Palatine of Durham* (Harvard Historical Studies, Vol. VIII; Cambridge, Mass., 1900), pp. 166–167, 313–316. A similar complaint was brought against the mayor of London during Henry III's reign (CRR, XIV, 222, no. 1081, Hilary 1231; also *Note Book*, II, 384–385, no. 489).

[17] Glanville, p. 148, lib. xii, cap. 25.

[18] *Pipe Roll 6 John,* ed. Doris M. Stenton (Pipe Roll Society, N.S.; London, 1940), Michaelmas 1204, pp. 44–45; he paid 20 marks.

had possessed this privilege. The roll is mutilated at this point, but it appears that the justices ordered a jury of twelve knights from Yorkshire, twelve from Northumberland not of the bishop's liberty, and twelve from his liberty—a total of thirty-six knights —to make the inquiry. The case had proceeded this far by the morrow of Low Sunday (3 May 1204), but two weeks after Trinity Sunday (5 July), when the bishop and Geoffrey appeared for judgment, King John ordered the case adjourned until he could consult his magnates.[19] The advice of the king's men is not recorded, but the problem raised by this proceeding ceased to be pressing, since the bishopric of Durham fell vacant and remained in the king's hand from 1208 to 1217. Besides, in 1208 the knights of the bishopric purchased a charter granting them the right of being impleaded only according to the customs and legal assizes of the kingdom and granting them the right to use these new forms of action in the bishop's court.[20] The larger question of royal rights within the liberty of Durham remained unsettled.

It is significant that two of the three cases found in which John sought the advice of his magnates come from the summer of 1204, the time of the loss of Normandy. The king's consultation of the barons and prelates is doubtless connected with this event: he must have felt that his position demanded caution in his dealings with the great men of his realm. If this does represent an attempt to conciliate the barons by giving them a role in judgments involving them, it was a short-lived effort; after 1204 the plea rolls record no other cases postponed for their consideration.

It is unlikely that the barons were happy with this situation, which left them hardly any part in the administration of justice, even though the judicial clauses of Magna Carta indicate that they generally favored the legal innovations of Henry II. The phrase *judicium parium* in chapter 39 reveals their desire for some voice in judgment. They did not reject the judicial system devised by Henry and his sons, and they were usually satisfied to

[19] CRR, III, 131. There is no further reference to the case in the plea rolls.
[20] Lapsley, Durham, pp. 167, and 313–316, app. 1.

have their suits settled by the same assizes that were available to all freemen. But they did wish for some role for themselves in cases involving members of the baronage if the law was doubtful or if the king failed to do justice.[21] Further evidence of dissatisfaction with the limited part that the great men of the realm played in judgment is found in the anonymous interpolation of the *Leges Edwardi Confessoris*, written by London jurisprudents during the early years of the thirteenth century. This compilation includes the statement that the king ought to render justice *per consilium procerum regni sui*.[22] Since the early years of Henry III were marked by an attempt to implement the Great Charter, the magnates might be expected to take a greater part in the decisions of the royal courts.

During Henry's minority his council did not find it necessary to afforce the court of the bench at Westminster with barons and prelates because the members of the council, themselves great men in the kingdom, could advise the justices informally. An example of this was seen in the decision of the bishops of London and Winchester concerning the hearing of the plea of the excommunicate count of Aumale.[23] The great men became accustomed to sharing in the work of justice. After Henry III attained his majority, he continued to consult them, for they took

[21] The "baronial interpretation" of Magna Carta, perhaps best represented by G. B. Adams, *The Origin of the English Constitution* (new ed.; New Haven, 1920), pp. 266–268, is that in seeking judgment by peers the barons rejected all the Angevin legal innovations and demanded a return to the feudal court as the only tribunal for trying barons. More moderate is the interpretation of Barnaby C. Keeney, *Judgment by Peers* (Harvard Historical Monograph Series, Vol. XX; Cambridge, Mass., 1949), p. 68: "The court of peers, then, was a court of great men deciding cases between king and subject." Similar is the view of F. M. Powicke, "Per iudicium parium vel per legem terrae," in *Magna Carta Commemoration Essays*, ed. H. E. Malden (London, 1917), p. 120: "The 'judicium parium' ran through a good part of English procedure, but was not universal. From the baronial standpoint it was especially important as a last resort, in cases where justice had not been done, and where the law was uncertain." For Bracton's views, see Chapter 8, pp. 237–238.

[22] *Die Gesetze der Angelsachsen*, ed. Felix Liebermann (3 vols.; Halle, 1903–1916), I, 635–636; and Bertie Wilkinson, *The Constitutional History of England 1216–1399* (London, 1948–1958), III, 84–85, 100–101.

[23] See Chapter 3, pp. 113–114.

part in judgments in several cases. In five of the cases, one of the litigants was a bishop or an abbot. In 1228 contention arose between the king and Stephen Langton, archbishop of Canterbury, about which court—the royal courts or the archbishop's court—should try pleas of the crown involving the archbishop's men.[24] When Henry came to agreement with the archbishop on this question, it was recorded that the king did so "at the instance of and by the petition of his magnates." A few years later a case between the king and another prelate, the bishop of Norwich, was postponed for hearing *coram domino rege et consilio suo.*[25] About the same time, however, the king wrote to the barons of the exchequer commanding them to join with the justices of the bench in deciding the case.[26]

Other evidence of the magnates' part in judgments comes from an action before the bench in 1229, when Katherine de Montague sought from the abbot of Grestain in Normandy land at Marsh, Buckinghamshire, held by her late father.[27] The abbot maintained that her father had granted the land to the church of Grestain by his charter. Katherine objected that her father could not have enfeoffed the abbot because he held land of him, and one cannot be both lord and tenant of the same person. She further objected that the transfer ought not to be binding because it was a deathbed grant, but the abbot replied that her father had suffered no infirmity at the time unless perhaps from goiter. The case was adjourned for judgment "before the lord king at Westminster in the presence of the justiciar and the earl marshal and other great men," where the judgment was in favor of the abbot. In effect, then, the court ruled that a tenant can grant a part of his land to his lord, becoming both lord and tenant, although Glanville earlier and Bracton later expressed a

[24] CRR, XIII, 105, no. 453, Hilary 1228; also in Note Book, II, 229–230, no. 277.

[25] CRR, XIV, 384, no. 1793, Trinity 1231.

[26] Close Rolls (1227–1231), p. 503, 15 May 1231, Teste Rege.

[27] Note Book, II, 292, no. 354, Michaelmas 1229. Katherine was the heiress of John de Montague, baron of Chiselborough, Som. (Sanders, Baronies, p. 34).

contrary view.[28] In 1233 a question about the liberty of the bishop of Carlisle was heard in the magnates' presence; and in 1237 the abbot of Osney was accused in their presence of having forged a charter.[29]

Suits involving important laymen could cause the king to take counsel with his magnates too. The question of the succession to the earldom of Chester in 1237–1238 was a difficult one that required such consultation.[30] When John the Scot, earl of Chester, died in 1237 leaving as his heirs two nieces, who were the daughters of his eldest sister, and three other sisters, the normal practice should have been to divide the inheritance equally among the cosharers, his two nieces sharing a quarter and each of his surviving sisters receiving a quarter.[31] They would all hold their shares in chief of the king. However, William de Forz II, son of the count of Aumale, to whom the title of earl of Chester passed because of his wife's right of primogeniture, claimed first that the other cosharers should hold of him rather than directly of the king, that is, that the Norman custom of *pariage* be followed. Later he claimed that the earldom was indivisible and, therefore, it rightfully belonged to him and his wife alone.

[28] Glanville, pp. 71–74, lib. vii, cap. 1. Marginal comment in *Note Book* notes this decision as meaning that one can be both lord and tenant, but Bracton, II, 84, f. 24, states definitely that this cannot be.

[29] *Note Book*, II, 564, no. 741, Hilary 1233, bishop of Carlisle; and III, 203–206, no. 1189, Trinity 1237, abbot of Osney.

[30] *CRR*, 117, m. 10, no. 136C (also in *Note Book*, III, 242–243, no. 1227; pp. 280–283, no. 1273). The problem is discussed in Ronald Stewart-Brown, "The End of the Norman Earldom of Chester," *E.H.R.* XXXV (1920), 26–53. A genealogical chart helps to clarify the issues:

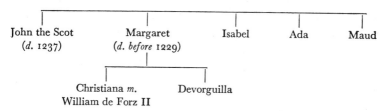

| John the Scot | Margaret | Isabel | Ada | Maud |
| (d. 1237) | (d. *before* 1229) | | | |

Christiana *m.*   Devorguilla
William de Forz II

[31] The rule set forth in a royal letter to the justiciar of Ireland, *Close Rolls* (1234–1237), pp. 375–376, 30 Aug. 1236; Pollock and Maitland, II, 277; Stewart-Brown, "End of Chester," p. 42.

Naturally, the other heirs opposed William and favored dividing the heritage according to the custom of England. The magnates and members of the king's council assembled at London were unable to advise the king: "All said that they had never seen such a case. Neither was it certain to them, nor did they know of anything in the charter of liberties concerning such a case, nor did they wish to judge it by examples used in overseas regions, nor had they ever seen such a case in written law." [32] Why this case should have been more difficult to judge than any other case involving female heirs is not clear; perhaps it was because it involved a palatinate rather than an ordinary lordship. The only solution was to postpone the case until the court could be afforced with more great men of the realm. When the plea was renewed, it was held at Westminster before a virtual parliament: the king, the papal legate Otto, the two archbishops, five bishops, and a number of earls and barons. This great assemblage judged that the traditional custom of England should prevail; that is, the earldom of Chester should be divided equally among the cosharers, all holding directly of the king. Such a decision could not have been displeasing to Henry III, for the son of the troublesome count of Aumale might have been as difficult as his father had he gained the earldom palatine. Later, as a result of the partition, the king was able to gain both the title and the county for the crown.

Another case that came into the king's court in 1237 involved a great baron and had to be settled *coram consilio domini regis*. This time the baron was Gilbert Marshal, earl of Pembroke. He was called to warrant lands that Henry III was claiming against several persons as his "escheat of the Flemish" because of Baldwin de Bethune's death.[33] Gilbert Marshal had a part to play in the proceedings because his brother, William, had been married to Baldwin's daughter, Alice.[34] He denied the king's claim that the lands should escheat to the crown. He admitted that Alice

[32] *Note Book*, III, 243.

[33] CRR, 117, m. 1, no. 8, Trinity 1237, pleas *coram rege;* (also *Note Book*, vol. II, no. 1220).

[34] Painter, *King John*, p. 41.

had died without leaving an heir, but maintained that Baldwin's lands should pass to his nephew, Robert de Bethune.[35] Later the king and his council accepted Gilbert's account, and their judgment was that the lands should not escheat to the crown but that Robert should inherit them.

An earlier case centering around a great baron that Henry III submitted to the magnates of the kingdom had far greater constitutional significance; it is the proceeding in which they considered his outlawry of Hubert de Burgh, the former justiciar.[36] The *magna curia regis* met at Gloucester a week before Ascension Sunday (23 May 1234), called, according to the court clerk, "because the lord king wished justice to be exhibited to anyone in his court." The assembled magnates advised him that the outlawry was contrary to the law of the land, in effect judging the king's deeds in his own court. Such an action is in marked contrast to the role of the great men in the courts of King John.

One criminal accusation that was heard before the king and his great council in 1235 concerned neither ecclesiastical officials nor barons, but Jews. It was removed from the court of the itinerant justices for hearing "before the lord king and the lord archbishop of Canterbury and the greater part of the bishops, earls, and barons of England." The reason for its removal there was "because such a case had never before come into the lord king's court and because it concerned God and Holy Church and

---

[35] Sanders, *Baronies*, pp. 141–142, makes possible the construction of a genealogical chart to clarify the succession:

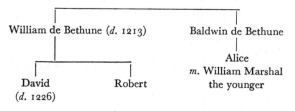

[36] *Note Book*, II, 664–667, no. 857, Easter 1234. Hubert's effort to recover lands seized by the king also came before the magnates; these cases are considered at greater length in Chapter 8, pp. 263–265.

because circumcision and [Jewish] baptism are injurious to the faith." [37] A group of Jews at Norwich were accused of seizing a Christian boy, circumcising him, and giving him a Jewish name, before he was able to escape and tell his story. According to widespread myth in the Middle Ages, this was the prelude to the boy's ritual murder re-enacting Christ's crucifixion.[38] Thus the accusation was not simply one of the crime of kidnapping, but the more serious crime of attempted murder and contempt for the Christian religion. Eventually, the case was returned to the itinerant justices for trial, and four prisoners were found guilty and executed.

Another plea heard before Henry III, the archbishop of Canterbury, and other great men was an action of debt against the London agent of some Florentine merchants.[39] His accounts were some £250 in arrears. Apparently, the king took special interest in the case because he wished to demonstrate to the Italians the high quality of English justice. He and his magnates decided that the agent should find men in Florence to stand as securities (*fidesjussores*) for his payment of the debt to his employers.

The plea rolls of Henry III, then, do record some cases that were heard in the presence of the great men of the kingdom. Here there is a contrast with the rolls from the reign of King John, for Henry sought the counsel of his great men more often than did his father: only three instances are found in John's reign and at least ten in the years of Henry III. The magnates did have a larger part in the work of the royal courts under Henry than under his father, a step toward the high court of parliament. Not simply difficult legal questions, but combinations of legal and political matters were raised. A list of the persons concerned in the cases submitted to the barons and prelates reveals the role of feudal politics: under John there was

---

[37] *CRR,* 115B, m. 22, no. 1320, Hilary 1235; also in *Select Pleas, Starrs, and Other Records from the Rolls of the Exchequer of the Jews,* ed. J. M. Rigg (Selden Society, Vol. XV; London, 1902), pp. xliv–xlvii.

[38] Rigg, *Select Pleas,* p. xxii.

[39] *CRR,* 115B, m. 16d, no. 1187, Oct. 1234.

the earl of Chester, the earl of Pembroke, the earl of Devon, and the bishop of Durham; under Henry there was the archbishop of Canterbury, the bishops of Carlisle and Norwich, a Norman abbot and an Irish abbot, the count of Aumale, the earl of Pembroke, and the earl of Kent.

It should be noted that the initiative for consultation of the great men in these cases came from the monarch and not from the magnates involved in the disputes. Both John and Henry III afforced their courts by calling on their barons when they desired advice that their familiar counselors could not supply. Henry made no serious attempt to provide for *judicium parium* in suits involving barons, and he seems to have resented talk of their right to it, in spite of Magna Carta. In 1227 his brother, Richard of Cornwall, announced in answer to a simple case of novel disseizin that he would submit to the judgment of the great men of the realm; Henry lost his temper on hearing his brother's reply, and he demanded that Richard either restore the land or leave England.[40] The king's tutor and trusted adviser, Peter des Roches, later replied to baronial demands for recognition of their right to judgment by peers that "there are no peers in England." [41] The judgment of the *magna curia regis* was sought in some cases, not because it was a court of peers, but because it was a body of the wise men of the kingdom, learned in the law and custom.

[40] Roger Wendover, *Flores historiarum*, ed. Henry G. Hewlett (Roll Series; London, 1886–1889), II, 320–322; *Rot. lit. cl.*, II, 191b; discussed by Keeney in *Judgment*, pp. 75–76.
[41] Powicke, *Henry III*, p. 76.

6

The King Corrects the Errors of the Royal Courts

With the establishment of judicial branches of the *curia regis* in the late twelfth and early thirteenth centuries, the king found himself in the position of an appellate judge. He was the "author of justice," and he was chosen "that he might do justice to everyone." [1] Consequently, he retained responsibility for the judgments of his courts whether he was present or not. Miscarriages of justice in the royal courts could always be corrected by appeals to the monarch.

English judges had before them the example of canon law with its machinery for appeals from lower courts to higher courts. This hierarchy of ecclesiastical courts culminating in the papal *curia* at Rome became familiar to increasing numbers as appeals from the English church courts multiplied. The English king and his royal servants must have envied the pope's position at the head of a graduated hierarchy of courts having a regular process of appeal, and indeed parallels were drawn between the role of the pope in the system of church courts and that of the king in the lay courts.[2] Despite the example of the ecclesiastical courts, the English royal courts failed to develop a rational system for the appeal of judicial decisions. Maitland clearly expressed the problem facing medieval English legal minds when he wrote, "The idea of a complaint against a judgment which is

---

[1] Bracton, II, 305–306, f. 107.
[2] *Ibid.*, IV, 281, f. 412; Pollock and Maitland, II, 664.

not an accusation against a judge is not easily formed." [3] Thus at the beginning of the thirteenth century the regular procedure for challenging judgments of a lower court was to convict that court of false judgment in the royal court. In cases where this process was not available, the only remedy was to appeal to the king, the source of all justice, for the correction of errors.

Glanville's treatise indicates no means of appealing a decision by the royal justices. That the judgments of the royal courts were final is indicated in the *Dialogus de scaccario* too. The author expressed the authority of the exchequer in a way that makes this clear: "For it shares with the King's court in which he administers justice in person the privilege that its records and judgments may not be impugned." [4] But, after Glanville wrote, the number of cases coming before the royal justices increased, and there were many men making judgments in the king's name. John and his son would have to provide remedies for the correction of their mistakes.

By the end of the twelfth century, machinery existed for reversal of decisions in the local courts—county and borough, and private jurisdictions—by the king's court. Royal control over these courts had been the rule since the time of King Henry I, when it was declared that only the *curia regis* could hear accusations of false judgments. In the *Leges Henrici Primi,* one of the duties listed for the itinerant justices on their visits to the county courts is punishment for *injustum judicium* or *defectus justiciae.*[5] According to Glanville, an unsuccessful litigant in an inferior court could purchase a writ *recordari facias,* which ordered the presiding officer of the incriminated court to have four knights bring a record of the proceedings before the royal justices. Then an action would take place between the accuser and the four knights representing the court.

Pleas of false judgment from local courts were not unusual

---

[3] Pollock and Maitland, II, 668.   [4] *Dial. de scac.,* p. 14.

[5] Pollock and Maitland, II, 666, n. 7; Maitland found this rule in the *Leges Henrici Primi,* cap. x. 1. The most convenient edition of the *Leges* is *Die Gesetze der Angelsachsen,* ed. Felix Liebermann (3 vols.; Halle, 1903–1916), I, 547–611.

during the reigns of John and Henry III, and they generally proceeded without requiring the king's attention. Yet even in such cases his intervention sometimes can be noted. The justices might find it necessary to consult the king about a plea of false judgment. Early in John's reign the prior of Coventry brought an action of false judgment against the county court of Leicester.[6] He charged that when a plea of land was brought against him, he sought view of the land in question, but that the county court had refused it and had forced him with threats to defend his right by wager of duel. He immediately complained to the justices that the county would render a false judgment, causing him to lose his land. After hearing the testimony of the prior and representatives of the county court, the justices of the bench marked the plea *loquendum cum rege* and postponed it for hearing at Winchester when King John would be present. The king's decision is unknown, for the prior of Coventry eventually gained undisputed right to the land by means of a final concord made with the plaintiff.[7]

Later during the minority of Henry III, the young king's council took part in a plea of false judgment heard before the justices at Westminster. The plea came from the court of the "count of Brittany," that is Earl Ranulf of Chester, who had a right to the title as a result of King John's grant of the count of Brittany's English fiefs.[8] No doubt, the council's interest in the proceedings was due to its wish to protect the rights of the earl of Chester while he was overseas on a Crusade.[9] He had great prestige among the young king's advisers, for he had been first in dignity among the royalists during the baronial revolt and the war with Prince Louis of France. Otherwise, it would be difficult

[6] *CRR,* I, 445–446, Easter 1201; discussed in Flower, *Introduction,* pp. 67–68.

[7] *Pipe Roll 3 John,* ed. Doris M. Stenton (Pipe Roll Society, N.S.; London, 1936), Michaelmas 1201, pp. 241–242. The prior offered a half-mark for the concord. In another case of false judgment, this time against a hundred court, the record was ordered produced before King John (*CRR,* III, 163, Trinity 1204; also in *Select Civil Pleas,* ed. W. P. Baildon [Selden Society, Vol. III; London, 1890], p. 73).

[8] Powicke, *Henry III,* p. 177, n. 1.

[9] "Ranulf de Blundeville," *Dict. Nat. Bio.*

to account for the interest of the council in this plea, which centered on possession of a stolen mare. The appealor had maintained that one of the warrantors of the appealed was a hired champion, but the court had not acted on his charge.[10] The council's judgment was that the count of Brittany should retain his court, but that the hired warrantor should lose his foot. A word of explanation concerning this penalty was added to the record: "And be it known that he has this merciful judgment by the council of the lord king, since he merits a greater punishment."

The action of false judgment as described by Glanville proceeded against the court that had given judgment, but this remedy was not available for judgments of the royal courts. The need for machinery to prevent miscarriages of justice there became pressing with the institution of the grand assize and the petty assizes and the resulting increase in their activity. Since the judgments in the assizes were based upon the findings of juries, it was possible to challenge their decision without accusing the king's court of false judgment. One could proceed against the jurors by charging them with swearing falsely. At the institution of the grand assize, according to Glanville, provision was made for the possibility of false oath by the jurors, and a severe punishment was prescribed.[11] But his treatise gives no indication of the means of convicting the jury in one of the petty assizes; presumably the person suffering from their false information could complain to the king.

A definite procedure for convicting jurors of false oath first appeared during the early years of King John—the jury of attaint, a panel of twenty-four to decide whether the earlier jury had sworn falsely. The earliest reference in the plea rolls to such a jury dates from the autumn of 1202, when the roll records the postponement of a jury "taken by the writ of the lord king from

---

[10] *CRR*, VIII, 271–272, Hilary 1220; also in *Select Pleas of the Crown*, ed. F. W. Maitland (Selden Society, Vol. I; London, 1888), no. 192. For another plea of false judgment that received the council's attention, see *Rolls for Lincs and Worcs.*, pp. 513–514, no. 1036, in which Alfred the tailor complained of a judgment in the county court of Worcester.

[11] Glanville, pp. 35–36, lib. ii, cap. 19.

beyond the sea for convicting the jurors who had made an assize of novel disseizin." [12] The fact that this writ came from the king in Normandy rather than from the justiciar, as would have been the case with a writ *de cursu*, indicates that it was an innovation.[13] Further evidence that the attaint jury was due to King John's initiative is found in another case from the same term. He sent a writ ordering that the jury of twenty-four concerning a grand assize proceed unless *ratio et consuetudo regni nostri* should stand in the way.[14] In the same year, 1202, a roll of the justices on eyre records an oblation of forty shillings to have the oath of twenty-four knights to convict the jurors of an assize of mort d'ancestor.[15] The new procedure evidently filled a need, for entries relating to attaint juries occur regularly both in the plea rolls and in the pipe rolls for the years following 1202.[16]

Under John, juries of attaint were allowed against both juries of the grand assize and juries of the possessory assizes, but under Henry III came a change in this practice. A grand assize had come to recognize whether the prior of St. Vaast or Thomas de Canville had the greater right to the advowson of a church.[17] The decision of the jurors was for Thomas, but the prior complained that they had sworn falsely because they had ignored a

[12] *CRR*, II, 97–98, fifteen days after Michaelmas 1202.

[13] *Proc. without Writ*, pp. lxxxvii–lxxxviii.

[14] *CRR*, II, 113, five weeks after Michaelmas 1202, is the first reference to this case; p. 223, Easter 1202, gives the text of the writ.

[15] *Lincs Assize Roll*, p. 7, no. 43; also p. 27, no. 173, where 20 shillings is offered. There are no references to these cases in the Pipe Roll for 1202; however, an oblation is recorded which may be a reference to an attaint jury: "And one mark from Robert de Worcester that the recognitors who made a recognition of novel disseizin against Roger the physician and Fina de Buckland concerning land she held of Robert be convicted" (*Pipe Roll 4 John*, ed. Doris M. Stenton [Pipe Roll Society, N.S.; London, 1937], Michaelmas 1202, pp. 91–92).

[16] E.g. *Pipe Roll 6 John*, ed. Doris M. Stenton (Pipe Roll Society, N.S.; London, 1940), pp. 185, 245; *Pipe Roll 7 John*, ed. Sidney Smith (Pipe Roll Society, N.S.; London, 1941), pp. 59, 230, 274; *Pipe Roll 8 John*, ed. Doris M. Stenton (Pipe Roll Society, N.S.; London, 1942), pp. 41, 82, 97, 101, 123, 202, 203, 208, 213, 223; *CRR*, III, 134, 138, 192, 194, 248, 315, 332; IV, 81, 96, 118, 173, 177, 230; V, 39, 211, 224.

[17] *CRR*, XIII, 69–70, no. 312, Trinity 1227 (also in *Note Book*, II, 216, no. 262).

number of charters that proved his right to the church. The justices would not grant a jury of twenty-four until they had consulted the king and the justiciar. Consequently, they postponed the case until a later date, but the prior of St. Vaast failed to appear on that date to hear the king's decision, and so the verdict of the grand assize in favor of Thomas de Canville stood. Bracton's marginal comment on this case is that there can be no attaint of a grand assize, and this is the teaching in his treatise on the laws of England.[18] This marks a departure from earlier practice, for there are examples of juries of attaint against the knights of grand assizes in the plea rolls from John's reign.[19] Apparently the precedent was set simply by the chance absence of the abbot, not by the king's decision.

The regular forms of action for questioning the judgments of a court were two—the plea of false judgment against an inferior court and the jury of attaint against an assize. Undoubtedly, miscarriages of justice occurred that could not be remedied by either one of these procedures. The problem was most acute in the royal courts, since no charge of false judgment against the king's court was permitted, but where no other remedy was available there was always the possibility of appeal to the king. The monarch, "the likeness on earth of the divine majesty," could redress the grievances of his subjects if regular process failed them.[20] If no known writ would right an individual's wrong, as was the situation in instances of error in the royal courts, he could appeal to the king, beginning proceedings by plaint or *querela*.[21] The rolls of the royal courts under John and

[18] Bracton, III, 341, f. 290b.

[19] E.g. the case recorded in CRR, IV, 17, 58–59, 118, 141, 173. For a discussion of this problem, see G. E. Woodbine, "Cases in New Curia Regis Rolls Affecting Old Rules in English Legal History," *Yale Law Journal*, XXIX (1930), 505–513.

[20] John of Salisbury repeatedly described the prince as the "image of divinity" in his *Policraticus*, ed. C. C. J. Webb (Oxford, 1909), I, 236, lib. iv, cap. 1; II, 74, 80, lib. vi, capp. 25–26; II, 345, lib. viii, cap. 17. Bracton wrote of the king's "likeness to Jesus Christ, whose vice-regent he is on earth" (II, 33, ff. 5b–6).

[21] The subject of proceedings by plaint in the royal courts has been examined by Richardson and Sayles in the introduction to *Proc. without Writ.*

Henry III reveal several examples of complaints concerning the correctness of a judicial decision which received the king's personal attention, and in other cases the king acted on his own initiative to remedy a miscarriage of justice in his courts. A comparison of cases in the two reigns reveals a contrast: a greater concern for justice for its own sake was shown by Henry III and his council.

First, the king's supervision of the various lower courts must be considered. As has been shown, the writ *recordari facias* was available for litigants in the inferior courts who questioned the judgment they had received. However, one of the parties to an action might complain of a miscarriage of justice without proceeding by writ, or he might offer a fine to have the case removed to the king's court. Such a case has already been met in connection with cases referred by the king to his magnates—the complaint of Geoffrey son of Geoffrey against the bishop of Durham's court for proceeding in a plea of land without a royal writ. Another case from Durham came before the king in 1211–1212. The court was then in the custody of the king due to the vacancy of the see, and the knights of the county palatine had purchased the privilege of enjoying the royal assizes in the court of the bishopric. The right to hold five carucates of land had been contested by Gilbert Hansard and Brian son of Alan and his wife Alice, who was also Gilbert's sister, in the court of Durham and later transferred to the king's court.[22] The record of the action brought by knights from the court at Durham was faulty, for they offered the king forty marks to have an inquest made by other knights. The case then went back to the court of the bishopric, and the knights making the inquiry were supervised by the bailiffs of the bishopric, but they were unable to reach a decision. First, they said that they did not know who had the better right to the land, Gilbert or Alice; later, with other knights and in the king's presence at Durham, they found for Gilbert. Alice then complained that this inquiry ought not to injure

---

[22] *CRR*, VI, 170, Michaelmas 1211, origin of the case; continued on pp. 188, 220; ending in Easter 1212, pp. 241–242. Discussed in Flower, *Introduction*, pp. 138–139.

her, since she had not placed herself on it, since it had not been made on oath, and since the men making it were untrustworthy. She placed herself on the grand assize; but King John would not allow a grand assize, pointing to the earlier inquest as an excuse. It hardly seems fair to deny a grand assize and to determine the right to land solely on the basis of an inquiry not even made by men under oath. The king's action doubtless is explained by an oblation of £100 to have seizin of the five carucates that Gilbert Hansard had offered earlier.[23] In this case, King John's intervention appears to have contributed more to the perversion of justice than to a safeguarding of it. Neither Gilbert Hansard, nor Brian fitz Alan, nor Alice could have had a very high opinion of royal justice after this experience in court, and it is not surprising to find the two men later among the rebels against the king.[24]

A case that moved back and forth in similar fashion from one court to another is one in which a miscarriage of justice in the halimote of Winchester was reviewed in the court *coram rege*.[25] These cases illustrate how easily pleas could be removed from the franchisal courts in order to be heard in the royal courts. Transfers from the county courts to the court of the bench at Westminster were accomplished just as easily by means of the writ pone. A case from the minority of Henry III offers an example of this common process, but in other ways it was an unusual proceeding. Appeals, that is criminal proceedings begun by the accusation of a private individual, were actions normally held in the county courts, and the royal justices at Westminster did not often hear criminal proceedings. In 1220, however, a group of persons appealed of homicide offered a fine to have their case heard, not simply before the royal judges, but "before H. de Burgh the justiciar and the council of the lord king at

---

[23] *Pipe Roll 13 John*, ed. Doris M. Stenton (Pipe Roll Society, N.S.; London, 1953), Michaelmas 1211, p. 34.

[24] Holt, *Northerners*, pp. 46, 48.

[25] *CRR*, VI, 290–292, Trinity 1212, a plea between Herbert son of Parnell and Nicholas son of Nicholas concerning a house in Winchester; discussed in Flower, *Introduction*, pp. 25–27. Nicholas had paid a half-mark to have the plea *coram rege* on the king's coming to Winchester (*Rot. de obl. et fin.*, p. 362).

Westminster." [26] They offered a relatively modest oblation of twenty shillings. Eleanor de Bayeaux, her sons John and Thomas, and others had been appealed of the death of William de Tilbrook; and they had been detained in the king's prison until they could secure pledges.[27] But they responded that the appeal had been made *de odio et atia,* not in good faith but through malice. By procuring this writ they were entitled to have the question decided by a jury, and they wished to have this inquiry held before the king's council.

When the action came to Westminster, the judges in the interest of justice reviewed the entire case from the beginning.[28] There the accusers told how the appealed parties had conspired to get William de Tilbrook drunk. Once he was in a drunken sleep they had struck him with an axe so that they brained him. They added that after the accused had killed him, they took his ruby ring and other valuables, and then tried to destroy the evidence of their crime by burning his body. For some reason, the judges never called for a jury to give a verdict on the question *de odio et atia.* Instead they adjourned the case until a later date, when they ordered two of the accused and their accusers to appear prepared to do combat. On that date, the king and his council gave them leave to agree, and then the appealors promptly appealed others of the same crime.[29] Their action would indicate that the appeal had indeed been made for reasons of hate and malice, and perhaps the judges realized that a threat of combat would reveal this without the necessity of calling a jury. Just why the council should have concerned itself with this criminal case involving obscure persons who could not offer large oblations is not clear. The only explanation is the council's desire to see justice prevail for all people regardless of their condition.[30]

Later in Henry's reign an appeal brought against three Lon-

---

[26] *Exc. e rot. fin.,* I, p. 45, 11 Mar. 1220.

[27] *Rot. lit. cl.,* I, 410b, 30 Jan. 1220.

[28] CRR, VIII, 381–383, Easter 1220.

[29] *Ibid.,* IX, 27, Trinity 1220, license to agree given; pp. 167–168, 307, 329, other appeals. For an appeal to King John, this time unsuccessful, to reverse the judgment of a county court, see *ibid.,* III, 115–116, Easter 1204.

[30] See Powicke, *Henry III,* pp. 38–39, on the council's sense of responsibility in the sphere of justice.

don Jews was postponed for hearing before him. In 1230 a Flemish merchant appealed the three Jews of breaking the king's peace. He charged that they had falsely accused him of paying them with counterfeit coins and had attacked and robbed him, biting his thumb until the blood ran. The Jews denied the accusation and placed themselves on a jury of both Christians and Jews. The case grew more complicated when the Jewish jurors who supported the defendants' version of the incident were convicted of swearing falsely. The Jewish community of London then paid the king sixty silver marks to have judgment postponed until he came to London.[31] What decision King Henry reached about the Jews' appeal is unknown. King John heard criminal cases involving Jews from time to time, although he was most interested in those in which the victim was a Jew.[32]

King John sometimes supervised criminal proceedings involving his other subjects. The pipe roll for 1206 records the amercement of two men, apparently justices of gaol delivery, "for dismissing men appealed of homicide without the warrant of the king or the justiciar." [33] In 1208 an appeal of homicide was referred to him. This time the appealed had already defended himself in the king's courts, so that an earlier decision of the royal justices was questioned. This draws attention to another phase of the monarch's correction of miscarriages of justice, the errors made in the royal courts by judges handing down decisions in his name.

In this case, William de Clendon, who had been a minor at the time of his father's murder, appealed Richard de Clendon of the crime, and he paid one mark to have the appeal removed from the county to Westminster.[34] There Richard denied the charge, claiming that he had already been acquitted of it as a

[31] CRR, XIV, 209–210, no. 1027, Michaelmas 1230.

[32] In Trinity term 1204, while King John was at Oxford, his court inquired into the murder of a Jew there, requiring suspects to undergo the ordeal of water (ibid., III, 144–145). In 1208, when he was at York, his judges heard an action concerning the death of a Jew's wife there (ibid., V, 256). Flower, Introduction, p. 49, states, "The murder of a Jew was a matter of searching inquiry by the king's justices."

[33] Pipe Roll 8 John, p. 134, Peter de Scudimor and Robert Belet.

[34] Pipe Roll 9 John, ed. A. Mary Kirkus (Pipe Roll Society, N.S.; London, 1942), Michaelmas 1206, p. 136.

result of an appeal brought by William's mother and uncle. He explained that Hubert Walter, then justiciar, had summoned an inquiry at Westminster to determine his guilt and that this inquest had found him innocent, as had another before the itinerant justices, and a third one at Westminster. Richard offered fifteen marks to have yet another inquisition, this time to attest to the truth of his story.[35] If Richard's account of his vicissitudes in court was correct, the judges were obviously at fault in entertaining another appeal against him for the same crime. The king commanded a postponement of the plea, and the justices consulted him in the interval.[36] When the case again came before the justices *coram rege,* they granted the two individuals license to agree, but only after the king had profited by fines of fourteen marks from Richard and six from William. Richard then conceded to William two virgates of land to be held by the service of presenting two pairs of white gloves, this in compensation for the supposed murder of his father.[37] The king's intervention saved Richard de Clendon from following an appeal that he had already defended several times; but it did not save him from heavy expenses, and it does not seem to have secured for William the punishment for bringing a false appeal that he doubtless deserved.

Turning from criminal actions to the possessory assizes, appeals to the king to right wrongs when no other recourse was available can be noted under both John and his son. An example of such an appeal can be found from the early years of King John, among the pleas before the king of 1200. The clerk added to the record of one plea the explanatory comment, "And it should be known that Hamo did not wish to proceed against the

[35] CRR, V, 50, Michaelmas 1207, pleas *coram rege;* discussed in Flower, *Introduction,* p. 258.

[36] CRR, V, 138, Hilary 1208, pleas *coram rege,* records the postponement. On p. 234, Trinity 1208, the name Richard de Clendon appears in a list of names headed *loquendum cum rege.*

[37] CRR, V, 249; also *Pipe Roll 10 John,* ed. Doris M. Stenton (Pipe Roll Society, N.S.; London, 1947), Michaelmas 1208, p. 179. King John later showed interest in another criminal appeal; in 1214 he ordered the coroners to investigate an appeal of rape, whereupon the appealor withdrew her accusation, claiming she had made it under compulsion (*CRR,* VII, 98).

jurors, but seeks that the lord king remedy that assize taken while he was a minor." [38]

In 1204, King John had to deal with a more serious grievance concerning the taking of an assize, one for which the jury of attaint did not provide a remedy, since irregular conduct by one of the king's justices was the issue. William Malesoures and Ivetta his wife complained that an assize of mort d'ancestor against them had been wrongfully taken by Hugh Bardolf's chaplain and constable.[39] Hugh Bardolf had died late in 1203 after long experience as a royal servant; he had served Henry II and his two sons as a royal justice since 1184.[40] Perhaps his final illness made him careless and prompted him to allow his servants to hear this case, but the result was a serious miscarriage of justice. The chaplain and constable proceeded with the assize and allowed the jury to decide against William and Ivetta in spite of the fact that they had vouched a warrantor and produced charters. Fortunately, four knights who were in court for another case witnessed the improper proceeding and were willing to swear to the truth of William and Ivetta's account. The couple succeeded in recovering seizin, which they had lost as a result of the judge's carelessness, but not until William had offered the king a mark to hasten judgment.[41]

Similar complaints against proceedings by the itinerant justices were made in the courts of Henry III. In 1224, Bishop William of Exeter came to Westminster seeking to have an assize of novel disseizin taken against his predecessor reversed on the grounds that it had been taken after his predecessor's death. The four justices acknowledged that the bishop had been dead at the time of the assize, but they thought that they could proceed because the king's writ said nothing of his death. The bishop was able to recover his possession "by precept of the lord

[38] *Pleas before King*, I, 323, no. 3251, morrow of St. Edmunds 1200; no further reference.
[39] *CRR*, III, 87, 97, Hilary 1204, pleas *coram rege*; discussed in *Pipe Roll 6 John*, p. xx, and in *Proc. without Writ*, p. lxxxix.
[40] Foss, *Judges*, pp. 54–55.
[41] *Pipe Roll 6 John*, Michaelmas 1204, p. 139.

king," since any action ended with the death of one of the parties.[42] Later a question concerning an inquiry where facts had been suppressed came before Henry III's court *coram rege*, when the bishop of Ossory, Ireland, showed the king that Alan son of Matthew de Rumilly had recovered possession of land because of his suppression of information. Alan denied the charge, and the rolls were searched; they revealed that Alan's father had been at fault, so that Alan escaped amercement, but lost seizin of the land in question.[43]

On other occasions appeals to the king were necessary to secure enforcement of the decisions of his courts. The holder of property at issue in an assize of novel disseizin might refuse to surrender possession of it to his successful opponent. Perhaps such action was to be expected when the holder was the stormy archbishop of York, Geoffrey Plantagenet.[44] The men of the town of Beverly had obtained a writ of novel disseizin against the archbishop, complaining of his invasion of their rights; but before the assize was taken he promised, in the presence of the justiciar and his justices, to restore to the townsmen all their liberties and rights.[45] Once the justiciar had departed, Geoffrey would do nothing to keep his promise. The men of Beverley again complained to the justiciar, who sent one of the royal justices and the sheriff of Yorkshire to correct his transgressions. They assembled the jurors, held the inquiry, and placed the townsmen in possession of all that had been taken from them. The archbishop's response to this was to excommunicate the justice and the men of Beverley. King John then intervened on behalf of the townspeople by seizing Geoffrey's barony, but this may not have been due entirely to his zeal in enforcing the

[42] *CRR*, XI, 293, no. 1459, Trinity 1224; p. 412, no. 2044, Michaelmas 1224; also *Note Book*, II, 690–691, no. 894.

[43] *Ibid.*, III, 189–190, pleas *coram rege*, 1236–1237.

[44] See Painter's characterization of the bishop, *King John*, p. 156: "Geoffrey was no easy man to get on with. He was arrogant and arbitrary with a high idea of his rights, liberties, and prerogatives and no inclination to compromise."

[45] *CRR*, I, 385, Hilary 1201, pleas *coram rege*; discussed in *Proc. without Writ*, pp. lxxviii–lxxix.

decisions of his court, for John and his half-brother had been quarreling ever since his accession to the throne.

King Henry III also received a complaint regarding failure to enforce the verdict of an assize of novel disseizin, although in this case the complainant rather than the offender was a prominent ecclesiastic. Jocelin bishop of Bath and Wells had an interest in the result of an assize of novel disseizin brought against the deacon of Wells, who had recently died and whose land was in the bishop's hands. He pointed out that the plaintiffs had been awarded the land, but that they had taken possession of the land awarded them without proper authority, and in doing so, they had damaged the deacon's property.[46] The bishop had been one of King John's servants, and he continued to serve Henry III, so that the king was willing to oblige him.[47] He called the plaintiffs and jurors before him for an investigation, and his inquiry resulted in an amercement of the trespassers and an order to the sheriff to establish seizin as the assize had determined.

The work of the council during Henry III's minority in overseeing justice has already been noted in connection with an action of false judgment against a private court and an appeal of felony. Its supervision extended over the royal courts as well. One of the grievances of the barons against King John was his administration of justice, for chapter 40 of Magna Carta, with its promise not to sell, refuse, or delay justice, constitutes an indictment of his judicial policies. The guardians of the new king felt that one way to secure the loyalty of the recent rebels was to restore their confidence in the royal courts, showing them that the new government would adhere to the "law of the land." [48]

Several examples of the council's correcting errors of the itinerant justices can be cited. One case in which they intervened is important because it shows the effects of the fourth Lateran Council's ban on clerical participation in ordeals. In 1219 the heirs of Peter de Aurre and John his son complained that these two men had been hanged *injuste et contra consuetudinem regni*, and the council commanded the justices who had heard

---

[46] *Note Book,* III, 185–186, no. 1170, pleas *coram rege,* 1235–1236.
[47] Foss, *Judges,* p. 717.   [48] Powicke, *Henry III,* p. 25.

the case to bring the record to Westminster.[49] Evidently, a jury of presentment had named the father and son for suspicion of harboring a criminal and receiving his stolen goods. When Peter and John were questioned before the justices, they said that they had received the thief as their son and brother, and they neither admitted nor denied receipt of his stolen goods. The justices could no longer send such suspects to the ordeal, so they summoned twelve jurors of the hundred to testify to their guilt. Because these jurors said that the two were of evil reputation and that they had heard rumors that the stolen goods had been divided in Peter's barn, they were hanged. When this record was heard at Westminster, it was adjudged that the heirs of Peter and John should not lose their inheritance, "because it seems to the council of the lord king and the justices of the bench that they were wrongly and unjustly hanged."

The review of this case illustrates the confusion that followed the abolition of the ordeal as a means of determining guilt. The instructions issued by the council to the justices on eyre in 1219 gave no rules for the trial of criminals presented by juries. They provided that those accused of serious crimes should be imprisoned, those accused of lesser crimes should abjure the realm, and those accused of only slight offenses should find pledges for their good behavior, "since it is uncertain and undetermined at the outset of your eyre what judgment should be imposed on those presented for robbery, murder, arson, and similar crimes, since it has been prohibited by the Roman Church to use judgment by fire and water." [50] Of course, this was only a temporary solution, for criminals could not be kept in prison indefinitely. Yet an accused person could only be subjected to a jury trial if he submitted voluntarily, if he "put himself on the country." The solution to this dilemma in the thirteenth century was to imprison criminals until they agreed to submit to a jury.[51] Then,

---

[49] CRR, VIII, 80–81, Michaelmas 1219 (also in Note Book, II, 58–59, no. 67); cited in Powicke, Henry III, p. 39.

[50] Pat. Rolls (1216–1225), p. 186.

[51] Pollock and Maitland, II, 650–652; Rolls for Lincs and Worcs., pp. lxix–lxx.

near the end of the century, the peine forte et dure was devised. In the above case, the justices had turned to a jury to decide the question even though Peter and John had not put themselves voluntarily on that jury; therefore, their action was reversed by the council when it was reviewed at Westminster.

The head of the itinerant justices, Jocelin of Wells, did not wish to share responsibility for such a serious miscarriage of justice, and the clerk took care to record that he had not been present when the judgment was given.[52] As an ecclesiastic—bishop of Bath and Wells—Jocelin had a legitimate reason for absenting himself from an action involving a "judgment of blood." Throughout the Middle Ages there was opposition to clerical participation in the work of the lay courts, but English bishops, abbots, and lesser clerics continued to serve as judges without their consciences being bothered too much.

One intervention of the council in the work of the justices on eyre aroused their vigorous protest. Gilbert de Ghent, the powerful Lincolnshire baron, had brought an assize of novel disseizin against William de Forz, count of Aumale, before the justices on eyre at Lincoln.[53] When neither the count nor his bailiff came to the court, the justices took the assize without them, and the jurors found for Gilbert. The count then sought a reversal of the decision by the council, and the members of the council surrendered to his demand. Perhaps they yielded because they feared a rebellion by William, perhaps because they remembered Gilbert's role as one of the enemies of King John in the barons' war. Whatever the reasons behind the council's judgment, it was a decision based upon political expediency. The justices who had taken the assize protested against this setting aside of their judgment in a letter addressed to three of the greatest men in the

[52] A year later, the council again corrected an error of the itinerant justices (CRR, VIII, 223, Hilary 1220; IX, 93–95, Trinity 1220). It reviewed a plea of false judgment against a county court heard by justices on eyre. The council ordered that a duel should not be waged and that the county should go free of any punishment because, if there had been any error, it was the fault of the justices rather than of the county court.

[53] *Rolls for Lincs and Worcs.*, p. 66, no. 151, 25 Nov. 1218. The case is discussed in the introduction, pp. lii–liii, and in Powicke, *Henry III*, p. 39.

realm, Peter des Roches, William Marshal, and Hubert de Burgh. In dignified language, they stated their position:

Since you chose us—we did not choose ourselves—and since you appointed us in this eyre for the peace of the lord king and his kingdom, bound to do justice to one and all, rich and poor without respect of persons, it would seem becoming and honorable, if it please you, that you should not so readily . . . believe evil of us. . . . We call Him who is witness of our conscience and the searcher of hearts and the knower of secrets that, sitting as a tribunal, we have done nothing of our certain knowledge according to our understanding and intelligence which ought to displease God or men of good will.[54]

The royal justices were distinguished men; among them were Hugh of Wells, bishop of Lincoln; John Marshal, the regent's nephew; Walter Mauclerc, formerly King John's agent at Rome; and William de Albini, one of the baronial leaders in the revolt. They were not obscure royal servants hopeful of gaining fortunes through loyal service. They took seriously their responsibility to give justice impartially to all men, regardless of how this related to the king's wishes. Evidently, their complaint led the council to reconsider its action; for shortly after William de Forz brought an action of attaint against the jurors in an effort to reverse the assize by legal means.[55] But ultimately the judgment of the itinerant justices prevailed, for William lost through default his attempt to convict the jury of false judgment.[56]

At the same time that the count of Aumale was resisting this decision against him, he was causing difficulties for the council in another case. William de Coleville had lost his lands because he had been King John's enemy during the baronial war, but later he secured a writ to have seizin of his lands as he had before the rebellion. William de Forz, who had come into possession of the estates, refused to give them up, and William de Coleville

---

[54] *Royal and Other Historical Letters Illustrative of the Reign of Henry III*, ed. W. W. Shirley (Rolls Series; London, 1862–1868), p. 21. The translation is Lady Stenton's, *Rolls for Lincs and Worcs.*, p. lii.

[55] *CRR*, VIII, 158, Michaelmas 1219, discussed in Chapter 3, above, where the question of the count's excommunicate status is raised.

[56] *CRR*, IX, 258, Michaelmas 1220.

was forced to bring an assize of novel disseizin against him to be heard before the justices on eyre.[57] The king's council intervened in this action too, commanding that it be placed in respite until the Whitsunday 1219 meeting of the council.[58] Evidently they decided to transfer the case to Westminster, for it later proceeded before the justices of the bench. Again political considerations took precedence over regular procedure, for the assize of novel disseizin was supposedly a speedy action without postponements. At Westminster, William de Coleville regained most of the lands he sought, and the count was assessed damages of fifty marks.[59]

The last case involving the count of Aumale indicates that the council's superintendence extended over the court of the bench as well as over the itinerant justices. The question of correcting errors made by the justices at Westminster is an important one. To call into question one of their decisions might be viewed as challenging the king's justice, as an attack on his majesty. Since Henry III's council was acting in the king's name, however, it could overrule the other courts, and it did interfere from time to time in the work of the court at Westminster. An early example comes from 1217, when an individual defending his land there in an assize complained to the earl marshal and the council that he should have the king as his warrantor, probably hoping to have the case postponed until Henry III came of age. He had to admit that he had no royal charters or other proof of a royal grant, and it was then commanded that the assize continue before the bench *secundum legem et consuetudinem regni*.[60]

Later, a plea to enforce a writ of prohibition to court Christian

---

[57] *Rolls for Lincs and Worcs.*, p. 203, no. 439, assizes at Nottingham, 18 Feb.–17 Mar. 1219; discussed in the introduction, pp. liv–lvi, and in Powicke, *Henry III*, p. 53.

[58] *Rolls for Lincs and Worcs.*, p. 350, no. 712, 29 April 1219.

[59] *CRR*, VIII, 30, 163–164, Michaelmas 1219. In 1220 the council had to deal with a similar question. Reginald de Braose sought land promised him by the council when he ended his revolt, but the holder of the land complained to the council that they had granted him the manor (*ibid.*, VIII, 365, Easter 1220).

[60] *Note Book*, III, 310, no. 1306, Michaelmas 1217.

heard before the justices at Westminster received the attention
of the council. Here the explanation for the council's supervision
is its desire to prevent any encroachment by the ecclesiastical
courts upon the jurisdiction of the king's court, a delicate matter
in England since the time of Thomas Becket. The widow of
Nicholas Duket was summoned to respond to his heirs why she
followed in the church courts a plea concerning a lay fee.[61]
Probably Nicholas, as a citizen of London, had bequeathed lands
by will, lawful for urban property but not for feudal tenures. His
heirs charged that after the judges of the ecclesiastical court had
been convicted before the council for holding such a plea, they
had made a precise estimate of the cash value of the land and
had proceeded with the case as if it involved money rather than
land. The king's council would have been alert to such a flagrant
attempt to bring real property under the jurisdiction of the
courts Christian. Before the truth of the charge could be established, however, they gave Nicholas' widow and his heirs license
to agree. The council undertook to enforce the agreement by
ordering the mayor and sheriffs of London to bring before it for
destruction Nicholas' seal and all charters sealed with it to prevent his executors from issuing charters under the seal of the
deceased to the disinheritance of his lawful heirs.[62]

After King Henry attained his majority, and after he reconstituted the court *coram rege,* it became the instrument for the
correction of errors by the justices of the bench.[63] Indeed, it is
not until this time that an example of an allegation of error
brought against the court of the bench can be found. The
proceeding is a complaint brought before Henry III in the twentieth year of his reign by the abbot of St. Augustine at Bristol.[64]
He had failed to appear before the justices on the day assigned
for a plea concerning a right of advowson, and they had given
judgment against him as a result of his default before exhausting

---

[61] *CRR,* VIII, 118, Michaelmas 1219 (also *Note Book,* II, 65–66, no. 73);
discussed in Flower, *Introduction,* pp. 110–111, and in F. W. Powicke's
review of *CRR,* Vol. VIII, in *E.H.R.,* LIV (1939), 711.
[62] *CRR,* VIII, 280–281, Hilary 1220.   [63] Bracton, II, 301, f. 108a.
[64] *Note Book,* III, 179–180, no. 1166, pleas *coram rege* 1235–1236.

the means at their disposal for compelling his appearance.[65] He then complained to the king that the justices had proceeded wrongly, and Henry took action to correct the error. As the plea roll records it, "And because it was shown to the lord king on the part of the abbot that the justices had proceeded badly, they were called before the lord king; and they acknowledged that they had proceeded wrongly, but that they did not know how better to proceed in the matter." The abbot regained his right of presentation, but there is no record of the fate of the erring justices. This case marks an important step in the development of the concept of "procedure in error," a complaint against a judgment that is not a complaint against the judges.

This survey of cases concerning errors in judgment does not reveal any great number of cases in which the king overruled judgments given in his courts; nevertheless, it does reveal a significant role for him in justice. In the absence of an appeals system, there was no means for correcting a wrong suffered in one of the royal courts except through an appeal directly to the monarch. Even injustices perpetrated in the local or franchisal courts sometimes could be corrected more readily by direct appeal to the king than through the regular process of false judgment. The English legal system of the early thirteenth century did not include an automatically functioning machinery for questioning decisions of the royal courts, for an accusation of false judgment against the king's judges was inadmissible. King John helped to remedy this situation by devising the jury of attaint to correct wrongful judgments in the possessory assizes. He was also active in superintending the work of his courts both through his encouragement of transfers of pleas to the court *coram rege* and through hearing plaints concerning judgments of his courts.

The question of John's reasons for supervising the work of his courts is a difficult one: one can attribute his activity to a genuine wish to see justice prevail, or to a selfish desire for financial gain, or to political scheming. Perhaps all these answers are true

---

[65] On this rule, see Pollock and Maitland, II, 593–594.

depending on the time and the circumstances, for John was a complex character moved by many interests. Certainly the oblations he received for juries of attaint are not large, if a half-mark or one mark is taken as the ordinary sum offered for a favor in the judicial sphere. However, some of the cases concerning miscarriages of justice that received the king's attention in the period beginning in 1208 do not inspire confidence in his administration of justice.[66] Litigants gave him large oblations, but these did not always ensure impartial administration of justice; on the contrary, they usually meant a distortion of it in favor of the person giving the fine. John seems to have been guided by self-interest in his supervision of the courts: in some cases, his motives were financial gain through offerings for favors; in others, his motives were political advantage through showing partiality to one party.

Supervision of the royal courts continued during the minority of Henry III through the work of the ruling council, but the purpose seems to have been a genuine desire to maintain high standards for the justice of the king's courts. The council did not hesitate to intervene in cases where there was little hope of financial gain, but sometimes political considerations did influence them, as the cases involving the count of Aumale indicate. This attitude toward the work of the courts continued during the early majority of Henry III, for it was at this time that the first example of the king's correction of an error by the justices of the bench at Westminster occurs. More and more, with the growth of several different branches of the *curia regis*, the court *coram rege* would be recognized as the tribunal for appeals from the decisions of the other branches.

[66] Lady Stenton, in her study of the pipe rolls for 1208–1209, notes a change in King John: "An examination of the King's activities as a judge during the years before 1209 reveals neither oppression nor indifference. What it suggests is a hardworking King, well served by able judges and their clerks. . . . But the pipe rolls of 1208 and 1209 give support to the chronicles which reveal another side of the picture: a suspicious ruler, keeping his subjects in hand through fear" ("King John and the Courts of Justice," *Proc. Br. Ac.*, XLIV [1958], 115).

7

The King Brings Actions

It is hardly surprising to find the king himself involved in litigation before the royal courts of justice, for he was not only the military leader and lawgiver for the kingdom but also a great feudal lord and a man of vast personal power, holding manors, advowsons of churches, monopolies, and other rights and privileges. The monarch was *dominus,* a territorial lord and feudal suzerain, as well as *rex,* a divinely appointed protector and judge of his people.[1] The king as a great landlord had to protect his property rights. Of course, he could use his executive instruments—his sheriffs, itinerant justices, or special commissioners —to protect these rights. But the medieval emphasis on customary procedures required that even as arbitrary a king as John proceed in his courts to recover possessions from other property holders.

Suits brought by the king presented a special problem. As *rex* he had no mortal superior in the kingdom, no one who could judge his acts; for he was the head of the judicial system, the source of all justice. This meant that the king was sometimes called upon to play a dual role in his courts: he and his servants were the judges, and at the same time he was one of the parties to the suit. The eventual solution to this problem in political theory was to separate the person from the office, the king from the crown, culminating in the sixteenth-century metaphysical conception of the king's two bodies, the body natural and the

---

[1] J. E. A. Jolliffe, *Angevin Kingship* (London, 1955), chaps. 1 and 2, pp. 13–49.

body politic.[2] But these concepts had not been fully developed in the twelfth and thirteenth centuries, and they had little effect on the practice of the time. Despite theories of the king's nature, the Angevin kings were men with wills of their own, whose personal favor and disfavor were facts of political life.[3] The king's subjects engaged in lawsuits against him in the royal courts had little hope of securing justice if they did not have his favor.

An examination of the royal justices' manner of proceeding in such cases should indicate what special privileges the king enjoyed in these proceedings to which he was a party. Further, it should reveal something of the relations between the king and his judges, whether they were subject to his will in such cases, or whether they were "servants of the law first and the king afterwards."[4] These pleas brought by the king may be divided into two groups for consideration: first, extraordinary proceedings or 'state trials,' and second, ordinary proprietary and possessory actions.

STATE TRIALS

The plea rolls of John and Henry III reveal many actions initiated by the two rulers to recover lands, liberties, custodies, and churches. The suits brought by the king in his common law courts were rarely spectacular cases of treason and *lèse-majesté*, but were usually the same proprietary actions or possessory assizes brought by his subjects. It must be noted that the records of the royal courts of justice offer little evidence that the king used the courts as instruments for persecuting individuals who had fallen from his favor. There are few proceedings that might be termed "state trials." There are no proceedings in the *curia regis* rolls or the assize rolls initiated by King John against such men as William de Braose, Robert fitz Walter, or Eustace de Vesci.

---

[2] Pollock and Maitland, I, 511–526. The most recent study of this concept is Ernst H. Kantorowicz, *The King's Two Bodies: A Study in Mediaeval Political Theology* (Princeton, 1957).

[3] Jolliffe, *Angevin Kingship*, p. 56.

[4] A statement of Sir Frederick Pollock's cited in Faith Thompson, *The First Century of Magna Carta* (Minneapolis, 1925), p. 57.

Neither is there anything to indicate that Henry III sought the judgment of royal justices before proceeding against Hubert de Burgh, Richard Marshal, or Gilbert Basset. This raises a question regarding the extent to which the monarch followed lawful procedures in dealing with his subjects. Does this absence of actions brought against his enemies mean that he never took measures against them, or does it mean that he always proceeded against them *sine judicio?*

Certainly King John disseized numbers of his subjects without any pretence of first obtaining a judgment. Indeed, he did this so often that disseizin *per voluntatem regis* seems to have been a normal administrative measure. Despite this harrying of individuals outside the law, the ruler found it possible many times to secure his goals without violating the letter of the law.[5] The court *coram rege,* the justices of the bench at Westminster, and the itinerant justices might not offer an opportunity for gaining his ends, but the king had a choice of courts in which he could pursue those persons who had fallen victim to his wrath. The exchequer, a branch of the *curia regis* that was "in part a judicial tribunal, in part a financial bureau,"[6] provided an instrument of discipline for those who happened to be in debt to the king. Judgments made under the *lex scaccarii* often amounted to no more than judicial reinforcements of the king's will, so that it was not necessary for him to proceed without judgment.[7] Debtors who lost the king's goodwill might find themselves imprisoned, their lands taken from them, or both. King John's infamous persecution of William de Braose began with distraint of his chattels for debt *secundum consuetudinem regni et per*

[5] See J. C. Holt, "The Barons and the Great Charter," *E.H.R.,* LXX (1955), 8–9, on John and due process.

[6] Pollock and Maitland, I, 191–192.

[7] J. C. Holt, *Magna Carta* (Cambridge, 1965), chap. 4, pp. 63–104; Holt, *Northerners,* chap. 10, pp. 175–193. Lady Stenton, in her introduction to *Pipe Roll 13 John* (Pipe Roll Society, N.S.; London, 1953), 1211, p. xxxii, discusses how King John modified exchequer procedure, reserving to himself the right to decide when a man imprisoned for debt should be released. Of course, the thesis of Jolliffe's *Angevin Kingship* is that John and his father constantly went beyond custom, yet Jolliffe admits that the exchequer was a vital agency for the exercise of the royal will (pp. 78–79).

legem scaccarii.[8] Similar to judgments of the exchequer were punishments for violations of the *lex forestae,* for the forest law too was simply an expression of the king's will.[9] Then the king could pursue his enemies by charging them with criminal acts in the county courts, for the solemn declaration of outlawry could be made only in the county courts, not in the king's central courts.[10] John proceeded against Robert fitz Walter and Eustace de Vesci in this way, having them outlawed in the county court following their plot against him.[11] Henry III proceeded against Hubert de Burgh in the same way.

Even though the king had available these other instruments, it does appear that he sometimes sought to use his common law courts to persecute individuals. Some of the pleas brought by private persons in the royal courts must have been inspired by the king as an indirect means of harrying his enemies. For example, William de Stuteville would not have brought suit against William de Mowbray for his barony without King John's tacit approval at least. There are other actions which probably originated as conspiracies by King John against powerful barons whom he hesitated to threaten openly.[12] The plea rolls of King John, then, record no dramatic state trials, no confrontations with his enemies in his court, such as his father's prosecution of Thomas Becket.

Neither do the plea rolls of John record spectacular trials for treason. Perhaps the lack of such cases is explained by the fact that attempts on the king's life were extremely rare. Perhaps it is explained by the serious nature of such crimes: they could not be left to the professional judges, but required a hearing before the *magna curia regis,* a tribunal that qualified as a court of peers.[13] Whatever the explanation, all the court records of John exam-

---

[8] Holt, *Northerners,* pp. 184–186; also Painter, *King John,* pp. 242–250.

[9] *Dial. de scac.,* pp. 59–60; Holt, *Northerners,* pp. 159–160; Holt, *Magna Carta,* p. 72.

[10] Pollock and Maitland, I, 554.   [11] Holt, *Magna Carta,* p. 92.

[12] See Chapter 4, pp. 157–165, for a fuller account of these cases.

[13] Bracton, II, 337, f. 119; Barnaby C. Keeney, *Judgment by Peers* (Harvard Historical Monograph Series, Vol. XX; Cambridge, Mass., 1949), p. 82.

ined yield only one case in which treason is charged. In 1214 some of King John's household knights appealed Baldwin Tyrel of a treasonous offense, of spreading the rumor that the king had been killed while fighting in Wales.[14] Apparently his story was part of a baronial plot against the king's life, planned for the Welsh campaign in the summer of 1212, but the plot had miscarried because John canceled his expedition.[15] In spite of this, the case does not seem to have received any special attention either from the judges or from the king, and it went through several postponements without a conclusion being recorded.

The two other cases of treason in the royal courts come from the time of King Henry III. One of them concerns an appeal against three men for plotting to poison the king in 1225.[16] Among those accused was a baron, Vitalis Engaine, heir to half the honour of Bulwick in Northamptonshire.[17] Vitalis vigorously denied the charge, offering to prove his innocence "either by the oath of twenty knights or a hundred or in any way at all which would please the lord king, as a faithful man of the king, and as the court should consider." It is clear that the accuser in this case was mad. When it was charged that he was an escaped prisoner, he admitted that he had broken out of gaol; but he said that it was to flee the devil, who had appeared in his cell in the form of a foul black monk (*nigri monachi scabiosi*). It did not take the judges long to decide that the accusation was false and to sentence the accuser to death by drawing and hanging.

In 1233 a man in possession of a forged writ sealed with a false royal seal was brought before the justices at Westminster. He admitted that he had forged the seal, that he had forged one of King John's, and that his wife had forged the seal of the judge William Raleigh. Forgery of the king's seal was an act of treason,[18] and death was the punishment. But in this case, King

---

[14] *CRR*, VII, 94–95, 168–173, 257, Hilary and Trinity 1214 (also in *Select Pleas of the Crown*, ed F. W. Maitland (Selden Society, Vol. I; London, 1888), pp. 67–75, no. 115).

[15] Holt, *Northerners*, p. 82; Painter, *King John*, pp. 266–267.

[16] *CRR*, XII, 215–216, no. 1055, Michaelmas 1225.

[17] Sanders, *Baronies*, p. 23.   [18] Pollock and Maitland, II, 504.

Henry III acted mercifully and "by his grace he conceded to him his life and limb, provided that he abjure the realm." [19]

Another time, several knights were summoned before the king charged with something bordering on treason, the disruption of a hundred court, "impeding irreverently the king's business and in contempt of the king's dignity." They had been so disorderly at the court that the sheriff of Devonshire had been unable to proceed with its business. The reason for their anger was his decision to place in respite a plea against the abbot of Caen. The abbot had first gained a postponement by calling the king to warrant. Then, when he failed to produce his warranty, the sheriff again postponed it, provoking an outburst by the knights. The knights came to the court *coram rege* in 1237, and the king released them until he should see how they conducted themselves in the future, and then they might escape his anger. [20]

Henry III, like his father, sometimes proceeded against persons who did not have his goodwill without first securing a judgment. The fall of Hubert de Burgh and the king's pursuit of those who took up Hubert's cause provide notable illustrations. But Henry, unlike his father, also used the common law courts as an instrument against his enemies. The barons' demands for "due process of law" warned the young king to give at least an appearance of legality to his proceedings against his enemies. The rolls of his courts record some "state trials," proceedings at which great men were called to account. The sixteen assizes of novel disseizin brought against Fawkes de Breauté before the itinerant justices in June 1224 provide an early example. [21] Fawkes was a great soldier who had served the royalist cause faithfully in the civil war, but he had become so powerful that he had felt himself beyond the law, and he had defied the king's council and courts, ignoring their writs and judgments. [22] An earlier entry in the plea rolls described Fawkes in this way: "For

[19] *CRR*, 113, m. 13, no. 508, Michaelmas 1233.

[20] *Ibid.*, 116B, m. 8, no. 1983, pleas *coram rege*, Easter 1237.

[21] *Ibid.*, XI, 383–388, nos. 1914–1934.

[22] F. M. Powicke, *The Thirteenth Century 1216–1307* (*Oxford History of England*, Vol. IV; Oxford, 1953), pp. 25–27.

he is against the lord king and is his enemy." [23] The assizes were brought by private persons, but there can be little doubt that they were part of the pressure that the royal council was exerting on Fawkes. Indeed, they were not strictly assizes of novel disseizin, since one of them was brought concerning a servile tenure, and that assize was not normally available for tenants in villeinage.[24] The title of the roll indicates that the proceedings were extraordinary, for the heading reads not *placita et assisa* but *inquisicione*. At the same time that these assizes were being taken before the itinerant justices, outlawry proceedings were being brought in the county court of Bedford. All these proceedings may have been completely within the law, but they convinced Fawkes that the king's council was attempting to crush him. They succeeded in goading him into outright rebellion.[25] When judgment in all sixteen assizes went against Fawkes, his brother kidnapped one of the judges. The king and his court followed him to Bedford Castle, which they besieged for most of the summer. Although Fawkes' life was spared in consideration for his past services to the king, he lost all his lands and was banished from the kingdom.

A more striking example of a state trial is Henry III's prosecution of Peter des Rivaux, one of the "Poitevins" who dominated the royal household during the years 1232–1234. F. M. Powicke says of him, "For a short time this comparatively obscure official had more authority than any of Edward I's great officers ever acquired or than Thomas Cromwell exercised at the height of his career as the agent of Henry VIII." [26] But Peter suddenly fell from royal favor. In the winter of 1233–1234 there was opposition to the rule of Henry and his Poitevins, led by Richard the earl marshal. Henry declared Richard and his companions traitors and commanded that their castles be besieged and that they be hunted down. Then, just as the king was about to be reconciled with the earl marshal, he was killed in a way that raised

---

[23] *CRR*, XI, 325, no. 1626.
[24] *Ibid.*, p. 383, no. 1914; discussed in *Proc. without Writ*, p. c.
[25] Kate Norgate, *The Minority of Henry III* (London, 1912), p. 237.
[26] *Henry III*, p. 86.

suspicions that the king had played some part in his death, so that he felt his honor threatened. Henry suddenly turned on his advisers—Peter des Rivaux, Stephen Segrave, and Robert Passelewe—in great anger for placing him in such a position.[27] They were deprived of their offices, and they were hunted and hounded as if common criminals.

Much of the story of the king's pursuit of Peter des Rivaux can be read on the *coram rege* roll for 1234. In May, Henry summoned Peter to appear before his court *coram rege* on the octave of Trinity to present his accounts for the many offices he had held, to surrender his castles, and to return the custody of a youth he had from the king.[28] While this action was continuing, several others against Peter were initiated. There were official inquiries into his financial dealings with the London Jewish community, and there were complaints by private individuals about his arbitary seizures of their property.[29]

Peter, fearing for his life, refused to come to the king's court without letters guaranteeing his safety, but Henry answered his messengers with *aspera verba per iram*. He rejected his request for a safe-conduct, claiming that none was necessary for a clerk traveling on the king's business in time of peace. After Peter failed several times to appear on the days appointed to him, the court on June 30 declared him in mercy and ordered him distrained by his body, his lands, and his chattels. Later, some of the bishops intervened on his behalf, and the king released him into their custody.[30] When Peter was again summoned—for 5 September 1234—the bishop of Winchester informed the judges that Peter said that he "dared not come to the lord king on account of danger to his body." The bishop added that he had sequestered all Peter's benefices in his diocese, that he had cited him before the judges-delegate of the archbishop, and that he

---

[27] *Ibid.*, pp. 124–138.

[28] *CRR*, 115B, m. 1d, no. 1031; *Close Rolls* (1231–1234), p. 412.

[29] *CRR*, 115B, mm. 13–14, nos. 1110–1118, 1119–1124, inquiries about his relations with the Jews; *ibid.*, m. 3, no. 1038, complaint that he took a warhorse valued at 28 marks and a ruby ring worth 20 marks; no. 1042, complaint that he took a horse of 15 marks' value.

[30] *Ibid.*, m. 7d, no. 1064, 14 July 1234.

could do no more to compel his appearance.[31] Finally, the king agreed to give Peter des Rivaux his safe-conduct,[32] and he came to the *curia regis* at Woodstock on the eve of All Souls. But Henry III declared that because he did not have adequate counsel he could not pass judgment.[33] Peter offered the king a fine of 1,000 marks for recognition of his clerical privilege, an extension of his safe-conduct, justice according to his charters, and a hearing before the magnates. Peter again came to the court two weeks after All Souls, this time at London, where the king accepted his fine.[34] Then in December 1234 at Reading, "before the lord of Canterbury and many other great men," judgment was again postponed.[35] The conclusion to all these proceedings was well phrased by F. M. Powicke, when he wrote, "So Henry's wrath, which was mainly due to wounded pride, passed away." [36] He and Peter des Rivaux were reconciled by 1236, although Peter never regained his high offices at the English court.

Along with Peter des Rivaux, the justiciar, Stephen Segrave, and the deputy treasurer, Robert Passelewe, felt the force of the king's fury. He commanded that justices be appointed to hear evidence of their misdeeds; [37] he had an investigation made into their dealings with the Jews of London; [38] and he demanded the return of lands they held of him.[39] The king also summoned Stephen to his court to answer charges concerning his conduct as justiciar.[40] Stephen came to the court at Westminster, where he stated that he did not wish to enter into a legal action against the king but only sought his grace and mercy. He surrendered all his

---

[31] *Ibid.*, m. 9d, no. 1091, and m. 4, no. 1126.

[32] *Cal. Pat. Rolls* (1232–1247), p. 74, 18 Oct. 1234.

[33] *CRR*, 115B, m. 18d, no. 1225.

[34] *Ibid.*, m. 24d, no. 1289. The extension of his safe-conduct is in *Cal. Pat. Rolls* (1232–1247), p. 82.

[35] Until the octave of Hilary, Jan. 1235 (*CRR*, 115B, m. 24d, no. 1289).

[36] *Henry III*, p. 138.   [37] *Close Rolls* (1231–1234), pp. 573–578.

[38] *CRR*, 115B, mm. 13–14, nos. 1110–1118, 1119–1124.

[39] *Royal and Other Historical Letters Illustrative of the Reign of Henry III*, ed. W. W. Shirley (Rolls Series; London, 1862–1868), I, 444, no. ccclxxii; *CRR*, 115B, m. 4d, nos. 1136–1137; m. 11, no. 1102; m. 27, no. 1363; m. 28, no. 1384.

[40] Shirley, *Royal Letters*, I, 445, no. ccclxxiii.

manors to Henry, and he agreed to judgment by the *curia regis*.[41] But Henry's anger against Stephen Segrave and Robert Passelewe cooled too, and they regained his favor and returned to posts in the government.[42]

Here is a definite contrast between the common law courts of Henry III and those of his father. One can conclude that because King John failed to use the common law courts to harry his enemies, he never took any action against them. But this bears hardly any resemblance to the portrait of John painted by other sources. Other records picture the king's will, the king's wrath, as something very real and as something to be feared. There can be no doubt that John was a jealous guardian of royal rights and privileges, taking all steps necessary to preserve them, even to expand them. John must have found some other way to protect his interests. Sometimes he acted arbitrarily.[43] At other times he was able to act within the letter of the law, but the law of the exchequer and the law of the forest proved much more serviceable to him than did the law of the courts of justice. Henry, too, sometimes lost his temper and proceeded without judgment, but more often he used the courts of justice for the pursuit of enemies, as in the cases of Peter des Rivaux and Stephen Segrave. Doubtless, he was more concerned than his father to provide an appearance of legality. The baronial revolt of 1215–1217 and the reaction in 1232–1233 to his harrying of Hubert de Burgh were warnings to him. Whatever the explanation, state trials of high government officials in the regular royal courts are something that appear in the time of Henry III but not in that of John.

REGULAR PROCEEDINGS

The pleas brought by the king before his justices were generally the same proprietary and possessory actions brought by his subjects. The system of writs and assizes by which these courts

---

[41] *CRR*, 115B, m. 7d, no. 1059, 10 July 1234.
[42] Powicke, *Henry III*, pp. 138, 152–153.
[43] Jolliffe, *Angevin Kingship*, pp. 50–186; Holt, *Magna Carta*, pp. 68–70.

operated proved as convenient for the ruler as a means of recovering his possessions as it did for his subjects. The plea rolls for the reigns of King John and Henry III reveal many regular actions brought by the monarch. He sued in his courts to recover his rights of wardship and marriage; [44] he sought to recover judicial rights that had been alienated; [45] he even brought actions concerning financial matters that might have been heard at the exchequer. [46] Questions of reliefs, aids, and other feudal payments were the concern of the barons of the exchequer. The bulk of the king's suits in the common law courts related to property in land, presentation of priests, custodies of minors, and jurisdictional rights. Such proceedings exist in sufficient numbers to indicate that the royal courts of justice provided an important instrument for the maintenance of royal rights. Indeed, they are so numerous that it would be impossible to consider all the various types of actions in which the king appeared as plaintiff. However, a survey of two categories—the pleas of land and actions relating to presentation to churches—should provide some insight into how the royal courts dealt with such matters.

Before turning to these cases, it is necessary to consider the theories governing the king's relations with his courts when he was one of the parties to an action. Bracton wrote of the king, "Therefore there ought to be no one greater than he in the administration of justice, but he ought to be the least, or nearly

---

[44] E.g. *CRR*, I, 165, II, 62, IX, 379, individuals summoned to Westminster to answer why they married girls in the king's gift; XI, 157, no. 782, individual summoned to respond why he withheld from the king half of a vill which belonged to him as part of his custody of heiresses.

[45] E.g. *ibid.*, VII, 158-159, suitors of the hundred of Plympton summoned to show why they had refused to appear before the sheriff at his tourn and do those things which belonged to the peace and security of the kingdom; XII, 434-435, no. 2142, two individuals accused of preventing the sheriff of Lincolnshire from holding his county court and tourn.

[46] E.g. *ibid.*, I, 390, agreement concerning a fine for custody of a widow and her three daughters; pp. 118-119, the king seeking a tallage of 102 marks from the citizens of Lincoln; VII, 34, payment of relief for half a knight's fee; XIII, 249-250, no. 1139, the king asking why persons prevented his reeve from taking a toll at Dorchester.

the least, in submitting to judgment if he seeks it." [47] His meaning was that in spite of the monarch's general superiority, he should enjoy no special privileges when he was the plaintiff in a lawsuit.[48] Bracton faced the problem of how to put this theory into practice in his discussion of the crime of treason. There he wrote that the king ought not to judge, "otherwise he would be plaintiff and judge in his own case"; but neither should the king's justices do the judging, "since in judgments the justice represents the person of the king whose place he takes." Bracton concluded that in such cases the court and the peers should render judgment.[49] He applied this principle of judgment by peers only to the crime of treason, however, and not to ordinary proprietary or possessory actions brought by the king.

Bracton made one important exception to the general rule that the king should not have special privileges in an action in which he was plaintiff. That was in connection with suits to recover rights and privileges that normally belonged to the monarch; there the principle *nullum tempus occurrit regi* applied, and the burden of proof rested with the defendant. Two groups can be distinguished among the property rights pertaining to the king. Bracton says of the first group, "Matters of jurisdiction and peace and what is bound up with justice and peace belong to no man save only to the crown and the royal dignity. They cannot be separated from the crown since they make the crown what it is." [50] Elsewhere Bracton describes these matters as no more to be

---

[47] Bracton, II, 33, f. 5b. He makes a similar statement in II, 305, f. 107: "Nevertheless, he [the king] ought to be compared, in receiving justice, to the lowliest one in his kingdom."

[48] Fritz Schulz, "Bracton on Kingship," *E.H.R.*, LX (1945), 149; Pollock and Maitland, I, 517.

[49] Bracton, II, 337, f. 119b.

[50] *Ibid.*, p. 167, f. 55b; the translation is Helen Cam's in *Law-Finders and Law-Makers in Medieval England* (New York, 1963), pp. 40–41. The question of the king's privileges in matters of jurisdiction is discussed in Ludwik Ehrlich, *Proceedings against the Crown, 1216–1337*, ed. Sir Paul Vinogradoff (Oxford Studies in Social and Legal History, Vol. VI; Oxford, 1921), pp. 40–41; and in C. H. McIlwain, *Constitutionalism: Ancient and Modern* (rev. ed.; Ithaca, N.Y., 1958), pp. 75–77.

alienated than the holy possessions of the Church.[51] The second group consisted of things that could be granted to others:

> On the other hand those things known as privileges, though they pertain to the crown, may be separated from it and transferred to private persons, but only by the special grace of the king himself. Unless his grace and special concession should intervene, then lapse of time does not exclude the king from such a claim. For time does not run against him in this case where there is no need of proof. For it ought to be clear to all that things of this kind pertain to the crown unless there is someone who can prove the contrary by producing a special grant. In other matters, where proof is necessary, time runs against the king just as it would against any others.[52]

There was a double standard, then, to be applied in actions brought by the king: in suits to recover jurisdictional rights—things that normally belonged to the royal power—he had certain advantages, while in suits concerning land or other property, he was to have no special privileges. The question remains concerning the extent to which this principle that the king should have no special privileges as plaintiff in ordinary pleas was reflected in the pleas that he brought in his courts. The judges were the king's servants, and they must have been hesitant to give judgments against their master.

In practice, neither King John nor Henry III was bound to the regular forms of action in the proceedings that they brought before their justices. Many questions concerning royal rights were put to jurors in the royal courts which did not fit into the categories of novel disseizin, or mort d'ancestor, or one of the other established procedures. A remarkable statement of this royal privilege comes from the year 1258, when a woman complained that she ought not to be required to answer a writ of the king because she resided in the liberty of Southampton. The justices replied:

[51] Bracton, II, 57–58, f. 14; discussed in Kantorowicz, *The King's Two Bodies*, p. 168.

[52] Bracton, II, 167, ff. 55b–56.

The king has this privilege regarding the pleas and plaints from the town of Southampton, that he impleads in his court wherever he wishes by any writ, as well for plaints as for trespasses and for every kind of plea of land and debt, and many examples of this were shown to her which she could not gainsay.[53]

The rolls from King John's reign reveal a number of actions relating to land brought by him. While he did not necessarily begin proceedings by one of the writs *de cursu,* he did use juries of recognition in his courts to inquire into diminutions of royal rights to lands, particularly at the beginning of his reign. One of these proceedings, held before the justices at Westminster in Trinity term 1200, was an inquiry of general nature. A jury of recognition was called to determine what had been alienated from the royal demesne at Kingston on Thames since the first coronation of Henry II.[54] At other times the proceedings resulted from complaints made by the king against private persons, and the justices decided these actions too by means of juries of recognition. In Michaelmas term the same year, a jury came to recognize whether the abbot of Lilleshall had made a purpresture on the land and forest of the king at Edgmond.[55] The men who came proved unsuitable to the justices of the bench, and they postponed the case until the coming of the itinerant justices, so that the sheriff could select knights and upright men as jurors. That this case came before the justices at Westminster is evidence of the varied functions of the branches of the *curia regis,* for this was a forest plea that should have come before the justices of the forest.[56]

Again in 1200, King John brought an action against Robert de

---

[53] *Proc. without Writ,* p. 36, no. 34, Trinity 1258, pleas at Southampton.

[54] *CRR,* I, 209, 252, Trinity 1200, pleas at Westminster; cited in Flower, *Introduction,* p. 196.

[55] *CRR,* I, 287, Michaelmas 1200, pleas at Westminster; cited in Flower, *Introduction,* p. 435.

[56] *Pipe Roll 2 John,* ed. Doris M. Stenton (Pipe Roll Society, N.S.; London, 1934), Michaelmas 1200, p. 253. Under *"placita foresta"* it is recorded that the abbot of Lilleshall owed a half-mark for a mill and pond made in purpresture.

Beaumont, earl of Leicester, charging him with disseizin of two carucates of land and with damaging the king's millpond at Caldwell.[57] The king did not wish to give offense to so powerful a baron so early in his reign, and he gave the earl every opportunity to prove his case. A jury of recognition stated at the court *coram rege* that the earl's bailiff had come and seized the land and mill, but they did not know by whose authority he had done it. When the sheriff was questioned, he answered that he had given the earl seizin by command of the justiciar. A jury of knights was then summoned to come before the king for a further inquiry. The knights came the next spring, and they were asked to determine what lands at Caldwell the earl's father had lost on account of his support of the young King Henry in his rebellion against Henry II.[58] They stated that the earl of Leicester had never held any land at Caldwell, and that the millpond he was said to have damaged was actually on the fee of another person, who had broken it because the sokeman holding the mill had failed to make his yearly payment of eight pence. No conclusion to the case survives, but the jurors' statement would seem to acquit Leicester of any wrongdoing.

Not everyone had such opportunities to prove his rights against the king. A jury came before the royal justices in 1205 to recognize whether the hundred of Brixton, held by Pentecost de Wildsworth, was part of the king's demesne or a fee that Pentecost held of the king.[59] Pentecost, unlike the earl of Leicester, was a person of no importance in the kingdom, and the outcome of his case contrasts sharply with the previous one. Pentecost came and said that he could not endure a jury in opposition to the king, and he claimed nothing there save at the king's will. The justices then found him in the king's mercy because he had previously claimed that the land was his free tenement. In an age when persons who angered the king could lose their lands, it

[57] *CRR*, I, 259, Michaelmas 1200, pleas *coram rege*.

[58] *Ibid.*, p. 415, Easter 1201, pleas *coram rege*.

[59] *Ibid.*, III, 309, Easter 1205, pleas at Westminster; discussed in Flower, *Introduction*, p. 87.

is not surprising that Pentecost feared to contest a suit brought by the king.[60]

This method of asserting royal rights—bringing regular actions against individuals to be decided by juries of recognition—continued to be used by Henry III. Indeed, the number of such actions increased sharply during his reign.[61] Henry was being careful to protect his rights by lawful procedures. The examples that the plea rolls provide are similar in nature to those of John's reign. Sometimes the question was not a matter of a person's withholding land from the king, but was of a more general nature, as when a jury was called to recognize whether four and a half hundreds pertained to the royal manor of Bensington.[62] Again, the justices carefully supervised the selection of jurors. When none of those called to testify concerning Bensington appeared, they marked the case for consultation with the king's council. In a plea concerning land claimed by the king against Ralph Gernun in 1228, the justices ordered four of the jurors removed because they were men of the justiciar, Hubert de Burgh.[63] The reason for their removal is not clear—perhaps Ralph Gernun was also one of the justiciar's men. About the same time, the justices postponed an action by which the king sought recovery of the manor of Nacton in Suffolk because all the jurors had been removed as useless (*inutiles*).[64]

Henry III's jurors, once chosen, did not always decide in favor of their ruler. In one case, they were to consider the question of how land had passed to the tenant, whose right was being challenged by the king: had the land passed to him by hereditary

[60] The plea rolls of John's reign indicate that other juries also settled questions between the king and individuals; but, unfortunately, they cannot be traced. The rolls record postponements of actions against William de Warenne (CRR, IV, 159, Trinity 1206, pleas at Westminster) and against William de Esseteford and his son (VI, 246, Easter 1212).

[61] Just as under John, the plea rolls record the origin or postponement of a number of such actions without recording their conclusion.

[62] CRR, IX, 29, Trinity 1220. Rot. lit. cl., I, 476, 27 April 1221, identifies Bensington, Oxon., as a royal manor.

[63] CRR, XIII, 154, no. 684, Easter 1228.

[64] Ibid., p. 159, no. 709, Easter 1228. Henry III sought the manor from Andrew Peverel and Lucy his wife. The outcome of the case is not recorded.

right from his father, or was the land part of the royal demesne in his father's care through his office as sheriff? The jurors answered that the land had never been part of the royal demesne, and the court allowed the tenant to continue to hold it in peace.[65] Another time, jurors were asked if a manor had come into the king's hand in such a way that he could dispose of it: was it royal demesne, escheat of the Normans, or escheat of the Bretons? The jurors declared that it was neither the king's demesne nor his escheat, but belonged rightfully to a widow and child in his custody.[66] In another suit brought by Henry to recover land, the tenant was left in possession "because no one followed the plea against him, and because the jury was more against the king and for William [the tenant] than the reverse." [67]

In addition to actions in which the king put forth a claim in opposition to that of the tenant, the kings of England had another weapon available—the quo warranto proceeding. A quo warranto writ was a challenge, a demand that the tenant reveal by what right he held his possession; and it gave great advantage to the plaintiff, the king. The other original writs described clearly the plaintiff's claim, but the quo warranto writ forced the tenant to reveal his right, while leaving him in the dark about the king's claim. The basis for the king's claim was sometimes revealed at the outset of the proceedings, but not always.[68] A demand that the possessor prove his claim to hold liberties or franchises was justifiable because these were royal privileges that could be transferred to private persons only by the special grace of the king,[69] but use of a quo warranto writ in proceedings to

[65] *Ibid.*, XIV, 269–270, no. 1274, Easter 1231, land of John le Viscount claimed to be part of the king's vill of Shoreton.

[66] *Ibid.*, 115B, m. 19d, no. 1242, Michaelmas 1234, pleas *coram rege*, inquiry about the manor of Haunford, Dorset.

[67] *Ibid.*, XIV, 139, no. 696, Michaelmas 1230; the origin of the case is recorded in XIII, 364–365, no. 1735. The manor of Oakford was claimed against William Briwerre.

[68] Donald W. Sutherland, *Quo Warranto Proceedings in the Reign of Edward I, 1278–1294* (Oxford, 1963), pp. 7–8; T. F. T. Plucknett, *Legislation of Edward I* (Oxford, 1949), p. 36.

[69] Pollock and Maitland, II, 661.

recover land put the tenant at a distinct disadvantage. Bracton recognized the possibilities that the quo warranto offered for arbitrary action by the king. He protested that a man should not be required to reveal his right to one who has not revealed any superior right.[70]

The quo warranto was not among the writs *de cursu* available at the chancery for a small fee.[71] But occasional writs containing the words *quo warranto, quo advocatio,* or *quo jure* were issued for private persons. They were used in difficult situations, where none of the regular writs would apply. They differed from royal quo warranto actions, for the purchasers made clear the nature of their claims.[72]

The quo warranto action had its origin in the great periodic investigations into royal rights begun with the Domesday inquest by William the Conqueror and continued by the Angevin monarchs. King John commanded such an inquiry in 1212, an extensive investigation into all tenements held in chief of the king by knight-service or by serjeanty.[73] Later, the government of Henry III's minority undertook investigations into the liberties claimed by the king's subjects. Quo warranto proceedings appear on the eyre rolls from 1218, and in 1223 the sheriffs made a general inquiry into customs and liberties in their counties.[74] While these great investigations had both judicial and administrative aspects, they usually were supervised by the exchequer and conducted by the sheriffs. Besides these general investigations at the county courts and before the barons of the exchequer, individual actions were brought by quo warranto writs before the justices of the common law courts. These proceedings sometimes questioned rights to lands or churches, as well as to liberties.

---

[70] Bracton, IV, 167–168, f. 372, cited in Plucknett, *Legislation,* p. 36, n. 9.

[71] Powicke, *Henry III,* p. 114; Pollock and Maitland, II, 661, n. 5: "Sometimes when a subject brings a writ which contains the words *quo waranto* [*sic*], this is really a writ of intrusion (see Bracton, f. 160b) and the plaintiff's title is stated."

[72] Plucknett, *Legislation,* pp. 35–36.

[73] Painter, *King John,* pp. 208–211; Holt, *Northerners,* p. 81, n. 1.

[74] Cam, *Law-Finders,* p. 39.

A few examples of cases in which persons were summoned to answer "by what right" they held date from the reign of King John. Several of them concern ecclesiastical livings, but two are actions relating to possession of land. The earliest was in 1206, when Elias de Wimberville was called before the king to reveal his right to the third part of one-half a knight's fee; John maintained that the land was part of the escheat of the Normans, but did not spell out his claim any more exactly.[75] Elias explained that he had transferred his Norman lands to one of the knights who remained in Normandy after 1204 in exchange for the knight's English lands. It is not known if this explanation proved satisfactory to the king, for no judgment is recorded. Later, in 1213, Thomas de Feckenham was summoned to show by what warrant he held the vill of Boarstall, a part of the royal manor of Brill in Buckinghamshire.[76] Thomas offered a lengthy defense of his claim, basing it on hereditary right, which he traced back to the time of the Empress Matilda; but he must have been aware of the true purpose of the inquiry, for he offered twenty marks to have the king's confirmation of his rights. But the men of the king's manor offered the same amount to have the land in question recognized as a part of Brill. This was a time of great financial distress for King John, just before his campaign of 1214 on the Continent, and his justices struck a hard bargain. When the men of Brill increased their oblation to thirty-five marks, it was agreed that Boarstall be added to their holdings on the condition that they increase their annual rent for the manor by twenty shillings.

In contrast to the relatively small number of quo warranto proceedings in the plea rolls from John's reign, the *curia regis* rolls of Henry III record a vast number of such actions.[77] The first quo warranto action brought by Henry to recover land dates

---

[75] *CRR*, IV, 102–103, Easter 1206, pleas *coram rege*.

[76] *Ibid.*, VII, 20, Michaelmas 1213; discussed in Flower, *Introduction*, pp. 493–494.

[77] Plucknett, *Legislation*, pp. 37–38, described the *quo warranto* as "not very common" under Henry III, but he admitted that he was basing his finding only on *Bracton's Note Book*.

from Hilary term 1223.[78] The rolls for almost every term in the 1230's contain several quo warranto proceedings: roll 113 includes six; roll 115B includes eleven; roll 116B lists fifteen; and roll 117 lists thirty-one.[79] A list of essoins on roll 117 contains sixteen entries; the king is given as one of the parties to ten of these suits.[80] There was always an element of arbitrariness about these actions, since the tenant was forced to defend his right regardless of whether or not the king had a better right. Yet the justices did conduct them along the lines of regular judicial proceedings, offering the tenant numerous opportunities to prove his right.

[78] CRR, XI, 62, no. 337, land in Wallington, Sur.

[79] Ibid., 113, 17–18 Henry III: m. 5d, no. 310, land in Terreton, Som.; m. 6, no. 325, land in Octon, Yorks; m. 11d, no. 464, land in Hatfield, Dev.; m. 12, no. 474, land not identified; m. 13, no. 516, land at Gomshall, Sur.; m. 16, no. 583, place is illegible. Ibid., 115B, 18 Henry III: m. 9d, no. 1090, land in White Roding, Ess.; m. 12, no. 1144, land in Havering, Ess.; m. 18, no. 1211, manor of Brangston, Suff.; m. 19, no. 1241, land in Havering; m. 24, no. 1276 and 1280, land at Wootton, Oxon.; m. 25, no. 1292, land in Beleton, Norf.; m. 26, no. 1350, land at Havering, Ess.; m. 26d, no. 1361, manor of Watton; m. 27d, no. 1380, land in Gissich and Erchampton, Dorset; m. 35, no. 1444, land in Terreton, Som. Ibid., 116B, 20 Henry III: m. 1, no. 1882, land in Garboldisham, Norf.; m. 1, no. 1885, land in Chippenham, Wilts; m. 2, no. 1892, and m. 5d, no. 1952, land in Brimsgrave, Worcs.; m. 6, no. 1957, manor of Ringwood, Hants; m. 6d, no. 1965, land at Feckenham, Worcs.; m. 6d, no. 1964, vill of Torksey, Lincs; m. 7, no. 1970, land in Bingham, Notts; m. 7, no. 1971, land in Bemerton, Wilts; m. 7, no. 1972A, land in Up Wimborne, Dorset; m. 7d, no. 1972B, land in Brimsgrave, Worcs.; m. 8, no. 1985, land in Barton, Yorks; m. 8, no. 1986, 30 acres in Heref.; m. 8d, no. 1993, land in Norton, Worcs.; m. 8d, no. 1999, land of manor of Gomshall. Ibid., 117, 21–22 Henry III: m. 1, no. 1, land in Ringwood, Hants; no. 2, land in Netham, Hants; no. 3, land in Merrow, Sur.; no. 5, manor of Purle, Ess.; no. 6, land in Acornburgh, Heref.; no. 7, land in Ringwood, Hants; no. 8, manors in several counties; m. 1d, nos. 9, 10, land at Ditton, Kent; no. 24, Denham; no. 25, wood in Bray, Berks; no. 29, land in Chadenwick, Wilts; m. 3, no. 33, land in Up Wimborne, Dorset; no. 34; land in several vills in Hants; no. 35, land in Melksham, Wilts; m. 5, no. 75, La Manasse, Kent; no. 77, land in Merrow, Sur.; no. 79, land in Ringwood; m. 5d, no. 84, land in Netham, Hants; no. 86, land in Ringwood, Hants, no. 87, land in Merrow, Sur.; m. 6d, no. 105, Sherwood forest, Notts; m. 8, no. 110, land in manor of Merrow, Sur.; no. 111, manors in York; no. 113, land in Ringwood, Hants; m. 9d, no. 132, land in several vills; m. 11d, no. 146, land in Norton, Worcs.; no. 147 and 148, land in Ringwood.

[80] Ibid., 117, m. 4, nos. 47–62.

A typical case, that of John the parson of Nettlestead, Suffolk, illustrates the judicial nature of the process. He was summoned to Westminster in 1229 to show by what warrant he held twenty-six acres of land at Nettlestead, which the king claimed as escheat of the Normans.[81] Philip de Pirie offered himself against the parson as the king's attorney, or as the court clerks phrased it, *sequitur pro domino rege*.[82] John alleged that he had successfully defended his right to the land in an earlier proceeding in the royal court, and he placed himself on the record of the plea roll for that case, heard earlier in King Henry III's reign. The roll was searched, but it did not support John; on the contrary, it revealed a suit against him for chopping down a wood and carrying away grain. Therefore, the court ruled that he should answer the present plea. The parson then responded by producing a charter showing that he held the land in fee of Albert de Willisham. The king's attorney challenged the charter as evidence by maintaining that Albert had not held the land in such a fashion that he could enfeof another. The judges then called a jury of recognition to determine whether Albert had held the land in fee or at farm; the jurors swore that he had held it in fee. No final decision is recorded, but the jurors' statement indicates that the parson's charter was lawful and that the land did not belong to the king.

The tenants sometimes raised exceptions to the king's questioning of their right to avoid a defense. If they were bold enough, their exceptions could be quite original, as those that Gilbert Marshal, earl of Pembroke, raised in 1237 show. He was summoned *coram rege* to warrant several manors that Henry III claimed as escheat of the Flemish. Gilbert first argued that he ought not answer because the plea was a common plea, and that Magna Carta would be violated if it were heard before the king. When this exception was rejected by the judges, he tried others. Then when all had failed, he demanded that "the lord king show by what right and for what reason those manors ought to be his

---

[81] *Ibid.*, XIII, 373, no. 1176, Easter 1229; pp. 470–471, no. 2009, Trinity 1229.

[82] On the king's suitors, see Flower, *Introduction*, p. 407.

escheat." The king then gave an account of his claim, but later judgment was given *coram consilio domini regis* that the manors were not part of the king's escheats.[83] When another great baron Roald fitz Alan was summoned to answer quo warranto concerning three manors, he brought a charter of King John which stated that he should not be disseized *nisi per judicium curia domini regis,* and he asked whether he needed to respond further.[84] Clearly, these great barons were unhappy about the opportunities for oppression that the quo warranto offered the king.

On several occasions individuals sought support in proving their right to land by vouching to warranty their grantor or their lord. The usual rules concerning warranty prevailed even in cases to which the king was a party.[85] Robert de Hilton, summoned to show by what right he assarted a pasture to the injury of the king's forest, called to warrant his nephew, a minor. The justices then postponed the action until the boy should come of age, and Bracton's comment on their decision was, "Note that he who is under age ought not to respond to the king any more than to any private person." [86] He set forth a different view in his *De legibus,* however, for there he wrote that a minor must sometimes answer if the matter touched the king.[87]

Warranty of another's lands was something to be avoided whenever possible, for it meant the expense and inconvenience of a lawsuit for the warrantor, when he replaced the tenant as defendant in the suit. Further, if he lost the suit and the land was adjudged to the plaintiff, then he had to compensate his tenant with other land equal in value to the land he had lost.[88] Thus it is hardly surprising that persons sought to escape acting as warrantors, and they seized upon the fact that the king was

[83] *CRR,* 117, m. 1, no. 8, Trinity 1237 (also *Note Book,* III, 233, no. 1220).

[84] *CRR,* 117, m. 8, no. 111.

[85] *Ibid.,* XIII, 154–155, no. 687. The prioress of St. James of Huntingdon sought the warranty of the daughters and heirs of Simon le Cornur. For additional examples, see *ibid.,* XIII, 183, no. 613; p. 300, no. 1380; p. 403, no. 1923.

[86] *Ibid.,* XIV, 128, no. 647, Michaelmas 1230 (also *Note Book,* II, 358–359, no. 449).

[87] Bracton, IV, 313, f. 422b.   [88] Pollock and Maitland, I, 306; II, 662.

their opponent as an excuse. In 1223, Henry III sought the manor of Watlington in Oxfordshire from Peter fitz Herbert, who vouched to warranty Henry d'Oilly, from whom he had received the estate by charter.[89] Henry acknowledged his charter, and then, according to the record of the case, "he freely warranted him against all men except the lord king, and he asked if he ought to warrant him against the lord king." Peter retorted that "in that charter it is written that he should warrant that land against all men, so that neither the lord king nor any other ought to be excepted." The justices agreed with Peter, and when the manor was adjudged to the king, they instructed Henry to make an exchange at value.[90]

At other times the force of the royal will can be seen in these cases, as tenants conceded the king's right without a defense of their own right. In 1222 the dean of the cathedral of Chichester was summoned before the royal justices to prove his right to a certain marsh near the king's castle there. He replied that the earl of Arundel had given him to understand that the king had returned it to him as his right and inheritance. Obviously, the dean had no firm proof of his right, for the entry concludes: "But since it is not pleasing to the lord king, he returns to the lord king his right to whatever he had in that marsh."[91] Similarly, in 1226 a plea brought by the king against William Briwerre concerning a manor was postponed indefinitely by royal command "because William Briwerre acknowledged before the lord king that he claims nothing unless at bail of the lord king at his will."[92] On roll 117 there are two cases in which the tenants of

[89] *CRR*, XI, 7, no. 43, Hilary 1223. Henry de Oilly was baron of Hook Norton, Oxon. (Sanders, *Baronies*, p. 54).

[90] A similar situation arose in a plea of service, when an individual called to warrant sought the judgment of the court whether he ought to warrant against the king (*CRR*, XII, 155–156, no. 755, Michaelmas 1225; also *Note Book*, III, 513–514, no. 1665). The plea was dismissed without a decision on this question.

[91] *CRR*, X, 276, Trinity 1222.

[92] *Ibid.*, XII, 448, no. 2227, Easter 1226. *Ibid.*, p. 168, no. 826, Michaelmas 1225, records a similar statement by William, but for some reason the action continued.

the land sought by the king refused to plead against him, but threw themselves on his mercy.[93]

The king did not recover in every suit that he brought. A count of cases won and lost is difficult because quo warranto actions were subject to the same delays as other proceedings. But an examination of *curia regis* roll 117 for 21 and 22 Henry III, which contains an unusually large number of quo warranto actions, shows that of the nine cases that came to a conclusion the king's claim was upheld in five, the tenant's in four.[94] Why some persons should have been afraid to contradict the king when others were successful in their contests is difficult to know. One explanation is that some actions were brought by private persons simply using the king's name, so that he had no concern about their outcome.[95] The quo warranto proceedings were conducted by attorneys for the king, and the attorneys may have been the actual claimants in some cases.

The plea rolls of Henry III sometimes reveal surprising carelessness in the prosecution of the king's cases. The decisions of the judges in two quo warranto proceedings illustrate this: "And because no one follows against him [the tenant], and because we know nothing of the lord king's right, therefore the plea should be dismissed." [96] On other occasions, the action was dismissed because the defendant was able to prove his right to the satisfaction of the judges. In 1228, John de Estley was asked to prove his right to land, and he replied that he held it of the king in return for a farm of eight pounds ten shillings as had his

---

[93] *Ibid.*, 117, m. 2, no. 19, and m. 5, no. 77, land at Merrow, Sur.

[94] *Ibid.*, 117, nos. 19, 77, 146, 148, for the king; nos. 24, 29, 33, 84, for the tenant.

[95] Plucknett, *Legislation*, p. 36.

[96] CRR, XIII, 339, no. 1598, Hilary 1229, Paul Pievre summoned to show by what warrant he held one carucate of land in Todenham, Bucks. For identical conclusions, see the case of Robert Trussebut in *ibid.*, XIV, 29, no. 152, Trinity 1231 (also in *Note Book*, II, 449–450, no. 582). Similarly, a plea of advowson brought by the king against the bishop of Llandaff was postponed to be heard before the barons of the exchequer, "because no one knew anything to say for the lord king" (CRR, XI, 100, no. 525, Hilary 1223).

ancestors.[97] A jury of recognition then confirmed that his ancestors had held the manor for the same annual payment, but they did not know through whom they had entry or by what warrant they held the land. Evidently John had no stronger proof of his right than the long tenure of his family, but neither did the king have any stronger disproof. The record of the case notes that later "the lord king commanded that John should be dismissed because he [the king] did not wish to hold that plea at present, saving his right in the future, if he should wish to speak thereof."

While the main purpose of the quo warranto proceedings may have been to safeguard the king's legitimate interests, there is little doubt that the profits derived from sale of royal confirmations of rights formed a subsidiary motive. The financial factor has already been noted in the case of the manor of Brill during the reign of King John, and the plea rolls of Henry III offer added evidence of this factor. William de Brickville was asked by what right he held the manor of Bentley, part of a royal serjeanty held by William le Archer.[98] He replied that the brother of William le Archer had subinfeudated it to him; the brother was present in court and acknowledged this. William de Brickville's title to the manor was incomplete without a royal confirmation of the grant, for the English kings had been attempting to restrain the alienation of their serjeanties since 1198, and the 1217 issue of Magna Carta contains a chapter aimed at limiting tenants' alienations of their lords' lands.[99] It was clear that he had not obtained such a confirmation, for he stated that "if in any way he entered without the lord king, he would correct it at the king's will." He then offered the king two marks to have a royal charter of confirmation. Henry III eventually did confirm him in his possession of the manor, but not until he had raised his oblation to one hundred shillings.[100]

[97] CRR, XIII, 232–233, no. 1070, Michaelmas 1223, land at Nordley, Salop.

[98] Ibid., p. 21, no. 91, Easter 1227.

[99] Charter of 1217, chap. 39; Pollock and Maitland, I, 332–335.

[100] Pipe Roll 14 Henry III, ed. Chalfont Robinson (Pipe Roll Society, N.S.; London, 1927), Michaelmas 1230, p. 196.

The largest groups of actions brought by the king in his courts were those relating to churches, and these proceedings conform most closely to the regular forms of action used by all litigants in the royal courts. No doubt, the monarch took care to adhere closely to legal forms in actions relating to churches because an autonomous and almost equal power watched over such cases. The Church with its own system of courts had been in rivalry with the king and his courts for jurisdiction over questions of presentation since the time of the Constitutions of Clarendon. The plea rolls of both John and Henry III provide numerous regular actions of *quare impedit,* which demanded why one impeded the right of presentation of another; *quare admisit personem,* which demanded why one had admitted a parson to a church in the gift of another, and assizes of darrein presentment, in addition to quo warranto or *quo advocatio* actions.[101] The

---

[101] E.g. actions *quare impedit: CRR,* V, 43, church of Wembworthy, Dev.; VII, 46, church of Graston, Norf.; VII, 121–122, St. Clement of Ipswich; VII, 144–145, church of Thornhaugh, Northants.; XI, 160, no. 803, church of Marden, Heref.; *Note Book,* II, 603, no. 785, church of Bedingham, Norf. Actions *quare admisit: Pleas before King,* I, 297, no. 3116, church of Halesowen, Salop; *CRR,* XII, 7, no. 44, church of Shalford, Sur.; XII, 72, no. 379, church of Stamford, Notts. Assizes of darrein presentment: *RCR,* II, 64, church of Eure, Dorset; *Pleas before King,* I, 85, no. 3230, church of Salisbury; *CRR,* II, 145, church of Arley, Staffs; IV, 115, church of Coldred, Kent; VI, 28, chapel of Hereford Castle; VI, 93, church of Ashwell, Herts; VII, 185, church of Costessey, Norf.; VIII, 305–306, church of Little Tynton, Lincs; IX, 54, church of Combe, Oxon.; X, 70–71, church of Cavendish, Suff.; X, 141–142, church of Akeley, Bucks; XI, 407, no. 2027, deanery of St. Probus; XII, 522, no. 2617, church of Eyling, Hants; XII, 442–443, no. 2186, church of Hathill, Norf.; XIII, 247, no. 1128, church of Morebath, Dev.; XIII, 331–332, no. 1556, church of Newton, Hants; XIII, 399–400, no. 1906, church of Hurstbourn, Hants; XIV, 98, no. 495, church of Beckley, Oxon.; *Note Book,* II, 153–154, no. 187, Bokinton, Staffs; II, 308–309, no. 1300, church of Swynnerton, Staffs; II, 406–407, no. 519, church of Lillingstone, Oxon.; III, 231–232, no. 1219, church of Medbourne, Leics; III, 251–255, no. 1238, church of Great Walsingham, Norf.; III, 337, no. 1364, church of Bottesford, Lincs; III, 568–569, no. 1732, church of Linton, Devon. Actions *quo warranto: CRR,* III, 113, St. Helen, Garstang, Lancs; III, 118–119, church of Binstead, Hants; IV, 12, church of Shebbear, Dev.; VI, 213, church of Chelmondiston, Suff.; VI, 308, church of Skegness, Lincs; *Note Book,* III, 285, no. 1275, church of Canewdon, Ess. Actions *quo advocatio: CRR,* I, 384, church of Marton, Lincs; XII, 18, no. 96, St. Issey, Cornwall.

reason for the great number of pleas concerning churches is easily explained: the right of advowson to churches was an important financial resource of the monarchy because ecclesiastical livings provided incomes for the clerks who staffed the royal secretariat.

Sometimes proceedings concerning churches were begun by the king for the express purpose of gaining a living for one of his clerks. King John once brought suit for a prebend at the collegiate church of Morton against the bishop of Hereford, summoning the bishop to show why he had given the prebend without the king's consent.[102] A letter from King John to his sheriff reveals that he appointed a royal clerk, Henry Luvel, to the prebend; he commanded the sheriff to give Henry possession of a manor held of the king by the canons of Morton, "until he recovers his prebend of Morton."[103] In addition, this writ illustrates John's use of distraint to force submission to his will. If his clerk could not receive the prebend, then the canons would lose the manor they had from the gift of the king. Furthermore, King John was not above using churches in the gift of others to provide livings for clerks in his service. In 1203 a suit was brought in the royal court between the constable of Normandy and the abbot of Crowland concerning the last presentation to a church, but the king sent a writ to the justices commanding them to dismiss the case because they had agreed to accept his beloved clerk, Thomas of Branchester, as parson.[104] Another Branchester, John, the archdeacon of Worcester, served King Richard as vice-chancellor and was one of King John's senior chancery clerks.[105] Perhaps Thomas was a relative inspired by John's success to seek a career for himself in the king's service. King Henry III continued to claim advowsons in an effort to find livings for clerks in his service. In Easter term 1221 he brought an assize of darrein presentment against the prior of St. Frides-

---

[102] CRR, I, 262, Michaelmas 1200, pleas *coram rege.*

[103] Rot. lit. cl. I, 77, 6 Feb. 1207, *Teste me ipso.* The manor was Langford, which the canons held of the king for an annual return of 50 shillings.

[104] CRR, II, 191, Easter 1203, pleas at Westminster; cited in Flower, *Introduction,* p. 177. The church was at Easton, Northants.

[105] Painter, *King John,* p. 79.

wida concerning a church in Buckinghamshire.[106] The jurors found for the king, and in the next term he wrote the bishop of Lincoln that he had presented his clerk, Ralph of Norwich.[107]

It comes as no surprise that the decisions declared in these cases were more often than not in favor of the king's right of presentation. Several times judgment was given for the king simply because those whose right he contested withdrew rather than defend their right against him. For example, King John once summoned the abbot of Pershore to show why he had admitted a clerk to a church said to be in the king's gift.[108] The abbot was ill, and he sent two monks to defend the abbey's right. They presented charters as evidence that the church had been given to the abbey, and they called to warrant the persons who had given it. The case was postponed until the warrantors could be summoned, but the plea did not go forward. A note added to the record of the case explains: "Afterwards the abbot came in his proper person and withdrew and put himself in the king's mercy and gave up to him his charters." Similarly, in 1206, King John brought an assize of darrein presentment against the prior of Dover to recover the church of Coldred, which he claimed by reason of his custody of the archbishopric of Canterbury during its vacancy.[109] The prior conceded the presentation to John because he could not endure a suit when the king was the other party; he reserved his right to subsequent action, however, stating that he would seek recovery when the see was no longer in the king's hands. An action between Hugh, archdeacon of Wells, and the abbot of Leicester concerning presentation to a chapel ended in a similar fashion.[110] The archdeacon was one of

[106] CRR, X, 141–142, Easter 1221 (also Note Book, III, 436, no. 1545), church of Akeley.

[107] Pat. Rolls (1216–1225), p. 291, May 1221.

[108] Pleas before King, I, 297, no. 3116; discussed in introduction, pp. 62–63. Also in RCR, II, 156–157, Hilary 1200, pleas coram rege at Woodstock. The church in question was Halesowen, Salop.

[109] CRR, IV, 115, Easter 1206, pleas at Westminster.

[110] Ibid., V, 165, Easter 1208, pleas coram rege; discussed in Flower, Introduction, pp. 208–209. The chapel was at Wanlip, Leics, and Hugh claimed that it belonged to the church of Rothley, a church in the king's gift. Later the abbot claimed that his warrantor was a minor, but he would allow

King John's clerks, who later earned an appointment as bishop of Lincoln through his service to the king.[111] Clearly, possessors of churches claimed by the king were sometimes hesitant about defending their rights.

These withdrawals cannot be credited solely to fear of King John's wrath, for they continued during the reign of his successor. In 1226, Henry III brought an assize of darrein presentment against William de Warenne, earl of Surrey, and his wife. After the earl and his wife failed to appear once, he came to the court *coram rege* and said that he did not wish to plead against the king, and he returned the presentation to him. Yet the earl did not escape without an amercement. Because his wife had also been summoned but had not come with him, she was considered to have made a default; and the assize was taken against them by default in spite of his attempted withdrawal.[112] Henry III won an action *quare non permittit* by default, when the justices bore witness that the advocate of the church in question had left on a pilgrimage and had no wish to contest the king's claim.[113] But King John and Henry III did not win every action they brought by default, for some persons attempted to defend their claims against the king.[114]

Not every suit brought by the king resulted in his gaining the right of presentation that he sought. Out of thirteen actions brought by King John which can be traced to a conclusion, he

---

the king to present to the chapel until his warrantor came of age (*ibid.*, pp. 253–254, Trinity 1208, pleas *coram rege*).

[111] Painter, *King John*, pp. 79–80.

[112] *CRR*, XII, 442–443, no. 2186, Easter 1226, an adjournment; *Note Book*, III, 586, no. 1755, Easter 1226, the conclusion of the case. The same year Henry Hose, one of the defendants in an assize of darrein presentment, remitted his right and claim to the king (*CRR*, XII, 522, no. 2617). For a similar case, see an action against the bishop of Salisbury (*CRR*, XII, 466, no. 2196, Trinity 1226).

[113] *CRR*, XIV, 530–531, no. 2451, Easter 1232.

[114] E.g. persons who unsuccessfully defended their rights to churches against the king: *ibid.*, VI, 308, William Wibian; VII, 144, Geoffrey Gibbon; X, 70–71, prior of Hertford; X, 141–142, prior of St. Frideswida; X, 276–277, John son of Philip; XIV, 158–159, no. 795, abbot of Cormeilles, Normandy; *Note Book*, II, 406–407, no. 519, Ralph de Kareville and William de Oseville; III, 231–232, no. 1219, abbot of Luston.

was successful in seven and unsuccessful in six.[115] Sometimes the king freely conceded his right to another or withdrew from his suit before a judgment was reached. In April 1200 an assize of darrein presentment brought by King John against the church of Salisbury concerning the church at Hurstbourn was dismissed by his command because "he quitclaimed that church forever to the church of Salisbury."[116] Since that date was just before John's return to the Continent for a meeting with the king of France, this possibly represents an act of propitiation made for the success of his negotiations. Four years later a jury came before the king to recognize whether the chapel of Binstead in Hampshire was in his gift or was a pensionary of the church of Alton. Evidence to support the chapel's connection with Alton was given by the clerk, who had been its incumbent for fifty-five years. His testimony must have convinced the king of the weakness of his case, for the jury was postponed indefinitely at the command of the justiciar.[117]

At other times, when the suit brought by the king did come to a judgment, the decision was not always in his favor. In 1204 a jury came to the court *coram rege* to recognize whether a chapel belonged to a church in the king's gift. The jurors swore that it had never been a chapel in their time, but always a church; and they added that many juries had inquired about this before, and

---

[115] *Staffordshire Suits Extracted from the Plea Rolls, temp. Richard I and King John*, ed. George Wrottesley (Wm. Salt Soc., Vol. III, pt. 1, 1882), p. 74, church of Arley, Staffs, won by the king; *Pleas before King*, Vol. I, no. 3116, church of Halesowen, won by the king; no. 3230, church of Hurstbourn, the king withdrew; *CRR*, II, 145, church of Arley, won by the king; III, 118–119, church of Binstead, Hants; p. 113, church of St. Helen, Garstang, Lancs, the king lost; IV, 115, church of Coldred, Kent, won by the king; V, 39, church of St. Peter at Cambridge, lost by the king; V, 43, church of Wembworthy, Devon, the king lost; V, 174, church of Brayles, War., the king won; VI, 308, church of Skegness, Lincs, won by the king; VII, 46, 116, church of Graston, Norf., the king lost; VII, 144, church of Thornhaugh, Northants., won by the king.

[116] *Pleas before King*, I, 320, no. 3230; discussed in introduction, p. 85.

[117] *CRR*, III, 118–119, Easter 1204; pleas *coram rege*; discussed in Flower, *Introduction*, pp. 41–42, 207–208. Similar is *ibid.*, p. 343, which records that Simon de Eckingham had leave to withdraw from a plea concerning a prebend *per preceptum domini regis*.

none had ever found that this church belonged to the king. In the face of such a definite statement in opposition to the king's contention, the judges had no choice but to declare that the king should take nothing by that jury.[118] In 1207 a jury of recognition was summoned before King John to determine whether a church at Cambridge was in the gift of the king or of others. The jury found neither for the king nor for his opponents, but stated that the church was rightfully in the gift of the Hospital of St. John in Cambridge.[119]

The rolls for the years of Henry III's reign reveal additional illustrations of suits in which the king did not gain the church he sought. In eighteen cases in which a conclusion can be found, he failed in five, succeeded in eleven, and divided two with their possessors.[120] Once during his minority, the justiciar and the council commanded that an assize of darrein presentment between two private individuals be dismissed. They alleged that the church in question was in the king's gift, and they brought an action *quo advocatio* against the priest.[121] A jury of twelve

[118] *Ibid.*, p. 113, Easter 1204; discussed in Flower, *Introduction*, p. 277; church of St. Helen, Garstang, Lancs.

[119] *CRR*, V, 39, Michaelmas 1207, pleas *coram rege*.

[120] *Ibid.*, VIII, 305–306; IX, 5, 122–123, 232, 356, church of Little Tynton, Lincs, lost by the king; VIII, 364–365; IX, 11–12, church of Bottesford, Lincs, lost by the king; IX, 54, 187; X, 226, church of Combe, Oxon., won by the king; X, 70–71, church of Cavendish, Suff., won by the king; X, 141–142, church of Akeley, Bucks, won by the king; X, 276–277, church of Bokinton, Staffs, won by the king; XII, 522, no. 2176, church of Linton, Dev., lost by the king; XII, 442–443, 521–522, nos. 2186 and 2616, church of Hathill, Norf., won by the king; XII, 522, no. 2617, church of Eyling, Hants, the king won against two of three possessors, but conceded his right to the third; XIII, 331–332, no. 1556, church of Newton, Hants, the king lost; XIII, 399–400, 466, nos. 1906 and 2196, church of Hurstbourn, Hants, the king won; XIV, 112, 158–159, nos. 572 and 795, church of Kingsland, Heref., the king won; XIV, 530–531, no. 2451, church of Drayton, Bucks, the king won; *Note Book*, II, 406–407, no. 519, church of Lillingstone, Oxon., the king won; *CRR*, 113, m. 12d, no. 493, church of Epworth, Lincs, lost by the king; 113, m. 30d, no. 848, and 115B, m. 19, no. 1239, church of St. Keverne, Corn., won by the king; 116B, m. 6d, no. 1965, three churches in Torksey, Lincs, one taken by the king; 117, m. 1, no. 4, church of Medbourn, Leics, won by the king.

[121] *CRR*, VIII, 305–306, Easter 1220.

knights was summoned for the inquiry, but the recognitors failed to come, causing three adjournments, and causing great annoyance to the justices. The plea roll entry recording the third adjournment voices their anger: "Be it known that the sheriff acts warmly in the business of others since becoming so negligent in the king's business." [122] When the knights finally did come to make the recognition, they found that the father of the plaintiff in the original assize had presented the last parson, and the justices then directed that the plaintiff be given seizin of the church.[123]

This survey of cases indicates that while the king in theory might not have possessed any privileges in actions that he brought, in actual practice he did enjoy certain advantages. Perhaps the most striking advantage was the hesitation on the part of some persons to defend their claims against him, either through fear of provoking him to extralegal action or for some other reason. Of course, the king enjoyed other practical advantages. Because of his position as the head of the judicial administration, the time and place of pleas could be arranged to suit his needs or the needs of those prosecuting the case for him. There are several examples of postponements of pleas touching the king made *per preceptum domini regis*.[124] Sometimes, too, the principle *coram rege terminari debet placitum quod ipsum tangit* was

---

[122] *Ibid.*, IX, 232, Michaelmas 1220. Earlier postponements are: IX, 5, Trinity 1220; and IX, 122–123, also Trinity. The case was concluded in Michaelmas 1220, *ibid.*, IX, 356.

[123] In an assize concerning the church of Linton in Devonshire, the abbot of Ford said that he did not wish to plead against the king, but that he wished to tell the truth. He then explained how he had come to possess the church, and the justices gave judgment for him (*ibid.*, XII, 440, no. 2176, Easter 1226, and *Note Book*, III, 568–569, no. 1732; discussed in Ehrlich, *Proceedings against the Crown*, p. 13).

[124] E.g. *CRR*, II, 159, and IV, 231, pleas relating to churches in the king's gift postponed until they could be heard *coram rege*. *Ibid.*, XII, 2, no. 12; XIII, 105, no. 454; and XIII, 542, no. 2567, actions brought by the king relating to land postponed by his command. *Ibid.*, XIV, 98, no. 495, assize of darrein presentment brought by the king placed in respite by his writ. *Ibid.*, 113, m. 18, no. 600, plea between the king and the prior of Holy Trinity, Canterbury.

applied; and this caused delays and inconvenience for the defendant, sometimes meaning travels up and down the kingdom
following the king on his eyre.[125] The king could command
special types of juries to decide cases to which he was a party.
Once the itinerant justices gave the sheriff special instructions
for choosing the jurors in an assize of darrein presentment,
adding the explanation, *quia negocium illud pertinat ad dominum Regem.*[126] Furthermore, the king was not bound by the
regular forms of action, but could make any complaint that he
brought proceed in his courts. Other litigants could have special
juries and could proceed without writ by plaint, but usually
these dispensations from the ordinary procedures were made in
exchange for oblations.

In spite of the advantages the monarch enjoyed, the cases in
which he appeared as plaintiff do not reveal an autocratic ruler.
Indeed, the fact that John and Henry III were willing to submit
questions relating to their rights to their courts shows that these
medieval English kings had respect for custom and law. The
royal privilege of proceeding by writ quo warranto had potential
as a means of oppression, since the king did not have to show any
superior right before forcing an opponent to reveal his right. Yet
even this action did follow judicial process with opportunity for
the possessor either to prove his right promptly or to delay a
decision in the many ways that customary procedure allowed.
Judgment could go against the king, and it sometimes did. Cases
concerning lay tenures lost by the king may have been in reality
private pleas brought in the king's name. Those concerning
rights to churches may not have been pursued too vigorously by
the king because he feared a confrontation with the Church, or

[125] This was the reply made by the justices to a complaint that an action in
which the king was called to warrant was a common plea and ought not to
follow the king (*Note Book*, III, 233, no. 1220). The principle was not
followed consistently, however, because a number of pleas brought by the king
were heard by the justices of the bench under both John and Henry III. For a
fuller discussion, see Chapter 1, pp. 33–36.
[126] *Staffordshire Suits* (Wm. Salt Soc., Vol. III, pt. 1), p. 124, assizes at
Hereford, 5 John, church of Broom, Staffs.

possibly because he feared for his soul. Still there is no denying that the king had real advantages over his opponents in practice if not in theory in lawsuits in the royal courts.

Finally, some comparison of the reign of John with that of his son and heir, Henry III, is necessary. The plea rolls provide evidence that Henry brought a far greater number of actions in his courts to recover royal rights and possessions than did his father. Even though it was during Henry's reign that the quo warranto proceeding developed, an instrument that did have an element of arbitrariness about it, he did submit his claims to the "law of the land." The number of cases seems to indicate that Henry III was more zealous in asserting royal rights than was his father, or at least that he made greater use of the common law courts in asserting them. Perhaps King John was too preoccupied with his struggles against his enemies on the Continent to devote his attention to this problem. But more likely, he passed over the courts of justice in favor of more reliable executive instruments.

8

Pleas against the King

One of the maxims of medieval English political theory was that the king was under the law. This conception was the very heart of Magna Carta, and Bracton expressed this view of the ruler's subjection to a higher authority when he wrote, "Moreover, the king ought not to be under man but under God and the law, because the law makes the king." [1] Another aspect of kingship recognized by English thinkers in the Middle Ages was the monarch's position as the "author of justice," the head of the legal system, whose primary duty was to give justice to his subjects. Yet in addition to being the supreme judge and lawgiver of the realm, the king was an active chief executive, the feudal suzerain, and a private person with vast power. Obviously, in an age when the ruler combined all these functions, he was bound to take action at times that violated the rights of his subjects. Indeed, exploitation of their purely personal power was one of the bases of strength for the Angevin monarchs, enabling them to achieve "a kind of unrealized absolutism" unimpeded by traditional law and custom. [2] For their subjects, the *ira* or *malevolentia regis*, the king's personal ill-will, was a real danger that could bring them ruin.

It is easy to see how conflicts might arise between the king's interests as a feudal lord, or simply as a man, and his duty to render justice to all impartially. The king was a great and often greedy property holder, and he had the strength to threaten the

---

[1] Bracton, II, 33, f. 5b.
[2] The view of J. E. A. Jolliffe, *Angevin Kingship* (London, 1955), pp. 56, 87; the quotation is from p. 341.

property of others, if he chose. Medieval legal thinkers were aware that the king could do wrong, yet they acknowledged that he had no mortal superior who could judge his actions. A statement by a prominent royal servant, the author of the *Dialogus de scaccario,* expresses this view well. Speaking of the king's wealth, he says, "And although this wealth is not theirs by strict process of law, but proceeds . . . sometimes even from their mere arbitrary power, their subjects have no right to question or condemn their actions." [3] Political theorists might declare that the monarch did have a superior in God and the law, but this must have been small satisfaction to an individual who had suffered at the hands of the king. In thirteenth-century England the king was the head of the legal system, the judge ordinary of the realm, yet one who had a grievance against the king had to secure redress in the king's own courts.

DIRECT ACTIONS

The system of writs and assizes ordinarily available to persons seeking justice offered no remedy for those who had a grievance against the king. The royal clerks of the chancery could hardly issue a writ compelling their master to appear and answer charges before his justices. Bracton in the section of his treatise considering novel disseizins set forth clearly the rule concerning proceedings against the king:

But if it is a prince or a king who has no superior except God, there is no remedy against him by assize. In such a case, there is only place for a petition that he amend and correct his act. And if he will not do this, it must suffice as a punishment for him that he shall stand ultimately before God, who says: "Vengeance is mine, and I will repay"; unless it may be said that the *universitas regni* and his baronage can and ought to do this [amend the king's action] in the king's court.[4]

[3] *Dial. de scac.,* p. 1.

[4] Bracton, III, 43, f. 171b; for a similar statement, see II, 33, f. 5b: "If, however, action is taken against him, since no writ runs against the king, there is place for a petition that he will correct and amend his action. If he does not do this, it suffices as a punishment for him that he may await the vengeance of God."

Thus Bracton allowed two possible ways to seek justice against the king: there was the possibility of a judgment of the king by the earls, barons, and great men who composed the *magna curia regis;* or a subject could appeal to his ruler to correct the wrong he had done.

This first opinion, the theory that there was within the kingdom a body legally competent to judge the king—the *universitas regni* or the *baronagium*—was well known in the thirteenth century. Whether it represents Bracton's own thoughts is a matter of scholarly controversy, chiefly because the strongest statement of the doctrine occurs in the clause concerning the king's bridle, "And one who has an associate [the barons and the earls] has a master; and therefore if the king is without a bridle, that is without the law, they ought to put a bridle on him." [5] There are doubts concerning the authenticity of this *addicio de cartis*. Study of the manuscripts of Bracton's treatise has led some scholars to regard it not as a statement by Bracton but as a later addition, probably made by some supporter of the baronial party against Henry III.[6] Even though the statement may not have come from Bracton himself, it is significant as an expression of a theory of kingship held by some in England in the mid-thirteenth century. But whatever its significance in the sphere of political theory, it had little import as a practical instrument for individuals seeking judgments against the king. As C. H. McIl-

[5] *Ibid.,* II, 110, f. 34.

[6] *Constitutionalism: Ancient and Modern,* pp. 69, 157–158, summarizes current scholarly opinion. Maitland thought it possible that the addition was made after the completion of the treatise by Bracton himself (*Note Book,* I, introduction, 30–33). Hermann Kantorowicz, *Bractonian Problems* (Glasgow, 1941), pp. 49–52, found "no passage more genuinely Bractonian." H. G. Richardson, in *Bracton: The Problem of His Text* (Selden Society, supp. ser., Vol. II; London, 1966), p. 31, writes, "In truth, the whole of the *addicio* is very Bractonian." He believes it to have been added by Bracton sometime between 1261 and 1264 (p. 35). For opposing views, see Woodbine's review of *Bractonian Problems* in the *Yale Law Journal,* LII (1943), 428–444; Fritz Schulz, "Bracton on Kingship," *E.H.R.,* LX (1945), 136–176; and Gaillard Lapsley, "Bracton and the Authorship of the 'Addicio de Cartis,'" *E.H.R.,* LXII (1947), 1–19. Brian Tierney, in "Bracton on Government," *Speculum,* XXXVIII (1963), 311, refuses to take a stand: "The point does not seem capable of proof one way or the other."

wain wrote in a discussion of the relationship between the theory of medieval monarchy and the actual facts, "Though the king was under the law in theory, there was little effective machinery in existence to make this theory a practical reality." [7] The mechanics for securing the judgment of the *universitas regni* simply did not exist. Only once did the great men of the realm judge the king's unlawful acts in the way described in the two passages from Bracton. That judgment came as part of a political crisis which had aroused the barons' anger against Henry III.

The regular course of the law provided no opportunity for recourse against an unjust ruler, except an appeal to him to amend his ways. Consequently, proceedings against the crown before the royal courts of justice normally took the form of petitions to the king. Because the king was not limited to the regular forms of action, the wronged person could appeal to him to correct the injustice by a plaint or *querela*, presented either in writing or orally. One who had a complaint against the king could seek redress of his grievance in the same manner. The aggrieved party could request that the king voluntarily allow his courts to weigh the merits of his complaint. Such petitions were matters of grace that the king might accept or reject as he chose, but if he accepted them, they were heard before the royal justices according to legal procedures and were recorded on the plea rolls. [8] By 1270 this procedure appeared fully developed as the petition of right, but more informal appeals to the king were frequent throughout the thirteenth century. The plea rolls of John and Henry III provide a number of illustrations of such actions. [9]

[7] C. H. McIlwain, *The Growth of Political Thought in the West* (New York, 1932), p. 197; Richardson and Sayles, in *Governance*, p. 145, express a similar view.

[8] *Proc. without Writ*, p. lxx.

[9] *Ibid.*, pp. lxx, clxxxvi; Powicke, *Henry III*, p. 116; Ludwik Ehrlich, *Proceedings against the Crown, 1216–1337*, ed. Sir Paul Vinogradoff (Oxford Studies in Social and Legal History, Vol. VI; Oxford, 1921), pp. 26–27; and W. S. Holdsworth, "The History of Remedies against the Crown," *Law Qtrly. Rev.*, XXXVIII (1922), 141–164. Ehrlich, pp. 26–27, argued that in the time of Henry III a person claiming a grievance against the king was required to appear in person and make his complaint orally, and that written petitions first

Most cases that came before the royal justices were the various proprietary and possessory actions, and most proceedings against the king that they heard were requests for recovery of some right, privilege, or property that had come into the king's possession. An examination of such proceedings under King John and Henry III should seek to answer two questions. First, the question of whether the royal justices had enough independence to act on their own initiative in such cases must be considered. It seems clear that they could not proceed to answer these petitions without the king's permission. Second, the rolls of Henry III should show whether Magna Carta caused any change in the courts' handling of complaints against the king. The attempt by means of the Charter to require procedure *per judicium* of the king had an effect upon the courts' treatment of such cases. The young king and his council admitted more petitions for hearing in the courts, and they admitted petitions that raised more significant questions about royal acts.

The records of three actions heard by King John's justices illustrate the informality with which appeals to him for correction of his misdeeds could be made. They are also reminders that he could remedy such appeals by executive writ without recourse to the machinery of his courts. The first example comes from 1212, when the prioress of Amesbury brought an action to recover land from Eudes Patrick.[10] He maintained that the land was his rightful inheritance, which he had recovered from the king by means of a fine. The prioress denied that it was part of his inheritance, although she admitted that the sheriff at one time had seized it along with Eudes' inheritance. She explained that she had gone to the king and had shown him how she was disseized by his sheriff; she said that King John had commanded that if this were true he would have the sheriff return her land to her. An inquiry had then borne out the truth of her contention,

---

appeared under Edward I. Richardson and Sayles in *Proc. without Writ*, however, have proven conclusively that written petitions were presented as early as the time of King John. For a convenient summary of opinions, see Powicke, *Henry III*, p. 116, n. 2.

[10] *CRR*, VI, 242–243, Easter 1212.

and she had recovered seizin, but Eudes afterwards took it away from her. The prioress' account is in keeping with John's well-known kindness to nuns. Further, the account of the sheriff's deputy agreed with hers.

A similar story comes from the assizes taken before the itinerant justices at Lincoln in 1219. Alice the daughter of Stulli brought an assize of novel disseizin against Thomas de Moulton concerning her free tenement in Boston.[11] The jurors declared that she had only come into possession of the property at the time of the barons' war while Thomas was in the king's prison and his possessions were in the king's hand. When King John arrived in Boston, "she so cried upon the lord king that he gave her seizin." The only time that John ever visited Boston was on October 5, 1216, about two weeks before his death.[12] That King John found time to hear this plaint while engaged in a military campaign for the defense of his crown and while in ill-health may be a sign of stability unnoticed by other students of his character. Yet one wonders how Alice convinced him of her right to Thomas' tenement in Boston, for no other contemporary sources indicate that John was a man easily moved by a woman's tears.

A third example of application to the king for restoration of land comes from the verdict of a jury of recognition held during the time of Henry III. The king claimed the manor of Duddington in Northamptonshire held by Idonea de Canville and her husband as part of the escheat of the Normans.[13] The jurors were asked to determine whether Gerard de Canville and his wife—Idonea's grandparents—or William de Humez, constable of Normandy, had held the estate at the time of the loss of Normandy. The jurors stated that Gerard and his wife had held the entire manor in the time of King Richard, and five virgates of

---

[11] *Rolls for Lincs and Worcs.*, pp. 145–146, no. 319; discussed in Lady Stenton's introduction, pp. lx–lxi.

[12] *Ibid.*, p. lx. Lady Stenton says of the case, "It is pleasing to reflect that in the midst of a savage campaign of suppression John found time to listen to the plaint of one of the humblest of his subjects."

[13] *Note Book*, II, 437–438, no. 565, Easter 1231, pleas at Westminster. The origin of the case is found on pp. 391–392, no. 503.

land at Eston in addition. Later, following the loss of Normandy, other land held by William de Humez had escheated to King John; and, in taking possession of that land, he had disseized them of five virgates. They went to the king and showed him how he had disseized them by his will, and he then gave them other land in exchange for their land at Eston. It was easy for Gerard de Canville to approach the king with a request, for he had been one of John's men in the rebellion of 1193–1194 and later served him as a sheriff. Questioned whether the king gave them land in exchange or of his own will, the jurors stated that they did not know, but that they thought in exchange. The case concludes, "The record was sent to the lord king and he returned to them their seizin, but it is not known whether by judgment of his court or by his will." It is uncertain whether this is a continuation of the jurors' account of events during the time of King John, or whether it refers to Henry III's case against Idonea de Canville.[14]

King John could have dealt with each of these appeals for restoration of seizin by purely executive action, and none of them would have been recorded on the plea rolls had they not been cited during the course of other actions. No doubt, the king many times redressed grievances in this informal manner, leaving no record at all. Some other complaints against royal acts, however, were made before the court *coram rege* and were conducted along the lines of regular judicial proceedings. An example comes from 1204, when the prior of Holy Trinity, Canterbury, complained that a royal charter took away his right. Since only the king was competent to rule on questions regarding his charters, the prior's only recourse was to appeal to him. William of Wood had gone to King John in Poitou, where he offered him ten marks confirming his right to build a windmill at Monkton in Kent.[15] The prior complained that William had deceived the king when he obtained the royal confirmation. He

---

[14] Maitland in *ibid.*, p. 438, n. 2, assigns the first clause to the action between Henry and Idonea, the second to the description of the complaint made to King John.

[15] *Rot. de obl. et fin.*, p. 44.

pointed out that an earlier dispute of his with William in the court of King Richard had ended in a final concord, in which William agreed to destroy the windmill and not to rebuild it without the assent of the prior and monks.[16] William had deceived King John because, keeping silent about the suit and final concord, he had obtained the king's confirmation of his right. It was decided that the charter should be annulled and the windmill destroyed. The record of the case ends with a note that the prior gave twenty-five marks for hastening judgment; this, plus the fact that the plea touched the king, explains its speedy conclusion.

A similar case represented an attempt by an individual to recover from King John lands that his predecessors had taken. William Turpin offered the king forty marks to have possession of his lands and other property of which he had been disseized by the will of King Richard.[17] Before William regained possession, however, an inquiry into how he lost his land was held before the justices at Westminster.[18] There it was reported that William had been in seizin of his land until the earl of Arundel disseized him by his will because he knew of King Richard's *malevolentia* against him.

Other wrongs that individuals sought to have amended were actions by the men of royal manors. One of these cases was met earlier when the Knights Templars brought a plaint against the men of the royal manor of Woodstock, alleging that they had disseized them of four acres of land.[19] It was plain that the defendant in this action was really the king, and the royal justices recognized this, refusing to proceed until they had consulted him. Similar cases that merited the king's consultation were plaints by the prioress of Appleton, Yorkshire, and by the prioress of Moxby that the men of Huby, Yorkshire, made a

[16] CRR, III, 86–87, Hilary 1204, pleas *coram rege*. Discussed in Flower, *Introduction*, pp. 283–284, and *Proc. without Writ*, p. lxxxii.

[17] *Pipe Roll 1 John*, ed. Doris M. Stenton (Pipe Roll Society, N.S.; London, 1933), Michaelmas 1199, p. 225.

[18] CRR, I, 285, Michaelmas 1200.

[19] RCR, II, 157, Easter 1200 (also in *Pleas before King*, I, 297, no. 3117).

purpresture on the nuns' pasture.[20] In these cases too, the actual defendant was the king; otherwise, the nuns would have been required to proceed by one of the regular forms of action. The king complied with the requests of the prioresses for justice, and he sent commands to the sheriff of Yorkshire to ensure that justice was done.

Appeals to King John for restoration of property that are recorded on the plea rolls do not add up to a very impressive number—only eight; neither are they complaints against major injustices committed by the king. William Turpin's plaint comes closest to a true proceeding against the king, but in his case the action was against the former king, Richard I, not against the reigning monarch, John. The question remains: How could one who had suffered arbitrary and unlawful treatment at the hands of the monarch obtain justice? Perhaps there is a simple explanation. John may have heard such serious complaints informally and remedied them personally without use of the machinery of his courts, as he did in the cases of the prioress of Amesbury, Alice daughter of Stulli, and Gerard de Canville. When it is recalled, however, that John was the king whom the chroniclers called "tyrant," whose administrative records reveal numerous arbitrary seizures of land and extortions of money, and whose reign closed with a rebellion by his barons, it becomes difficult to accept this as a full explanation. Further, Magna Carta itself is an acknowledgment that there was no effective instrument for the king's subjects to secure redress of their grievances against him.

Doubts about the efficacy of petition as a means of proceeding against the king arise from one aspect of King John's rule in particular—his seizures of his subjects' lands without judgment. Temporary seizure of land into the king's hand—distraint to secure a defendant's appearance in court, for example—was a necessary part of the procedure of the royal courts. But John made disseizin *per voluntatem regis* into a normal administrative measure to discipline his servants, to punish his enemies, and to

<hr>

[20] RCR, II, 162–163, Easter 1200; and *Pleas before King*, I, 303, nos. 3136, 3138; discussed in Lady Stenton's introduction, pp. 68–69.

enforce payment of royal debts. The administrative records of his reign provide innumerable examples of this method.[21] The royal courts of justice offered no effective remedy to victims of John's arbitrary acts, as the absence of cases, even of plaints to the king, indicates. The only solution in such cases must have been to offer the king a large fine for his confession to an unlawful disseizin, as the oblations for recovery of lands seized by the king recorded on the fine rolls prove.[22]

This situation changed after the Great Charter placed the king under the law. The court records of Henry III indicate that the practice of petitioning the king for recovery of possessions seized by him or his agents continued and even increased. Such requests, once allowed by the king, were conducted much as ordinary judicial proceedings before the royal justices with the king defending his right much as any other tenant. An example of such a proceeding comes from the period of Henry III's early majority, when Walter de Godarville sought to regain his manor of Southhill, which had been taken from him by royal command.[23] The king had ordered all Walter's lands and chattels seized in August 1224 because he had been with Fawkes de Breauté when Fawkes defied Henry at Bedford Castle that summer.[24] Early in 1225 the king pardoned him for his part in the revolt and sent him on an expedition to Gascony; in return Godarville gave £100 to have the *gratia et benevolentia domini regis* and to recover seizin of his lands.[25] Evidently he did not

---

[21] See the references in Jolliffe, *Angevin Kingship,* chaps. 3–4. On pp. 72–73, for example, he discusses John's disciplining of Roger de Cressi for defying the wardship right of the crown and, on pp. 101–102, John's action against the Cistercians for their refusal to pay the carucage of 1200. See also J. C. Holt, *Magna Carta* (Cambridge, 1965), pp. 116–118, for examples of royal disseizin and payments to avoid it.

[22] E.g. *Rot. de obl. et fin.,* p. 513, offer by Richard Gubiun and Roger the Forester of 500 marks and a palfrey; p. 481, 200 marks offered by Robert of Castle Carrock; pp. 511–512, 100 marks and a palfrey offered by Isolde Biset.

[23] *CRR,* XIII, 422, no. 2014, Easter 1229.

[24] *Rot. lit. cl.,* I, 616. For an account of Fawkes' abortive revolt, see Powicke, *Henry III,* pp. 61–65.

[25] *Rot. lit. cl.,* II, 20, 25 Feb. 1225.

receive Southhill at this time, for in 1229 he brought suit against the earl of Gloucester for it. Since the earl replied that he only held it at bail of the king, Walter had to approach Henry III in order to regain it. The king ordered an inquiry made into the facts of the case, and the inquiry was held before the justices of the bench. Their decision was that Walter should have possession of the manor, "because the lord king commanded that Walter should have judgment according to the tenor of the inquiry."

Several other examples can be seen of persons pressing claims against the king in his own court. The bishops of England could easily approach the king with their complaints. In 1230 the bishop of Norwich appeared before the royal justices claiming a right to the amercements of his tenants throughout his liberty, whether imposed in the county court or by the justices on eyre.[26] Liberties usually gave their holder some profit—amercements in this case—which normally went to the king. King Henry was present in court, and he asked the bishop by what warrant he claimed a right to those amercements. The bishop replied that he had them by charters from King John. At first, he agreed to a judgment of the court on the basis of those charters, in which he would lose any right to the amercements forever if the judgment went against him. Afterwards, he reconsidered and said that he did not wish a judgment without the archbishop and other bishops and their counsel. Whether the bishop succeeded in gaining an afforcement of the court is unknown, for no conclusion to the case can be found in the plea rolls. The roll for Trinity term 1231 does record a postponement of a plea between the king and the bishop for hearing before the king and his council, but it describes the case as a "plea of land." [27]

Another bishop, Jocelin of Bath and Wells, came to Henry III in January 1235 to show the king that he had been wronged by

---

[26] CRR, XIII, 550–551, no. 2612, Hilary 1230; also in Note Book, II, 320, no. 391. Cited in G. B. Adams, Council and Courts in Anglo-Norman England (Yale Historical Studies, Vol. V; New Haven, 1926), p. 180, n. 2; and Ehrlich, Proceedings against the Crown, pp. 35–36.

[27] CRR, XIV, 384, no. 1793.

him.[28] The king had given away twenty-five oak trees in the bishop's wood, although he held only rights of vert and venison, the rights of cutting green wood and of hunting. The bishop presented charters of King Henry and John as evidence of the limited royal rights. The king replied that he had not remembered the charters when he granted the trees, but he recognized Jocelin's right. He personally pronounced judgment that the bishop's right to the woods should remain unimpaired, and letters patent were drawn up stating this.[29] Unfortunately, fifteen of the oaks had already been cut down.

A discreet manner of putting forth a claim against the king is illustrated by the case of Richard Siward in 1231. He was an able soldier and had served the king as an administrator; furthermore, he had powerful friends in the Marshal family and in Gilbert Basset, his brother-in-law.[30] Richard believed that he was entitled to jurisdictional rights over the hundred of Bullingdon, Oxfordshire, through the hereditary right of his wife, but it was uncertain whether his predecessors had exercised those rights in his capacity as sheriff or as lord of the hundred.[31] Richard showed (*monstravit*) the king that the sheriff impeded his exercise of his liberty; he did not complain (*queritur*), but he simply wished to know to what rights he was entitled. The king allowed him an inquest into his rights, and its findings supported his claim.

Not all petitions to the king concluded so happily. In 1237, William Longsword, son of the late earl of Salisbury and a cousin of Henry III, sought from him custody of the castle of Salisbury and recognition as hereditary sheriff of the county of Wiltshire.[32] His plea was heard by the court *coram rege* in the presence of the papal legate and other great men, and it was

[28] *Ibid.*, 115B, m. 25d, no. 1305. The bishop's wood was on the manor of Cheddar, Som.

[29] *Cal. Pat. Rolls* (1232–1247), pp. 90–91, 31 Jan. 1235.

[30] Powicke, *Henry III*, pp. 128–129.

[31] *CRR*, XIV, 252, no. 1188, Hilary 1231 (also *Note Book*, II, 400–402, no. 513); discussed in *Proc. without Writ*, p. lxx.

[32] *Note Book*, III, 248–249, no. 1235, pleas *coram rege* 1237–1238; discussed in Ehrlich, *Proceedings against the Crown*, pp. 36–37.

conducted just as any suit between private persons. The king responded to his claim by placing himself on the record of his court; that is, he appealed to the verdict of a jury taken in the time of King John. William first sought to have this judgment invalidated on the grounds that his mother, one of the parties, had been under age at the time. When this failed, he produced a charter of Henry II in defense of his claim, but the court found that the charter was not contrary to the finding of the jury, since it contained no mention of succession or hereditary right. The judgment was that the king should remain in seizin. All the forms of legality were present in this case, and there is no evidence that the substance of legality was lacking either. Nevertheless, it must be noted that a decision against a hereditary shrievalty was to the king's advantage.

That same year, the death of John the Scot, earl of Chester and of Huntingdon, brought another claim against the king to the royal court. Immediately after the earl's death, Alexander II, king of Scotland, sent three envoys to Henry III to ask that he be recognized as overlord of the honour of Huntingdon because he had been John's overlord and had acted as his guardian during his minority.[33] The king and his council replied to the Scottish king's representatives:

This ought not to injure the king because if the earl John was ever in the custody of the king of Scotland, it was in the time of Hubert de Burgh, earl of Kent, who was the friend and relative of the king of Scotland and who had the kingdom of England in his hand, while the king of England was under age. And this custody ought to belong to the king rather than to anyone else because it is the law of England and the custom approved and held in England by great men as well as lesser ones, that if anyone was enfeoffed by the king at any time of a tenement held by military service the king should have custody of all of his lands by whomsoever he was enfeoffed.

[33] *CRR*, 117, m. 2, no. 18, Michaelmas 1237, pleas *coram rege*; also *Note Book*, III, 235, no. 1221. Noted in Ronald Stewart-Brown, "The End of the Norman Earldom of Chester," *E.H.R.*, XXXV (1920), 47, and in Sanders, *Baronies*, p. 118, nn. 3–4, where Sanders identifies the honour of Huntingdon as the probable barony of Fortheringay, Northants.

The court's answer is a remarkably clear statement of the custom of prerogative wardship, one of the special feudal privileges of the English king by which he gained custody of all the holdings of his vassals, not only the fiefs they held directly of him.[34] Despite the denial that the Scottish king had any claim by reason of his former custody, Henry did agree to recognize him as overlord of the honour. Since the honour was to be divided among coheiresses, this concession cost nothing; yet it was a friendly gesture, a step toward the establishment of good relations between the neighboring rulers.[35]

The proceedings against the crown that have the greatest constitutional and political significance are those which arose out of the crisis of 1233–1234. At that time, the king's court did sit in judgment of his acts, and it did declare them unlawful. The personal government of Henry III, organized in 1232 following the fall of Hubert de Burgh, provoked the crisis by arousing the opposition of the great men of the kingdom. F. M. Powicke considers this crisis "probably more important than the better known and more prolonged assertion of baronial opinion, under the leadership of Simon de Montfort and the earls of Gloucester, a quarter of a century later." According to him, the leaders of the opposition, Richard Marshal, earl of Pembroke, and his friends, reasserted "the conception of kingship which was implicit in the Charter of Liberties and was vigorously upheld in the schools and in all the numerous treatises on the rights and duties of a king."[36] The king responded to this challenge to his personal rule with actions that violated every word of chapter 39 of the Great Charter. He arbitrarily outlawed and disseized the earl marshal, Gilbert Basset, Richard Siward, and other leaders of the

[34] Pollock and Maitland, I, 321.

[35] See F. M. Powicke, *The Thirteenth Century 1216–1307* (*Oxford History of England*, Vol. IV; Oxford, 1953), p. 586, on Anglo-Scottish relations in 1237.

[36] Powicke, *Henry III*, pp. 143–144. Bertie Wilkinson, in *The Constitutional History of Medieval England 1216–1399* (London, 1948–1958), I, 109–110, does not share this view. For accounts of the crisis in 1233–1234, see chap. 4, pp. 123–155, of Powicke's work and chap. 2, pp. 99–116, of Wilkinson's.

malcontents. Henry's arbitrary acts were checked, however, by proceedings in his court that closely approached a judgment of the king by the incorporate realm represented by the baronage, as suggested by Bracton later in his treatise.

The judgment of the king's action came before his court in the form of a petition by those he had outlawed, asking that he allow his court to determine whether the outlawry was just and in accordance with the custom of the realm. On Ascension Sunday 1234 (23 May), Henry III called together in his court the archbishop of Canterbury, the bishops and earls, and other magnates to rule on this question because "he wished justice to be exhibited to anyone in his court." [37] The court found that the king's outlawry of Hubert de Burgh, the former justiciar, Gilbert Basset, and other companions of the late earl marshal was unlawful; and the judgment was pronounced by William Raleigh, one of the royal justices.[38] Outlawry by the king's command was serious because it amounted to a sentence of death; the outlaw could be killed by anyone simply on proof of his outlawry. A man could be outlawed legally only in the county court as a result of a private appeal or an indictment by a jury of presentment.[39] The outlawry of Gilbert Basset was reversed on the grounds that he had been outlawed because of an act committed in time of war and by irregular proceedings in the county court. Hubert de Burgh's outlawry was revoked because his crime—escape from prison—was not punishable by outlawry.[40] Clearly, these decisions mark an attempt by the barons to put the bridle of the law on the king. H. G. Richardson has written of them, "We could hardly hope for a better illustration of the doctrine in the *addicio* that, though the king has no human

[37] *Note Book*, II, 664–667, no. 857. Discussed in F. M. Powicke, "Per iudicium parium vel legem terrae," *Magna Carta Commemoration Essays*, ed. H. E. Malden (London, 1917), pp. 105–107; and Barnaby C. Keeney, *Judgment by Peers* (Harvard Historical Monograph Series, Vol. XX; Cambridge, Mass., 1949), pp. 62–63.

[38] *Note Book*, II, 667, Maitland's note.

[39] Bracton, II, 353–354, f. 125b; Pollock and Maitland, II, 449, 581.

[40] Henry III's writ pardoning Hubert de Burgh and others is found in *Cal. Pat. Rolls* (1232–1247), pp. 28–29.

superior, he yet has a superior in the law or that his court wherein his earls and barons sit is also—at least in a sense—his superior." [41]

Another victim of Henry's arbitrary action quickly gained a hearing before the royal courts in the summer of 1234. Eustace de Stuteville came to the king's justices at Wallingford seeking the manor of Cottingham in Yorkshire, which he maintained had been in his possession until he was disseized by the will of the king. [42] Two men, husbands of his cousins, then came and claimed that the manor belonged by right to their wives, and that the king had granted it to them, but that later he had come and disseized them. Henry III, in whose presence this plea was heard, recollected that he had disseized Eustace *per voluntatem suam* and *sine summonitione et sine judicio*. He recalled that he had then bestowed the land on the husbands of Eustace's cousins, but that he had taken it back into his hand on the advice of his magnates. The king had acted arbitrarily despite Eustace's offer to pay £1,000 in order that he not be disseized without judgment. Eustace repeated his offer of a fine of £1,000 to have a judgment—a large fine, but the price of an admission of error by the king in his own court was understandably high. [43] The king's justices gave the following decision:

And because he [Henry III] acknowledges that he first disseized Eustace without a summons and judgment by his will, it is considered that this first should be corrected and Eustace should regain his seizin, and then he should respond according to the law of the land to . . . [Eustace's cousins and their husbands] . . . by assize of mort d'ancestor or by writ of right. [44]

The decision is significant for two reasons: first, because it restored possession to one dispossessed by will of the king; and second, because it emphasized procedure *secundum legem ter-*

---

[41] Richardson, *Bracton*, p. 33.

[42] *CRR*, 115B, m. 7, no. 1026; also *Note Book*, III, 123–125, no. 1106, octave of Trinity 1234, pleas *coram rege*. Discussed in Ehrlich, *Proceedings against the Crown*, pp. 34–35; in Powicke, "Per iudicium parium," pp. 104–105; and *Proc. without Writ*, p. cli.

[43] *Exc. e rot. fin.*, I, 259.   [44] *Note Book*, III, 125.

rae. Clearly, it marks a departure from the attitude toward royal disseizin without judgment found in the courts of King John.

The plea rolls of Henry III, then, provide a number of illustrations of how one could approach the king through his courts for redress of grievances even in the case of acts by the king himself. In contrast to the plaints made to King John, which concerned relatively innocuous grievances, some of the appeals made to Henry involved serious charges against him, so serious that they may have been in the mind of the author of the *addicio de cartis*. Certainly the records of John's courts offer nothing comparable to the cases of Hubert de Burgh's outlawry or Eustace de Stuteville's disseizin. Further, these complaints received prompt attention from the royal justices, who reversed such arbitrary acts.

Yet it cannot be said that the courts of Henry III were less an instrument of the royal will than they had been under his father. These cases had to begin as petitions to the king for amendment of his unjust action, and they left unanswered the question of coercion: With what weapons were the barons to put a bridle on the king, if not with warfare? This time the king submitted to the judgment of his court, for he could not ignore the petitioners. Hubert de Burgh's request had the strength of the English baronage behind it, and Eustace de Stuteville's had the gentler pressure of an enormous fine. The courts still did not have the independence to judge the king's acts on their own initiative, but they did provide a channel for justice once he submitted to their judgment, whether voluntarily or because of pressure from his barons. The difference between the reigns of John and Henry III is that the young king did submit while his father never did. The lesson of Magna Carta had been learned.

PRIVATE PLEAS THAT QUESTION ROYAL ACTS

Disseizin *per voluntatem regis* is a phrase of common occurrence on the plea rolls of King John's and Henry III's courts. The Angevin kings made arbitrary seizure of their subjects' lands an administrative measure to punish their enemies, to discipline royal servants, and to collect crown debts. At the same time that these monarchs were taking arbitrary measures against some of their subjects, many other subjects were finding in the chancery writs and the assizes of the royal courts a convenient and equitable means of judging disputes. Pleas concerning lands seized by the king placed him in a dual role: he and his servants were judges, and at the same time his acts were being questioned. Obviously, the king's dual role meant that the common law courts offered no easy remedy to those disseized by royal command.

Most medieval thinkers could solve this problem only by stating that no true king, only a tyrant, would refuse to obey the law.[45] Or they could offer the king's victims consolation in the knowledge that he would one day face God's judgment. But were the victims of the king's will able to win any hearing before the royal justices? Was there any lawful means for relieving their plight, other than an appeal to the king's mercy? Bracton's suggested solution for those caught in this dilemma was for them to bring suits, not against the king, but against some third party —the sheriff, another royal agent, or the grantee. The monarch might then be forced into a trap, a situation in which he must either disavow his act or acknowledge its unjust nature and correct it.[46]

Because of this problem, it was only natural that the justices of the royal courts should have been called upon to hear proprietary actions and possessory assizes between private persons, which involved land seized by the king and which were indirectly proceedings against the king. Normally, persons whose lands were forcibly taken from them had recourse to the assize of novel disseizin; but the remedy was not available to those disseized by the king, since no action lay against him. Bracton wrote, "No person is entitled [to a writ of novel disseizin] who has been disseized by the king or his bailiffs in his name, unless the disseizin be evident, in which case the king's will is to be

---

[45] John of Salisbury, *Policratus*, ed. C. C. J. Webb (Oxford, 1909), I, 236, lib. iv, cap. 1; Bracton, II, 304–306, f. 107.

[46] Bracton, III, 43, f. 171b; cited in Tierney, "Bracton on Government," p. 316.

awaited." [47] Elsewhere he stated this in a slightly different way, "But if it be a bailiff or servant acting in the king's name, the assize must be held, but it should not proceed to judgment until the king's will is known." [48]

In any case, it was rare for the land to remain long in the king's hand. He usually granted it to another, and the victim might then attempt to bring an assize of novel disseizin against the person to whom the king had granted possession. Technically, the assize of novel disseizin did not lie against one who had received the land in question by royal grant; for the assize was applicable only against the disseizor, and it was the king, not the tenant having entry through him, who had seized the land. Bracton explained:

If the king has caused a disseizin and has afterwards transferred the property to another, each is the principal disseizor: the king is the first and principal one having done the act; and the other is also a principal because of his entry. And although he is a principal, he should not answer without the king, because he made the disseizin in conjunction with him. [49]

In another passage, Bracton hinted at a solution: "Indirectly and without a writ, however, the prince may be placed in such a position that he will amend his own act, or the injury will clearly reflect ill upon him." [50] He went on to explain that if an assize were brought against the person who had gained the land through the king, then he would seek the king's warranty. At this stage, the king would be placed in the position either of acknowledging his unlawful action and amending it or of refusing and placing himself openly in the wrong.

In the years before Bracton wrote his treatise, it proved difficult for the judges to determine the proper procedure in actions in which the king was the original disseizor. It was seen in Chapter 2 that sometimes the tenant's statement that he had possession *per preceptum domini regis* proved an adequate de-

[47] Bracton, III, 35, f. 168b.   [48] *Ibid.*, p. 43, ff. 171b–172.
[49] *Ibid.*, p. 118, f. 204, and similarly p. 43, f. 171b.
[50] *Ibid.*, p. 43, f. 171b.

fense of his right,[51] but other suits did proceed in which the complainant alleged that he or his ancestor had been disseized by a king, whether the reigning monarch or one of his predecessors. How the justices proceeded in such actions should provide an answer to the question of the amount of freedom from direct royal control enjoyed by the courts. These suits may be divided into two groups for consideration: first, cases in which disseizin by one of the king's predecessors was alleged; and second, actions in which disseizin by the reigning monarch was at issue.

A few proceedings were brought in King John's courts to regain lands seized by his father, Henry II, or his brother, Richard I—a half-dozen or so. The courts heard these cases, but John took an interest in them, and his judges were careful to consult him. One of the actions centered on an attempt to recover lands that King Richard had seized from John's allies in his rebellion in 1193–1194. William Bret made fine with King John for "such seizin of that land as Robert Bret his father had on the day on which he was disseized of that land and of his other lands." When William went to claim the lands in the summer of 1200, he found someone else, Geoffrey Mauduit, in possession, and he had to bring an action against him. The royal justices gave William's plea a hearing even though it questioned an act of Richard I. Geoffrey told the justices that the land was rightfully his because, while it was in King Richard's hand, he had purchased a writ for an inquest which had confirmed his right.[52] This case placed the royal justices in the awkward position of reversing seizin as commanded by a king, either the reigning monarch or his predecessor, whatever their decision. They postponed judgment until they could hear King John's will, and he commanded that the plea be heard before him at a later date.[53] Since the tenant neither came nor essoined himself on that day, William Bret gained seizin by default.[54]

[51] Chapter 4, pp. 70–71.

[52] CRR, I, 207–208, 245, Trinity 1200. For another case of disseizin by the will of King Richard, see ibid., p. 285, where William Turpin sought land, and Pipe Roll 1 John, p. 225, where he offered a fine of forty marks to regain the land.

[53] CRR, I, 287; and ibid., p. 338, Michaelmas 1200.

[54] Ibid., pp. 265–266.

In that same year, 1200, another tenant of lands seized following the rebellion of 1193–1194 found himself in litigation with one of John's former allies. The recognitors declared that the tenant had gained possession when the plaintiff was disseized "for service to the lord king," meaning for his support of John in the revolt against Richard.[55] The court clerk left a blank space for John's decision, which was inserted later: "The lord king commands that if he was disseized on that occasion, let him have his seizin." Neither of these cases proves much about redress of grievances against the king, for in both King John had an obvious interest in reversing his brother's action.

Two assizes in which litigants charged arbitrary disseizin by Henry II proceeded to judgment under John. In 1208, Roald fitz Alan, constable of Richmond, had to defend in the king's court his right to four manors and six and a half knight's fees against another claimant.[56] A jury of recognition supported Roald's contention that Henry II had disseized his grandfather unlawfully of those lands without judgment, although the loss of the lands was more the result of the anarchy of Stephen's reign than of any direct action by Henry II.[57] Roald made a point of stating that "he wished the court to know that he was not summoned as for a plea," as if to say that this was not a proper proceeding. The manors and knight's fees now disputed had been seized by King John because their holder sided with Philip Augustus in Normandy.[58] In 1205, they had been granted to Roald after he had given the king a fine of £100 and two warhorses. At that time, a jury had found for Roald, and John had given a charter pledging that neither he nor his descendants should be disseized of the lands *nisi per judicium curie domini regis*. Roald can hardly have been happy about having to defend his right three years

[55] *Pleas before King*, I, 299, no. 3123.

[56] *CRR*, V, 147–148, Hilary 1208, pleas *coram rege*; discussed in Flower, *Introduction*, pp. 157–158, and Holt, *Magna Carta*, pp. 88–89.

[57] Holt, *Magna Carta*, p. 88.

[58] They were the lands of William de Rollos according to *Pipe Roll 7 John*, ed. Sidney Smith (Pipe Roll Society, N.S.; London, 1941), Michaelmas 1205, p. 58, and Holt, *Northerners*, p. 179. For another account of how Roald gained the lands, see his reply to a *quo warranto* in 1237 in *CRR*, 117, m. 8, no. 111.

after this grant. Since he had been out of favor with King John since 1207 on account of recalcitrance in paying the thirteenth,[59] the suspicion arises that the suit was inspired by the king as an indirect means of pressuring him.

In another proceeding of this nature, King John again took an active part, but this time he seems to have been more interested in seeing justice prevail. Peter fitz Herbert, a prominent royal servant, came before the court in 1211 with an assize of mort d'ancestor against the abbot of Westminster.[60] Peter wished to gain seizin of land that his father had held in the time of Henry II before he was disseized *per voluntatem domini regis.* He offered King John two palfreys in order to have an inquiry determine whether or not his father had been dispossessed by Henry II, as he claimed. Such a large fine was offered because this was an extraordinary proceeding, not available through one of the writs *de cursu,* and because it was an attempt to prove arbitrary royal action. When the abbot opposed such an inquest and brought forward charters from the time of King Henry I in support of his claim, Peter added four Norwegian hawks to his oblation. The king refused the oblation, but nevertheless ordered an investigation to be made by a jury of twelve knights.[61] The jury found that Peter's father had been disseized, tactfully stating, "But they do not know in what manner, but, as they believe, by the will of the lord king Henry." [62] The abbot of Westminster protested that he had not placed himself on any jury, and he offered the king four palfreys to have judgment according to his charters. The court clerk left this final entry unfinished, so that the judgment is unknown, but a final concord ending another case years later indicates that the land was still in the abbot's hands.[63]

These cases indicate that it was possible through a third-party

---

[59] Painter, *King John,* pp. 70, 193, 331.

[60] *CRR,* VI, 176–177, Michaelmas 1211, pleas *coram rege.*

[61] *Ibid.,* p. 287, Easter 1212.   [62] *Ibid.,* p. 296, Trinity 1212.

[63] *Ibid.,* VII, 239, Trinity 1214. Final concord dated 30 Henry III, *An Abstract of Feet of Fines Relating to the County of Sussex, from 2 Richard I to 33 Henry III,* ed. L. F. Salzmann (Sussex Record Society, Vol. II, 1903), p. 114, no. 426.

action in King John's court to challenge unjust or unlawful disseizin by his father and brother. Yet these actions were rare, they were only brought by prominent persons, and they required special attention. The litigants who brought these actions were aware that they were unusual, offering oblations for a hearing; and the justices showed a similar awareness, seeking the king's counsel before pronouncing judgment.

More significant than these proceedings questioning acts of the king's predecessors are those that questioned his own acts. There is little evidence from the plea rolls that persons disseized by King John sought recovery of their lands by bringing actions against third parties. Indeed, in all the records of pleas in John's common law courts there appears only one such case. The presence of this single proceeding is explained by the prominence of the rival claimants: William Marshal, earl of Pembroke, against William de Reviers, earl of Devon, and his wife, the countess of Meulan. Both the earl marshal and the countess sought possession of the manor of Sturminster in Devonshire, which was in the king's hand.[64] The earl marshal claimed the manor on grounds that the count of Meulan had long ago granted it to him; the countess stated that she had held it but had been dispossessed *per preceptum domini regis*. King John was cautious in this case, and he sought his counselors' advice. They were unwilling to give an opinion, and the proceeding was postponed until a meeting of the *magna curia regis*. Apparently, the countess of Meulan's complaint went unheeded at the meeting of the great council, for King John later issued letters granting the manor to William Marshal.[65]

This survey of actions brought against private persons to regain lands seized by the king reveals only one plea alleging disseizin by John himself, and in that one plea the accusation was made by the wife of a great noble. Of course, there were other ways of approaching the problem. One could go outside the regular processes and petition the king, or one could seek a remedy through the exchequer, the tribunal for financial mat-

---

[64] *CRR*, III, 124, Trinity 1204.
[65] 9 Sept. 1204, *Rot. lit. pat.*, p. 45; *Rot. lit. cl.*, I, 7b.

ters. But the events of 1215–1216 force the conclusion that there was no effective means of challenging the king's arbitrary acts. Magna Carta was an attempt to supply a means. In chapters 52 and 56 of the Charter, King John promised to restore the lands, castles, privileges, and rights of persons whom he had disseized without judgment. He made a similar promise to the victims of disseizins by his father and brother. His promises were omitted in the versions of the Great Charter issued under Henry III. Nevertheless, they can be considered still binding, for they are simply a specification of chapter 39 of the Charter of 1215, the article protecting freemen from unlawful acts by their ruler.

A survey of cases from the courts of Henry III in which royal disseizin was alleged shows that these clauses of Magna Carta were taken seriously, for the number of cases in which arbitrary disseizin by one of Henry's predecessors was alleged increased greatly. In addition, the records of the cases contain little to indicate that they presented problems to the justices. A number of cases came into the courts in which arbitrary disseizin by the king's grandfather Henry II was an issue. Sometimes the reasons given for his seizures are bizarre. In a grand assize, jurors found that he had disseized a man because of a quarrel over a sparrow hawk.[66] Another grand assize gave an even more bizarre reason for disseizin by Henry II; supposedly he disseized a man because he refused to give dinner to a royal huntsman.[67]

Perhaps more significant are the pleas brought before Henry III's courts by persons seeking recovery of lands seized by his father, John. An assize of novel disseizin taken before the itinerant justices in 1221 shows Henry III's court acting to correct arbitrary action by John's chief forester, Hugh de Neville.[68] The jurors stated that the complainant had been disseized unjustly and without judgment by the forester's command. The justices adjourned the case to Westminster for judgment on receipt of a writ from Hugh, which informed them that:

[66] *CRR*, IX, 332–333, Michaelmas 1220, assize between Geoffrey Goldsmith, complainant, and Ralph Hopeshort, tenant.

[67] *Note Book*, II, 686–688, no. 769, Trinity 1233, assize between the prior of Newark and the prior of Sherbourne.

[68] *Rolls for Glos., War. and Staffs*, pp. 520–521, no. 1188.

Walter Hose [the complainant] was a malefactor in King John's forest when Hugh was forester, and by the lord king's command, he took that land into the hand of the lord king because bows and arrows and other things contrary to the assize of the forest were found in the house of Hugh Hose, and Hugh and the said Walter his man withdrew and would not stand to right.

The justices of the bench decided that disseizin for the offense of possessing bows and arrows contrary to the assize of the forest was an arbitrary act. They restored Walter's land to him, and they amerced Hugh for his part in the disseizin.[69] The justices' decision in this case is evidence of the effort made during the minority to implement the Great Charter and to protect the king's subjects from arbitrary acts.

Another action coming before Henry III's judges involved disseizin by the will of King John. In 1219 the tenant in a plea of land sought to place himself on the grand assize, but the complainant answered that the grand assize ought not to lie.[70] He explained that he had held the land in question by right of inheritance until his imprisonment by King John. He had made fine with the king to be released from prison, but had fallen behind in his payments, and the sheriff had then seized his land into the king's hand for debt. No jury was called upon to confirm this story of John's financial dealings, for the two parties settled the dispute by a compromise.

In another case, the knights of a grand assize did affirm that an individual had been unlawfully disseized by John. In 1223 an assize had to rule on the relative claims of two royal officials, William Briwerre and Geoffrey de Lucy, to one carucate of land.[71] The jury found that Rose, Geoffrey's sister, had granted him the land in question, but that the king had become angered with him and had seized it. Rose then offered the king a fine to have that land back, and she granted it to William Briwerre, probably in 1212. It seemed to the jurors that Geoffrey de Lucy

[69] *Ibid.*, p. xlvii.

[70] *CRR*, XIII, x, Trinity 1219; also *Note Book*, II, 16, no. 17. The tenant was the son of sheriff Reginald de Cornhill.

[71] *CRR*, XI, 77–78, no. 416, Hilary 1223; also *Note Book*, III, 466–467, no. 1593.

had the greater right, since he had been given the land first. The justices, however, did not pronounce judgment on the basis of the jurors' statement. Instead, they postponed the case for hearing before the justiciar and the barons of the exchequer. The fact that the case was removed to the exchequer might seem to indicate that it was marked for special attention, but Briwerre was a baron of the exchequer, and his post as baron gave the exchequer jurisdiction over his case.[72]

Another prominent person, Humphrey, earl of Hereford, claimed that King John had disseized his father "unjustly and without judgment" of a manor.[73] King John had seized the earl's lands in 1213, and he promised to restore them in 1215 as one of his concessions to the barons, but in the confusion of the barons' war the writs for restoration were forgotten. The suit was postponed to another date by Henry III's command, but the postponement was not due to Henry's anger at the accusation against his father. Rather it is explained by the tenant's presentation of royal charters and by his plea that he should not be required to respond without the king. The records of these pleas concerning arbitrary disseizin by King John, like the cases treating disseizins by Henry II, indicate that they were heard by the royal justices without undue difficulty.[74]

It seems clear from these cases that an effort was made during Henry III's early years to abide by the principles of the Great Charter, at least to the extent that those disseized by the king's ancestors could seek restoration of their lands in the royal courts. The question does arise concerning the disseizins of Henry III. Did his own victims find a hearing in his courts? Could they bring assizes of novel disseizin against the person to whom the king had granted the land? In Bracton's view, the assize of novel

---

[72] Powicke, *Henry III*, pp. 3, 57, 68. Briwerre had been a trusted deputy of King John as well.

[73] *CRR*, 115B, m. 25, no. 1293, 7 Jan. 1235. Earl of Hereford against Hugh the Dispenser for the manor of Ryhall, Rutl. For another plea in which Humphrey de Bohun sought to recover lands King John had seized from his father, see *ibid.*, XII, 528–529, no. 2646, Easter 1226.

[74] For other examples of disseizin by John treated in the courts of Henry III, see *ibid.*, X, 279–280, Trinity 1222, and XII, 65, no. 356, Hilary 1225.

disseizin did not lie against the tenant because it was not he who had made the disseizin, but the king.[75] The royal judges did hear these assizes from time to time, handling them in different ways, sometimes dismissing them and sometimes referring them to the king.

The plea rolls dating from Henry's minority offer examples of these assizes of novel disseizin. In 1219 the prior of the Hospitalers' assize brought a reply from the tenant that he held the land in question at the king's command. The sheriff produced a royal writ in support of the tenant's statement. But the prior refused to believe that the writ came from the royal chancery, and he maintained that if it did it was made *contra legem terrae et consuetudinem regis.*[76] The judges' reaction to the prior's statement is not known, for the plea rolls make no further reference to the case.

In another assize, dating from Henry III's early majority, the tenant produced a royal writ as evidence that the king had granted him possession.[77] The justices, when they saw this proof, decided in his favor and found the plaintiff in mercy. The reason that they gave for their judgment was that the tenant did not disseize the plaintiff, since he had entry *per preceptum domini regis.* Bracton knew both these cases, for he recorded them in his *Note Book;* the judges' dismissal of the second suit is in accord with the teaching in his treatise. The justices' dilemma can be seen in another case, a suit to recover custody of a manor in 1234–1235. When the tenant stated that he held the manor at bail of the king, they did not decide for him at once, but rather postponed the case until the king's will could be known.[78]

Bracton commented on another case in his *Note Book* in

---

[75] Bracton, III, 118, f. 204.

[76] *CRR,* VIII, 132–133, Michaelmas 1219; also *Note Book,* II, 68–69, no. 176. The tenant was Adam de Bereville.

[77] *Note Book,* II, 329–330, no. 401, Easter 1230, action by Walter de la Grava against Walter de Langford. Discussed by Ehrlich, *Proceedings against the Crown,* pp. 18–19, 25.

[78] *CRR,* 115B, m. 18d, no. 1222, Michaelmas 1234, case of Gerard Talbot; continued on m. 21, no. 1311, Hilary 1235, and on m. 8, no. 1466, morrow of Ascension 1235.

which the tenant claimed that he held at the king's will.[79] His suggestion was that the justices should not dismiss the assize at once, but should allow it to proceed and then postpone judgment until they could consult the king. Bracton repeated the suggestion in his treatise, when he discussed assizes of novel disseizin brought against the king's agents.[80] This solution seems to have been that most often used by the royal justices in solving the problem of these assizes.

Two assizes of novel disseizin concerning parts of the royal demesne illustrate the willingness of the judges to hear such cases. One of them, which came before the itinerant justices in 1221, contested arbitrary disseizin by one of Henry III's officers.[81] This case is interesting for two reasons: first, the jurors' evidence indicated that the complainant was a villein sokeman on the royal demesne; second, the jurors stated that the man named in the writ did not disseize the complainant, but that it was done arbitrarily by the king's agent, William de Cantilupe. If the judges had wished, either of these technicalities would have given them excuses for dismissing the assize. Instead, "by counsel of the court," they restored seizin to the tenant. Their judgment is evidence of the efforts made during Henry's minority to implement the Great Charter, protecting the English people from arbitrary acts by the government. Yet the justices were careful to safeguard the king's rights, stating that "the king, if he wishes, may deal with him according to the custom of the manor."

A few years later, in 1224, the royal justices reacted differently to an action touching the royal demesne. Richard de Percy, a Yorkshire baron, brought an assize of novel disseizin against a large number of men of a royal manor in Yorkshire.[82] The king's

---

[79] Note Book, III, 595, no. 1766, eyre in Kent 1227, assize brought by Richard fitz Roger against Joscelin de Oye. The jurors declared in favor of Richard, and the king then gave him seizin.

[80] Bracton, III, 43, f. 171b.

[81] Rolls for Lincs and Worcs., pp. 530–531, no. 1061.

[82] CRR, XI, 479–480, no. 2414, Michaelmas 1224; also Note Book, II, 697–698, no. 907. Sanders, Baronies, p. 148, identifies Richard de Percy as holder of half the honour of Topcliffe, Yorks.

men came and said that the assize should not be taken because the land named in the writ pertained to the royal manor. The judgment was: "And because the manor or Scarborough is demesne of the lord king and he does not wish to admit the assize, it is considered that a perambulation be made between the lord king and Richard by twelve knights." Thus Richard could not bring an assize against the king, but his complaint could be remedied in much the same way.

During Henry III's personal rule, the royal justices continued to allow possessory actions to proceed even though they indirectly questioned disseizin by the king. In 1235–1236 they heard an assize of novel disseizin against Walter Mauclerc, bishop of Carlisle.[83] The king had turned against Walter in 1233, depriving him of his office of treasurer and seizing his estates; but the bishop's fall from royal favor did not last long, and he was soon restored to his lands.[84] His bailiff maintained that the land now disputed had been returned to him by a royal writ at the time of his restoration to the king's favor. Consequently, he did not think that an assize of novel disseizin should lie, since responsibility for the disseizin lay with the king. The judges followed the procedure that Bracton recommended, that is, taking the verdict of the jurors and then delaying judgment.[85] The jurors found that the bishop had disseized the complainants, although they did not know whether he did so by the king's warrant or not. The justices withheld judgment until the king could give his warranty, if he wished. Henry III did acknowledge that the bishop had seizin through him, and the complainants were unable to regain their land by the assize.

Perhaps most significant of all indirect proceedings against the king are the actions brought by Hubert de Burgh, the former justiciar, in the summer of 1234. A consequence of Henry III's outlawry of Hubert, of Gilbert Basset, and of other companions of Richard Marshal, was his seizure of their lands. Once Hubert de Burgh's outlawry was declared unlawful, he began proceed-

[83] *Note Book*, III, 170–171, no. 1153.
[84] "Walter Mauclerc," *Dict. Nat. Bio.*
[85] *Note Book*, III, 595, no. 1766.

ings in the royal courts to regain the lands that the king had taken from him.[86] Since these lands had been granted by Henry III to others, Hubert's pleas were not proceedings against the king, but were private pleas against the tenants who had gained entry through the king. Yet the suits were not assizes of novel disseizin, nor were they regular proprietary actions begun by writ of right; rather Hubert demanded of the tenants by what right, *quo warranto,* they held their lands.

The king became involved in the actions when one of the tenants, Robert Passelewe, attempted to vouch him to warranty. Robert had been one of Henry's advisers at the time of Hubert's outlawry, but he was now out of favor. The king cannot have been eager to come to the defense of one of his "evil counselors." Henry replied to Robert with a strong statement of monarchical supremacy, much like the view of kingship that Bracton expressed in his treatise later:

And moreover no one who is vouched to warranty concerning any land is bound to respond to that warranty without a summons by writ of the lord king or by the precept of his justices; and the lord king can neither be summoned nor submit to the command of anyone, since he has no superior in the kingdom.[87]

Clearly, the king meant that he was not subject to the jurisdiction of his own courts. Nevertheless, he did acknowledge that he had seized Hubert's lands and granted them to others, although in one case he justified his act by explaining that he had been made to understand by his counselors that he could legally do this, since Hubert had been outlawed. Once the outlawry was declared null, Hubert had a very strong case, and judgment was given that the king's unlawful grants did not give their holders any rights. The justices restored Hubert's land to him in each case. Perhaps the pleas brought by Hubert de Burgh are the best illustration of Bracton's proposal that proceedings against some

---

[86] *CRR,* 115B, m. 18, no. 1207, and 116B, m. 2d, no. 1895; *Note Book,* III, 126–128, no. 1108, pp. 129–130, no. 1111, pp. 156–157, no. 1136, and p. 161, no. 1141.

[87] *CRR,* 115B, m. 6d, no. 1058 (also *Note Book,* III, 127–128).

third party be brought which would place the king in such a position that he must acknowledge his unlawful act.

Robert Passelewe's attempt to defend his land against Hubert de Burgh by drawing Henry III into the suit raised a question for the royal justices: Could the king be vouched to warranty? Henry clearly stated that he could not. Many times individuals did call upon King John and Henry III to warrant their charters and grants, but by the time that Bracton composed his treatise the courts were hedging individuals' right to seek the king's warranty. Bracton wrote that the king could not be called to warrant as could a private individual, but one who sought the king's warranty could say "with a certain courtliness" (*cum quidam curialitate*) that he could not answer without the king, from whom he held a charter. He added that this should not be allowed unless the royal charter included the king's promise to give warranty.[88] Yet the king's warranty of his charters did not mean that his acts were being judged in his courts, as would his being vouched to warranty. When a tenant's right to his land was challenged in court, he could "vouch to warranty" the person who had granted him his land. His grantor then replaced him as the defendant in the suit, and the remainder of the action was conducted in his name.[89]

Obviously, if Robert Passelewe had been successful in his attempt to vouch the king to warranty, the suit against him would have been converted into a proceeding against the king. His attempt was not the first time that the royal justices had faced this question. It was raised in an assize of novel disseizin against Robert de Mortimer taken before the itinerant justices in 1219. Robert's bailiff said that the assize ought to be dismissed because his master had seizin of the land from the earl Warenne at the command of King John.[90] If his statement was true, then the assize of novel disseizin did not apply. The complainant gave a complicated account of his loss of the land during the barons' revolt of 1215–1217 that indicated that Robert had seized the land during the war and had refused to surrender it when peace

---

[88] Bracton, IV, 197, f. 382b.   [89] Pollock and Maitland, II, 662.
[90] *Rolls for Lincs and Worcs.*, pp. 132–134, no. 297.

came. Robert's bailiff did not know how to respond to this account, so he vouched the king to warranty. Nevertheless, the justices proceeded with the assize because "he had no warranty through the lord king except the letters of the aforesaid earl [Warenne]," and because, "it is not customary for anyone to vouch the king to warranty concerning disseizin." Here the justices seemed to set forth the principle that the king could not be vouched to warranty in cases of novel disseizin.

The justices were still uncertain when the question arose once more in January 1235 in a suit by a chaplain to recover custody of a manor. He complained that he had been disseized *per voluntatem domini regis,* but the current custodian, Gerard Talbot, replied that he held the manor at bail of the king.[91] Gerard called the king to warrant, but because he had no charter or other proof of his grant, Henry was uncertain whether he ought to warrant him. Actually, Henry did not need to give his warranty, for Gerard was able later to present royal letters in proof of his grant of the custody.[92] The case was postponed until the king's will could be known.[93] His decision is not recorded on the plea rolls, but the close rolls record a letter indicating that the chaplain recovered custody of the manor.[94]

This survey of pleas brought against third parties by persons who had been disseized by the king reveals several points about the attitude of the judges. The plea rolls for King John's reign indicate that almost never did his victim have recourse to the courts, although in some cases victims of his father or brother brought suits to recover lands. The records of those cases reveal payments of fines and postponements for consultation with the king. It is apparent that John's justices were hesitant about hearing such cases, but the rolls for Henry III's reign reveal a change. Pleas for recovery of lands seized by his royal predecessors increased, and they proceeded with less difficulty. More

[91] *CRR,* 115B, m. 18d, no. 1222, Michaelmas 1234; continued on m. 21, no. 1311, Hilary 1235.

[92] *Cal. Pat. Rolls* (1232–1247), p. 39, 10 Feb. 1234.

[93] *CRR,* 115B, m. 8, no. 1466.

[94] *Close Rolls* (1234–1237), p. 294, 27 July 1236.

important, pleas in which disseizin by Henry himself was an issue were sometimes heard in court, even though the justices knew that the possessory assizes did not lie against the king. Most important, in the case of Hubert de Burgh, they did not hesitate to reverse the royal action. The royal justices understood the meaning of Magna Carta.

Yet their willingness to hear such suits does not mean that the justices were willing to pass judgment on their master's acts. Pleas brought by ordinary persons who did not have the baronage standing behind them were treated with the greatest circumspection by the royal justices. They would not allow the king to be drawn directly into disputes by being vouched to warranty, nor would they pronounce judgment without first knowing his wishes. Yet in many cases they did allow the assize to proceed to the jurors' statement, even though it sometimes amounted to an accusation of unjust or unlawful royal action and even though there were technical excuses for dismissing it. To this extent, at least, the common law courts did provide instruments for the correction of the ruler's wrongful acts.

Conclusion

At the beginning of this study of the plea rolls from the royal courts in early thirteenth-century England, three questions were raised concerning the king's relations with his courts: To what extent was the operation of the courts automatic and to what extent was it under the monarch's personal supervision? What was the nature of King John's judicial activity—a genuine attempt to improve the working of the courts, or a mere tampering with their operation for his own ends? Is there any contrast between the standards of justice in the royal courts before and after Magna Carta; that is, how seriously were its judicial provisions taken? Now that the organization of the royal courts, the king's instructions regarding procedural matters, his role in answering substantive questions, and the judges' activity in pleas that touched the king have been considered in the preceding chapters, it should be possible to answer these three questions.

Any picture of the Angevin monarchs wandering up and down their kingdoms patiently listening to the quarrels of their humblest subjects, wisely handing down judgments, and reconciling the disputing parties is false. The business of justice was too complex by the late twelfth and early thirteenth centuries for such a relaxed approach. The common law courts were tending to "go out of court," that is, to sit apart from the king and his courtiers. H. G. Richardson and G. O. Sayles's work, *The Governance of Mediaeval England,* emphasizes the growth in that time of an administrative system that could function without the king's intervention, so that they term the rule of Henry II and his sons an "impersonal monarchy." Their view is in direct opposition to J. E. A. Jolliffe's interpretation of Angevin monarchy. He has written of King John's activity, "Every membrane of the Curia Regis Rolls may, therefore, bear the impress of the King's intervention commanding his justices with a will and authority distinct from theirs, conveyed *per preceptum regis,* sometimes enforcing the course of law, sometimes denying, delaying, diverting or defeating it." [1] A careful examination of the surviving *curia regis* rolls leaves no doubt that John and Henry III did personally take an active part in the work of their courts, yet Jolliffe's statement is a bit too strong. The legal innovations of Henry II—his establishment of a permanent central court, his organization of the judicial eyres, his system of original writs and possessory assizes—did much to give England "an almost automatically working judicial machinery," in A. J. Carlyle's phrase. [2] The vast majority of cases were brought to a conclusion before the royal judges without the necessity of the king's interference. Most membranes of the *curia regis* rolls do bear the impress of the royal power in some fashion, for the king as the greatest landholder in England was a party to many actions, either directly or indirectly. But he did not intervene in the work of the courts so often that every membrane records some royal intervention. Indeed, by Henry III's time, the bench at Westminster was so close to functioning "automatically" that entire rolls lack any trace of direct royal influence.

At times there were questions the judges could not answer without reference to the ruler. He had a role to play in procedural questions, and both King John and Henry III sometimes gave instructions in routine matters of postponements of pleas or transfers from one court to another. The king had a share in settling substantive questions too. Medieval monarchs rarely pronounced judgments, but sometimes they did take part in deci-

[1] *Angevin Kingship,* p. 58. Richardson and Sayles disagree with Jolliffe. They emphasize the role of the justiciar in the administration before the accession of John (*Governance,* chap. 8) and are critical of Jolliffe for failing to take his role into account (see Richardson's review in *E.H.R.* LXXI [1956], 447–453).

[2] *A History of Mediaeval Political Theory in the West* (New York and London, 1903–1936), III, 31.

sions, as they advised the justices on difficult points of law or in suits involving powerful barons or important royal servants. At other times the king's advice was needed because he could modify the letter of the law. He could act mercifully to lessen the harshness of medieval English law, and he could provide remedies not supplied by traditional procedures. Even King John was occasionally "moved by mercy." Perhaps most important, the monarch could correct errors made in the courts of the kingdom on appeal from his subjects. The possibility of appealing to the king, the "fountain of justice," if all other efforts to correct an injustice failed, gave him an indispensable role in the judicial system.

The part played by John, Henry III, and Henry's council in the early thirteenth century contrasts with that of Henry II and Richard I in the last years of the twelfth century. At that time, the government of England had been often an absentee government under the justiciar's supervision; but following the loss of Normandy, the king became permanently resident in England. The administration of justice was then centralized and unified in the king's hands in a way that had not been possible in the twelfth century, when he was so often outside the kingdom. The phrases *dominus rex mandavit* or *per preceptum domini regis* occur often on the plea rolls, as the justices received instructions from him concerning the conduct of suits. The number of instructions sent from John and Henry III shows that there was no notion of an "independent judiciary" in medieval England. The royal justices were the king's servants and were responsive to his will. They were especially careful to consult him in pleas where royal lands or rights were at issue and in suits which questioned royal grants or charters. The judges never dared to interpret the terms of royal charters without first knowing the king's will. Suits arising out of the king's position as a feudal lord granting lands in return for services gave him opportunities to share in the judgments of his courts, for he could be drawn into the disputes as a third party. The king came closest to actually pronouncing judgment in such cases. *Loquendum cum rege* is a notation frequently found on the records of such cases.

Bertie Wilkinson was thinking primarily of the latter half of the thirteenth century when he wrote:

The judges were the king's. They were appointed by the king or council and held office during the royal pleasure. Their increasing separation from the royal presence did not change their loyalty and duty of obedience any more than in the case of other royal ministers, even though as in other cases it paved the way for a loyalty to the impersonal Crown.[3]

This summation states equally well the position of the royal justices during the reigns of John and Henry III. It is true that the system of writs and assizes normally brought private pleas to a conclusion without need for the king's intervention, but occasionally the ruler found it necessary to adjust the machinery of justice. Sometimes this was because the law was uncertain, but more often it was because royal interests were at stake. Suits involving the great men of the kingdom, royal favorites, or the king's enemies received the ruler's personal attention, as did pleas touching his lands or rights. Carlyle's definition of a civilized political system as one that has judicial machinery that functions almost automatically, as opposed to a barbarous society dependent upon "the chance of the presence of some exceptionally competent and clear-sighted individual ruler,"[4] is not fully applicable to England in the early thirteenth century. Many types of actions could proceed automatically with no need for the king's presence, yet other actions required the king's personal attention. He had an important role to play in making available remedies not provided by the system of writs and assizes and in granting dispensations from the law, that is, exercising equitable jurisdiction. He was sometimes consulted about difficult points of law, but this does not mean that he made rulings that formed precedents for future cases. Neither John nor Henry III seems to have influenced the development of the substance of the law.

The king's activity in the field of justice leads to the second

---

[3] *The Constitutional History of Medieval England 1216–1399* (London, 1948–1958), III, 155.

[4] Carlyle, *History of Mediaeval Political Theory*, III, 31.

question—the quality of justice that resulted from his supervision. Certainly this question is important for a proper evaluation of King John's reign because his interest in judicial administration was largely overlooked by contemporary chroniclers and by nineteenth-century historians, who preferred to concentrate on his more spectacular deeds of cruelty and tyranny. A typical chronicler's picture of John is a statement of the Waverley annalist, "He disinherited some without judgment of their peers, and he condemned others to a dire death; he violated their wives and daughters—his only law was his despotic will." [5] In the nineteenth century this one-sided portrait became the recognized scholarly interpretation when it was adopted by Bishop William Stubbs in his *Constitutional History* (Oxford, 1874–1878). [6] In recent years, historians have reacted against this interpretation, and they have been seeking a more balanced estimate of King John's rule through examination of the surviving legal and administrative records to counter the awful tales of the monastic chroniclers. [7] Perhaps some of them have gone too far in their attempts to rehabilitate John's reputation. Among these revisionists, Doris M. Stenton has turned to his work in the judicial sphere, and her studies have led her to conclude that he deserved praise rather than blame: "In any case, whatever may be the final judgment of history upon King John, if history can ever venture on a final judgment, his interest in legal development, his untiring activity in hearing pleas, and his readiness to admit litigants not only to his court but to his presence must be remem-

[5] *Annales Monastici,* ed. H. R. Luard (Rolls Series; London, 1864–1869), II, 282.

[6] E.g. "He was the very worst of all our kings: a man whom no oaths could bind, no pressure of conscience, no consideration of policy, restrain from evil; a faithless son, a treacherous brother, an ungrateful master; to his people a hated tyrant" (I, 534). For Stubbs's more detailed estimate of John's character, see his introduction to Vol. II of Walter of Coventry, *Memoriale* (Rolls Series; London, 1873).

[7] For valuable accounts of the historical interpretations of John through the years, see C. Warren Hollister, "King John and the Historians," *Journal of British Studies,* I (1961), 1–19; and J. C. Holt, *King John* (Historical Association Pamphlet; London, 1963).

bered in his favour." [8] Lady Stenton is able to cite evidence to back up her opinion of King John. She can point to his organization of an itinerant court *coram rege* as an additional permanent central court, his encouragement of transfers of cases into the royal courts, and his establishment of the jury of attaint; and perhaps most striking, she can show his constant close supervision of the work of his courts.

Unfortunately, there are dark shadows on this picture of John's supervision of his courts. Lady Stenton explains his activity in the sphere of justice as due to a genuine interest in the work of his courts, but another explanation for his close watch is the fear and suspicion that made him attempt to concentrate all power in his hands. Students of John's character agree that he was an unlovable person, mistrustful of others and himself untrustworthy.[9] His suspicious nature led to his closing of the court at Westminster for several years after 1209 in order to have all cases come before him. He did not hesitate to use his courts as instruments for his own policies, closing them to his enemies, expediting justice for his friends.

A number of persons who later joined the ranks of the Northerners rebelling against the king had reason to believe that he had tampered with justice in order to persecute them. Eustace de Vesci, one of their leaders, lost a plea of service in a decision that must have been due to the king's ill-will. William de Mowbray

[8] *Pipe Roll 6 John* (Pipe Roll Society, N.S.; London, 1940), 1204, p. xxxiii. See also her "King John and the Courts of Justice," *Proc. Br. Ac.*, XLIV (1958), 103–128.

[9] Hollister, "John and the Historians," pp. 16–19. Some typical recent views are Sidney Painter's and A. L. Poole's. Painter has remarked that "little can be said in favor of his private character. He was cruel, lecherous, and deceitful. His mind was always seething with jealousy and suspicion of his servants and vassals" (*King John*, p. 238). Poole is also extreme, maintaining that "almost any epithet might appropriately be applied to him in one or other of his many and versatile moods. He was cruel and ruthless, violent and passionate, greedy and self-indulgent, genial and repellent, arbitrary and judicious, clever and capable, original and inquisitive. He is made up of inconsistencies" (*From Domesday Book to Magna Carta 1087–1216* [Oxford History of England, Vol. III, 2d ed.; Oxford 1955], p. 425).

and Roger de Montbegon, members of the baronial committee of twenty-five, suffered injustices in the royal courts through the king's interventions. Even though Mowbray offered a fine of 2,000 marks to have a plea against him proceed "justly and according to custom," and even though it was a long-closed suit reopened on a technicality, he lost the case. Montbegon gave 500 marks to marry a widow, but when he brought suit to recover her lands, he found the courts closed to him. Among other rebel barons who had grievances against the king's courts were Roald fitz Alan, Roger Bigod, Henry de Bohun, Gilbert and Maurice de Ghent, Gilbert Hansard, and Simon de Kyme.

While it is true that the plea rolls provide few examples of actions initiated by the king in order to harry his enemies, there are some private pleas initiated that must have had his approval, if not his sponsorship; most obvious examples are the suits brought against Henry de Bohun, earl of Hereford, and Geoffrey fitz Peter, the justiciar. More spectacular royal suits are absent because most of John's quarrels with his barons centered around financial matters—their debts to him for reliefs and other feudal payments—and the appropriate tribunal was the exchequer, not the common law courts. The *curia regis* rolls fail to provide evidence that John was so contemptuous of the custom of the realm that he would openly violate it, but they fail to reveal that he had any great respect for it either, so that he sometimes managed to keep within the letter of the law while violating its spirit. King John's intervention in the courts was inspired by his own political ends in an effort to help those he favored or feared, or to hinder those he hated. He did not intervene in the conduct of cases of no interest to him, so that his ordinary subjects generally found a high standard of justice in his courts.

Unfortunately, even they might find themselves forced to offer fines to obtain justice. Most damning of John's interventions are those inspired by financial motives, as he extended his search for new revenues to include his courts. The number of times that fines or oblations lie behind King John's instructions to his judges leads to the conclusion that the old clichés about his "sale of justice" have some basis after all. The royal courts were opened or closed to suitors at the king's pleasure, and King John accepted oblations from litigants in return for dismissing suits that they were combatting. A baron, Gerard de Furnival, offered him the fantastic sum of £1,000 and fifteen palfreys to have a suit dismissed; another litigant offered forty ounces of gold. Just as the king could deny access to his courts, so he could slow or speed the course of justice, or remove cases from one court to another. One of the most frequent commands that King John's judges received was to postpone actions involving persons in his service. It was only right that men fighting for the king on the Continent should be safe from pleas, but as John's fortunes in Normandy declined in 1203, he issued commands not only postponing pleas involving his knights, but also those involving persons who contributed money to his cause. His postponements illustrate John's attitude toward justice: his interest in the smooth operation of his courts was subordinate to his interest in gaining victory in Normandy.

It is clear that a number of John's interventions in the work of his courts were due to financial considerations. King John was caught in an inflationary squeeze as government costs, especially the costs of military campaigns, rose while the royal revenues remained fixed. As Painter wrote, "The details of *Magna Carta* are largely a commentary on John's methods of raising money." [10] It is not surprising, then, that he sought to increase the profits of justice. Of course, a certain amount of venality in the administration of justice was normal in Angevin England and elsewhere in the Middle Ages, and not even the papal *curia* at Rome was entirely free from it.[11] Yet there can be no doubt that litigants with well-filled purses could purchase very real advantages over their opponents, occasionally managing to get the case against them dismissed entirely.

When these aspects of King John's administration of justice are taken into account, along with his more praiseworthy innova-

[10] *"Magna Carta," American Historical Review,* LIII (1947), 43.

[11] E.g. John of Salisbury's complaint of venality at the papal court made to Pope Adrian IV (*Policraticus,* ed. C. C. J. Webb [Oxford, 1909], II, 67–68, lib. vi, cap. xxiv).

tions, it seems as if his critics and his defenders have fought each other to a stalemate. Perhaps modern scholars reacting against the chroniclers have gone too far in their reassessment of the man. Careful examination of John's supervision of his courts reveals that his intervention in cases was due less to a wish that justice should prevail than to financial needs and political expediency. Possibly the most favorable adjective that can be applied to John's administration is "ambivalent." [12] His over-all supervision of justice, his expansion of the scope of royal justice, and his procedural innovations undoubtedly benefited many of his subjects; but these general advantages were often negated in individual cases by indirect measures taken for political or financial gain to deflect the course of justice. Certainly the chroniclers' picture of King John as all black is false, but this does not mean that the exact opposite is the correct picture. The legal records indicate clearly that justice was not rendered impartially or impersonally in cases that concerned the king. Even though such cases were only a minority, they cast shadows on his portrait. King John was far from the medieval political theorists' ideal of a monarch whose will was an impersonal force, dispensing justice with "even-handed equity" to all.

The judicial clauses of the Great Charter constitute an indictment of the administration of justice under King John. Chapter 40 with its accusation of the sale, delay, and denial of justice is a particularly serious charge, but the administration of justice was not so different under his father and brother. As Jolliffe has written, the Charter was "a judgment, a grand inquest upon the whole past of Angevin kingship." [13] This charge raises a third question, a comparison of the administration of justice after Magna Carta in the early years of Henry III with that in the time of his father. Certainly, close supervision of the work of the royal justices continued during the minority of the young king,

[12] This is Hollister's conclusion concerning John's reign as a whole, "John and the Historians," pp. 16–19.

[13] *Angevin Kingship*, p. 349. Cf. J. C. Holt, "The Barons and the Great Charter," *E.H.R.*, LXX (1955), 2: "The Charter must be read as a criticism of a system of government, not of the behavior of a single monarch."

as his council took command of the courts. Here, too, the justices continued to carefully protect the king's interests in cases affecting his rights or privileges. Some judgments were made because they were politically expedient, perhaps understandable in the case of troublesome barons such as Fawkes de Breauté and William de Forz who might renew their rebellion if provoked. Yet a number of the council's interventions in the work of the courts were due to a genuine desire to see justice prevail, often in cases involving poor people who could not afford large oblations. The number of amercements that were pardoned and the number of cases involving obscure persons that were reheard before the council are evidence of its interest in justice. F. M. Powicke has rightly written of the work of the council during this period: "Its sense of responsibility for the community was revealed most clearly, perhaps, in the administration of justice and the interpretation of difficult cases." [14] To the members of the council Magna Carta was no myth; they took its judicial clauses seriously, and they made a real effort to put them into effect.

Henry III's coming of age brought no sharp break with the practice of the courts that had prevailed in his minority. The court following the king was not even re-established until 1234. Indeed, the contrast with the administration of justice under his father continues to be noticeable after his coming of age. Perhaps most striking is the continued awareness of the principle of the Great Charter that the king must submit to the "law of the land." This lesson was taught to the young king by the crisis of 1233–1234, which ended with the reversal by his justices and the *magna curia regis* of his outlawry of Hubert de Burgh and other enemies. The action of the great men in this instance does not mean that the royal courts had become independent of the king with the right to judge him. The courts were still the king's, and no plea lay against the king. Although the courts were offering indirect ways of proceeding against the king, the only fully effective remedy available to Henry's victims was a petition to him, a prayer that he amend his wrongful act.

[14] *Henry III*, p. 38.

The contrast between the work of the courts under Henry III and their work under John is seen in other ways too. Both kings used their common law courts as instruments for the recovery of royal properties and other rights, but Henry made greater use of them than had his father, who had relied more on the laws of the exchequer and the forest. The king, however, had certain advantages in proceeding that his subjects did not enjoy, among them the quo warranto writ, which required the possessor to reveal his right without knowing the nature of the king's claim. This action presented opportunities for financial oppression, since those whose claims were uncertain had to buy the king's confirmation. But generally there was less effort to use the courts for raising revenues. Few fines offered to Henry III for favors can be considered exorbitant. The young king continued to promise in his reissues of the Charter that he would not sell justice, and the records indicate that he largely kept his promise.

In contrast to his father, Henry III made greater use of his courts as an instrument for disciplining royal servants. Great state trials of officials were held before the king's justices and recorded on the *curia regis* rolls, as the trial of Peter des Rivaux illustrates. Another contrast is that Henry III's courts were more receptive to appeals from his subjects to right wrongs committed by the king and his officers. The actions brought against royal servants or royal grantees were in fact if not in name proceedings against the crown. A single roll (*CRR*, 115B) records complaints by private individuals against three sheriffs, the constable of a castle, forest officers, and against the king himself.

Still another contrast is the greater participation of the great men of the realm in the work of justice. The barons who composed Henry III's council during his minority came to share responsibility for justice, and they could not be cut off completely from any part once he came of age. Although it was still unusual for the barons and bishops to be called to share in judgment, they did join with the professional judges in making decisions much more often in the reign of Henry than in that of John. Their participation is significant in setting the stage for the growth of parliament.

In spite of these contrasts, there is continuity in at least one aspect—the supervision of justice by the ruler. Henry III's re-establishment of the court *coram rege* early in the period of his personal rule shows his wish to watch closely the work of his courts. Although Henry III was perhaps less vigorous than John in his supervision, the royal courts could still be made to serve as instruments of royal policy, and the judges could still feel his personal will. The justices continued to be careful to protect the king's rights in cases touching his possessions, and they could still hand down judgments that must have been politically inspired. Indeed, in suits that hinged upon royal grants or charters, Henry sometimes joined his justices in pronouncing judgment. The common law courts under both John and Henry III were still subject to the monarch's personal supervision. In the sphere of justice, early thirteenth-century English government was not yet fully an "institutionalized monarchy" and was not yet headed by an "impersonal crown."

Bibliography

PRIMARY SOURCES

The surviving plea rolls, found at the Public Record Office in London, are the basic source for any study of the common law courts. These rolls are catalogued in Public Record Office, *Lists and Indexes* no. 4: *List of Plea Rolls of Various Courts, Preserved in the Public Record Office* (new and rev. ed.: London, 1910). Most of the *curia regis* rolls for the reign of King John and for the early years of Henry III are now available in published editions. Volume II of the *Rotuli curiae regis,* ed. Sir Francis Palgrave (Record Commission; London, 1835), contains the earliest pleas from King John's reign, those of 1199 and 1200. Doris M. Stenton has edited *Pleas before the King or His Justices, 1198–1200* (Selden Society, Vols. LXVII–LXVIII; London, 1948–1949), which includes the earliest surviving rolls of pleas heard *coram rege* as well as some pleas heard *de banco* and before the itinerant justices. The most complete collection of pleas for this period, published under the superintendence of the Deputy Keeper of the Public Records, is the *Curia Regis Rolls,* ed. C. T. Flower *et al.* (14 vols. to date; London, 1922——), which includes pleas of the bench and pleas before the king for the period from 1195 to 1232. The material for Vols. XV–XX has been transcribed, edited, and indexed, and the material for Vol. XXI is being prepared. Some pleas of Henry III's reign not found in the published *Curia Regis Rolls,* including pleas from the years 1217–1240, have been excerpted from both the *curia regis* rolls and the assize rolls in *Bracton's Note Book,* ed. F. W. Maitland (3 vols.; Cambridge, 1887). An old and badly edited collection of pleas from the time of Richard I through that of Edward II is *Placitorum in domo capitulari Westmonasterii asservatorum abbrevatio,* ed. William Illingworth (Record Commission; London, 1811). Several of the annual volumes of the Selden

Society consist of excerpts from the plea rolls of John and Henry III, and they contain valuable introductions by authorities in English legal history. In addition to Lady Stenton's volumes for 1198–1202, the society has published *Select Pleas of the Crown*, ed. F. W. Maitland (Selden Society, Vol. I; London, 1888); *Select Civil Pleas*, ed. W. P. Baildon (Selden Society, Vol. III; London, 1890); and *Select Cases of Procedure without Writ under Henry III*, ed. H. G. Richardson and G. O. Sayles (Selden Society, Vol. LX; London, 1941).

The Public Record Office has made no attempt to publish the rolls of the itinerant justices, but various local record societies have made available excerpts from the assize rolls relating to their particular counties. Among them are *Pleas of the Crown for the County of Gloucester, 1221*, ed. F. W. Maitland (London, 1884), and a number of volumes by Lady Stenton. Her editions include *The Earliest Lincolnshire Assize Rolls, 1202–1209* (Lincoln Record Society, Vol. XXII, 1926); *The Earliest Northamptonshire Assize Rolls, 1202 and 1203* (Northamptonshire Record Society, Vol. V, 1930); and three volumes for the Selden Society. *Rolls of the Justices in Eyre for Lincolnshire (1218–19) and Worcestershire (1221)* (Selden Society, Vol. LIII; London, 1934); *Rolls of the Justices in Eyre for Yorkshire in 3 Henry III (1218–19)* (Selden Society, Vol. LVI; London, 1937); and *Rolls of the Justices in Eyre for Gloucestershire, Warwickshire and Staffordshire, 1221, 1222* (Selden Society, Vol. LIX; London, 1940). Other printed assize rolls are *Roll of the Justices in Eyre at Bedford, 1227*, ed. G. Herbert Fowler (Bedfordshire Historical Records Society, Vol. III, 1916); *Roll of the Justices in Eyre, 1240*, ed. G. Herbert Fowler (Bedfordshire Historical Records Society, Vol. IX, 1925); *Calendar of the Roll of the Justices on Eyre, 1227*, ed. J. G. Jenkins (Records Branch of the Buckinghamshire Archeological Society, Vol. VI, 1942); *Northumberland Pleas from the Curia Regis and Assize Rolls, 1198–1272*, ed. A. Hamilton Thompson (Publications of the Newcastle upon Tyne Records Committee, Vol. II for 1921); *Somersetshire Pleas (Civil and Criminal) from the Rolls of the Itinerant Justices, Close of 12th Century–41 Henry III*, ed. E. H. Chadwych-Healey (Somerset Record Society, Vol. XI, 1897); *Staffordshire Suits Extracted from the Plea Rolls, temp. Richard I and King John*, ed. George Wrottesley (William Salt Archeological Society, Vol. III, pt. 1, 1882); *Plea Rolls, temp. Henry III*, ed. George Wrottesley (William Salt Archeological Society, Vol. IV, pt. 1, 1883); *Three Yorkshire Assize Rolls for the Reigns of King*

John and King Henry III, ed. Charles Travis Clay (Yorkshire Archeological Society, Vol. XLIV for 1910).

The careful records kept by the Norman and Angevin kings increased still more under King John, and a large part of the resulting administrative records are available in published editions with indexes of names and places, and often with valuable introductions. Perhaps most important are the publications of the Pipe Roll Society. Through its sponsorship, the pipe rolls for John's reign, 1199–1216, have been published under the general editorship of Doris M. Stenton. Volumes 1–6, 8, 10, 11, and 13 John (Pipe Roll Society, N.S.; London, 1933–1959) are edited by Lady Stenton, while *Pipe Roll 7 John* (1941) is by Sidney Smith, *Pipe Roll 9 John* (1946) by A. Mary Kirkus, *Pipe Roll 12 John* (1951) by C. F. Slade, and the rolls for 14, 15, and 16 John (1955–1959) are edited by Patricia M. Barnes. R. A. Brown is the editor of the final volume, *Pipe Roll 17 John* (1964). In addition, the Pipe Roll Society had published *Memoranda Roll 1 John* and *Memoranda Roll 10 John*, ed. H. G. Richardson (London, 1943, 1955), *Cartae Antiquae Rolls 1–10*, ed. Lionel Landon (London, 1939), and *Cartae Antiquae Rolls 11–20*, ed. J. Conway Davies (London, 1960). The *Rotuli de oblatis et finibus in turri Londinensi asservati*, ed. T. Duffus Hardy (Record Commission; London, 1835), records offers made for the king's good will and for favors. Unfortunately, the published financial records for Henry III's reign are less complete. Only two of the pipe rolls have been published: *Pipe Roll 14 Henry III*, ed. Chalfont Robinson (Pipe Roll Society, N.S.; London, 1927), and *Pipe Roll 26 Henry III*, ed. H. L. Cannon (New Haven, 1918). There is also the *Excerpta e rotulis finium in turri Londinensi asservati, A.D. 1216–1272*, ed. Charles Roberts (2 vols., Record Commission; London, 1835–1836).

Chancery enrollments began under King John, and many of these rolls have been published. Surviving charter enrollments can be found in *Rotuli chartarum in turri Londinensi asservati*, ed. T. Duffus Hardy (Record Commission; London, 1837), and in *Calendar of the Charter Rolls* (6 vols., Public Record Office; London, 1903–1927). The surviving patent rolls down to 1216 are available in *Rotuli litterarum patentium in turri Londinensi asservati*, ed. T. Duffus Hardy (Record Commission; London, 1835). For the period since 1216 there is the *Calendar of Patent Rolls, Henry III* (6 vols., Public Record Office; London, 1901–1913); the first two volumes

(1216–1232) contain Latin transcripts of the writs, while the later volumes are calendared in English. Also available in printed editions are the close rolls: *Rotuli litterarum clausarum in turri Londinensi asservati*, ed. T. Duffus Hardy (2 vols., Record Commission; London, 1833–1834), extending to 1227, and *Close Rolls of the Reign of Henry III* (14 vols., Public Record Office; London, 1902–1938), which completes their publication. Some of the surviving correspondence with Henry III is collected in *Royal and Other Historical Letters Illustrative of the Reign of Henry III*, ed. W. W. Shirley (2 vols., Rolls Series; London, 1862–1868).

A project for publication of the feet of fines was begun with *Fines, sive pedes finium, 1195–1214*, ed. Joseph Hunter (2 vols., Record Commission; London, 1835, 1844), but only fines from Bedfordshire alphabetically through Dorset were published. It is necessary to seek out other final concords in the publications of the English county record societies: *A Calendar of the Feet of Fines for Bedfordshire, Preserved in the Public Record Office, of the Reigns of Richard I, John, and Henry III*, ed. G. Herbert Fowler (Bedfordshire Historical Record Society, Vol. VI, 1919); *Calendar of Feet of Fines, 7 Richard I to 44 Henry III*, ed. M. W. Hughes (Records Branch of the Buckinghamshire Archeological Society, Vol. IV for 1940); *Cornwall Feet of Fines*, Vol. I: *Richard I–Edward III*, ed. Joseph Hambley Rowe (Devon and Cornwall Record Society Publications, 1914); *Devon Feet of Fines*, Vol. I: *Richard I–Henry III*, ed. Oswald J. Reichel (Devon and Cornwall Record Society Publications, 1912); *Feet of Fines, Northumberland and Durham*, ed. A. M. Oliver and Charles Johnson (Publications of the Newcastle upon Tyne Records Committee, Vol. X for 1931); *Final Concords of the County of Lancaster*, pt. 1: *7 Richard I to 34 Edward I*, ed. William Farrer (Lancashire and Cheshire Record Society, 1899); *Feet of Fines for Oxfordshire, 1195–1291*, ed. H. E. Salter (Oxfordshire Record Society, Vol. XII, 1930); *Pedes finium: Richard I to Edward I*, ed. Emanual Green (Somerset Record Society, Vol. VI, 1893); *Calendar of Final Concords*, ed. George Wrottesley (William Salt Society, *Collections for a History of Staffordshire*; Vol. III, pt. 1, 1882; Vol. IV, pt. 1, 1883); *An Abstract of Feet of Fines Relating to the County of Sussex, from 2 Richard I to 33 Henry III*, ed. L. F. Salzmann (Sussex Record Society, Vol. II, 1903); *Warwickshire Feet of Fines*, Vol. I: *Richard I–Edward I*, ed. Frederick C. Wellstood (Dugdale Society, Vol. XI, 1932); *A*

Calendar of Feet of Fines Relating to the County of Wiltshire, Remaining in the Public Record Office, from Their Commencement in the Reign of Richard I to the End of Henry III, ed. Edward A. Fry (Wiltshire Archeological and Natural History Society, 1930); *Feet of Fines for the County of York from 1232 to 1246,* ed. John Parker (Yorkshire Archeological Society, Vol. LXVII, 1925); *Pedes finium Ebor. regnante Johanne,* ed. W. Brown (Surtees Society, Vol. XCIV, 1897). Several collections of final concords from the reign of John have been published by the Pipe Roll Society: *Feet of Fines, Norfolk 1198–1202,* ed. Barbara Dodwell (Pipe Roll Society; London, 1950); *Lincolnshire 1199–1215,* ed. Margaret S. Walker (Pipe Roll Society; London, 1953); and *Norfolk 1201–1215* and *Suffolk 1199–1214,* both edited by Barbara Dodwell (Pipe Roll Society; London, 1958).

Two legal treatises are of great importance for the student of the laws of medieval England. The little book attributed to Ranulf de Glanville, *Tractatus de legibus et consuetudinibus regni Anglie,* ed. and trans. G. D. G. Hall (Medieval Texts; London, 1965), describes the law and procedures of the royal courts in the late twelfth century. Henry de Bracton's *De legibus et consuetudinibus Angliae,* ed. G. E. Woodbine (4 vols.; New Haven, 1915–1942), is a description of the law in the mid-thirteenth century. In addition, Bracton's treatise provides an insight into teachings about the duties of the king in thirteenth-century England. Another important source for doctrines of kingship is the twelfth-century work of that learned Englishman, John of Salisbury—*Policraticus,* ed. C. C. J. Webb (2 vols.; Oxford, 1909). The sections on political theory have been translated by John Dickinson in *The Statesman's Book of John of Salisbury* (New York, 1927). Richard fitz Neal, in *Dialogue de scaccario,* ed. and trans. Charles Johnson (Nelson's Medieval Classics; London, 1950), gives the view of kingship held by Henry II's courtiers, in addition to describing the law of the exchequer. Of course, the Great Charter of 1215 and its subsequent issues are of great value in any study of the law of the early thirteenth century. The various versions of Magna Carta are available in a number of publications, among them *Select Charters and Other Illustrations of English Constitutional History,* ed. William Stubbs (1st ed.; Oxford, 1870), which has gone through numerous editions. Stubbs's work contains the assizes of Henry II and other documents important for the study of the royal courts in the twelfth and thirteenth centuries.

SECONDARY SOURCES

The appropriate volumes of the *Oxford History of England* provide good general introductions to England in the twelfth and thirteenth centuries. They are Vol. III, A. L. Poole, *From Domesday Book to Magna Carta 1087–1216* (2d ed.; Oxford, 1955), and Vol. IV, F. M. Powicke, *The Thirteenth Century 1216–1307* (Oxford, 1953).

A number of works treating the constitutional and legal history of medieval England are useful. No list could fail to include the names of those two giants in the study of English constitutional history, Stubbs and Maitland. William Stubbs, *The Constitutional History of England* (3 vols.; Oxford, 1874–1878), is a pioneer work that cannot be overlooked, although many of his views have been superseded by more recent research. The fundamental work on the English law of the Middle Ages is Frederick Pollock and F. W. Maitland, *The History of English Law before the Time of Edward I* (2d ed., 2 vols.; Cambridge, 1898). This work has never been replaced. The first three volumes of W. S. Holdsworth's *A History of English Law* (13 vols.; London, 1902–1923) also treat the medieval period. T. F. T. Plucknett's *A Concise History of the Common Law* (5th ed., rev.; London, 1956), is a useful guide, organized for easy reference. Lady Doris M. Stenton, the editor of so many assize rolls, has examined an important period in the growth of English law in her Jayne Lectures for 1963, *English Justice between the Norman Conquest and the Great Charter 1066–1215* (Memoirs of the American Philosophical Society, Vol. LX; Philadelphia, 1964). J. E. A. Jolliffe, *The Constitutional History of Medieval England from the English Settlement to 1485* (3d ed.; London, 1954), is sometimes difficult to follow, but he has much that is important to say. Also difficult is *The Governance of Mediaeval England from the Conquest to Magna Carta* by H. G. Richardson and G. O. Sayles (Edinburgh, 1963), one of the most iconoclastic scholarly books to appear in years; the authors declare that it was written to refute Stubbs's *Constitutional History,* a work they feel has had far too much influence in its eighty years. A much easier guide is

Bryce Lyon's *A Constitutional and Legal History of Medieval England* (New York, 1960). Designed as a textbook, its bibliographies and its chapters on sources are extremely useful. Other useful guides to the sources of medieval English legal and constitutional history are two works by V. H. Galbraith, *An Introduction to the Use of the Public Records* (Oxford, 1934) and *Studies in the Public Records* (London, 1948). A valuable study of the administrative system that produced those records is S. B. Chrimes, *Introduction to the Administrative History of Medieval England* (rev. ed., Oxford, 1958).

A number of more specialized studies illuminate problems in the constitutional and legal history of medieval England. One of the great controversies of English constitutional history is the interpretation of Magna Carta. The fundamental work on the subject is W. S. McKechnie, *Magna Carta*, (2d ed., Glasgow, 1914), though now dated in its lawyer's approach. A new work by J. C. Holt, *Magna Carta* (Cambridge, 1965), brings McKechnie's study up to date. Holt's primary aim is to set the Charter in the context of the events and issues of 1215, but he does discuss its later role in English history in the seventeenth and eighteenth centuries. His appendixes reproduce the Charters of 1215 and 1225 and related documents. A number of valuable articles are collected in *Magna Carta Commemoration Essays,* ed. H. E. Malden (London, 1917). Barnaby C. Keeney discusses the background of the legal clauses of the Charter in *Judgment by Peers* (Harvard Historical Monograph Series, Vol. XX; Cambridge, Mass., 1949). Dealing with one aspect of the problem is L. W. Vernon Harcourt's "The Amercement of Barons by Their Peers," *English Historical Review,* XXII (1907), 732–740. Faith Thompson, in *The First Century of Magna Carta* (Minneapolis, 1925), considers the fate of the Great Charter under Henry III and Edward I.

There is no recent study of the king's council that makes use of newly published records, but some older studies are still useful. They include two works of James F. Baldwin: "The Beginnings of the King's Council," *Transactions of the Royal Historical Society,* N.S., XIX (1905), 27–60, which treats the role of the council during Henry III's minority, and *The King's Council in England during the Middle Ages* (Oxford, 1913), the bulk of which is devoted to the late Middle Ages. T. F. Tout's review of the second work, published in *English Historical Review,* XXX (1915), 117–

123, and reprinted in *Collected Papers* (Manchester, 1932) Vol. I, should be read to supplement Baldwin's views. G. B. Adams, in *Council and Courts in Anglo-Norman England* (Yale Historical Studies, Vol. V; New Haven, 1926), treats the period from the Conquest through the reign of Henry III. The king's personal role in the government, both in theory and in practice, is considered in J. E. A. Jolliffe, *Angevin Kingship* (London, 1955). Some scholars have strong reservations about his thesis; one of them is H. G. Richardson in his review in *English Historical Review, LXXI* (1956), 447–453.

The procedures and organization of the common law courts have been the subject of many specialized studies. The best short introduction to the procedure of the royal courts is Charles Johnson's "Notes on Thirteenth-Century Judicial Procedure," *English Historical Review,* LXII (1947), 508–521. Also useful are F. M. Powicke's reviews of the various volumes of the *Curia Regis Rolls* in the *English Historical Review.* He has reviewed Vol. I in XXXIX (1924), 264–272; Vol. II in XLI (1926), 281–286; Vol. III in XLII (1927), 604–606; Vol. IV in XLV (1930), 298–300; Vol. V in XLVII (1932), 661–665; Vol. VI in XLIX (1934), 111–113; and Vol. VII in LII (1937), 698–701. Less useful because they concentrate more on textual criticism than on legal and constitutional precedents are the reviews by G. D. G. Hall of the more recently published volumes. His reviews include Vols. X and XI in *English Historical Review,* LXXIII (1958), 481–484; Vol. XII in LXXIV (1959), 107–110; and Vol. XIII in LXXVII (1962), 103–106. Also useful in a study of law as reflected in the plea rolls is G. E. Woodbine, "Cases in New *Curia Regis* Rolls Affecting Old Rules in English Legal History," *Yale Law Review,* XXXIX (1930), 505–513. An invaluable guide to the work of the royal courts of justice is C. T. Flower, *Introduction to the Curia Regis Rolls* (Selden Society, Vol. LXII; London, 1944). He gives numerous illustrations of the various types of actions heard in the royal courts, drawn from the *curia regis* rolls, but he is not concerned with the constitutional or legal significance of these cases. The problem of proceedings against the king in the royal courts has been treated by Ludwik Ehrlich in *Proceedings against the Crown, 1216–1377,* ed. Sir Paul Vinogradoff (Oxford Studies in Social and Legal History, Vol. VI; Oxford, 1921); some of Ehrlich's findings, however, must be revised in the light of Richardson and Sayles's *Procedure without Writ.* A shorter study of the same problem is W. S. Holdsworth, "The History of Remedies against the Crown," *Law Quarterly Review*, XXXVIII (1922), 141–164.

Among the contributions of H. G. Richardson and G. O. Sayles to legal history are studies on the organization of the courts. Sayles's introductions to *Select Cases in the Court of King's Bench*, Vol. I (Selden Society, Vol. LV; London, 1936), and Vol. IV (Selden Society, Vol. LXXIV; London, 1955), contain excellent accounts of the origin of the court *coram rege*. Some of the views that Sayles expresses in Vol. I are modified in Vol. IV. H. G. Richardson also deals with the problem in his introduction to *Memoranda Roll I John*. A useful summary of his and Sayles's views on the origins of the three royal courts is found in Richardson's review of Lady Stenton's *Pleas before the King or His Justices* in *Law Quarterly Review*, LXX (1954), 568–575. The origins of the itinerant judicature are investigated by William T. Reedy in "The Origins of the General Eyre in the Reign of Henry I," *Speculum*, XLI (1966), 688–724. A number of historians' views on the beginnings of the common law courts are surveyed in R. V. Turner, "The Medieval English Royal Courts: The Problem of Their Origins," *Historian*, XXVII (1965), 471–497.

The introductions to the volumes of the Selden Society contain some of the most important studies of the English common law courts. Sayles and Richardson have studied the procedures of the royal courts as well as the organization; their *Select Cases of Procedure without Writ under Henry III* (Selden Society, Vol. LX; London, 1941) contains an introduction examining proceedings by plaint or *querela* in the royal courts. Another Selden Society publication, *Royal Writs in England from the Conquest to Glanville*, ed. R. C. Van Caenegem (Vol. LXXVII; London, 1958), is of fundamental importance in the study of common law procedures. H. G. Richardson has contributed to the knowledge of the itinerant judicature in his article "Richard fitz Neal and the *Dialogus de Scaccario*," *English Historical Review*, XLIII (1928), 161–171. The editions of the eyre rolls of John and Henry III prepared by Lady Stenton for the Selden Society and for other record societies contain valuable accounts of the work of the itinerant justices. W. C. Bolland, in *The General Eyre* (Cambridge, 1922), describes the work of the justices in the late thirteenth and early fourteenth centuries. The careers of many early justices are summarized in Edward

Foss, *A Biographical Dictionary of the Judges of England from the Conquest to the Present Time 1066–1870* (London, 1870). Francis West, *The Justiciarship in England, 1066–1232* (Cambridge Studies in Medieval Life and Thought, N.S., Vol. XII; Cambridge, 1966), includes chapters on the justiciars and the law courts.

There are a number of studies of King John and Henry III that are useful for understanding the environment in which the royal courts operated. A. L. Poole, in *Obligations of Society in the Twelfth and Thirteenth Centuries* (Oxford, 1946), describes the impact of fines and amercements on the people of those centuries. Perhaps no English king has aroused so much controversy among historians as King John. For an evaluation of the differing interpretations of his reign, see C. Warren Hollister, "King John and the Historians," *Journal of British Studies, I* (1961), 1–19. The best account of his reign is Sidney Painter, *The Reign of King John* (Baltimore, 1949). A recent personal biography that incorporates the findings of modern specialized studies is W. L. Warren, *King John* (New York, 1961). Particularly useful is his evaluation of the chroniclers' descriptions of John. Doris M. Stenton has studied King John's activity in the judicial sphere in her introductions to the pipe rolls of his reign, especially *Pipe Roll 6 John,* and in the introduction to *Pleas before the King or His Justices.* She has presented her conclusions in her Raleigh Lecture to the British Academy, "King John and the Courts of Justice," *Proceedings of the British Academy, XLIV* (1958), 103–128, reprinted in her *English Justice 1066–1215,* pp. 88–114. Other specialized studies that cast light on John's relations with his courts are C. R. Cheney, "King John's Reaction to the Interdict," *Transactions of the Royal Historical Society,* ser. 4, XXXI (1949), 129–150, and J. C. Holt, "The Barons and the Great Charter," *English Historical Review,* LXX (1955), 1–24. Holt has expanded his study of King John's baronage in *The Northerners: A Study in the Reign of King John* (Oxford, 1961), a detailed study of the events leading to the break between king and barons. A useful handbook for the study of the baronage in the twelfth and thirteenth centuries is I. J. Sanders, *English Baronies: A Study of Their Origin and Descent 1086–1327* (Oxford, 1960), which traces the history of more than two hundred baronies. H. G. Richardson, in *English Jewry under the Angevin Kings* (London, 1960), considers another group that played a part in litigation during John's reign.

Although the number of specialized studies on aspects of the early years of Henry III is not so great as that for John's reign, one work more than makes up for the lack. F. M. Powicke's *King Henry III and the Lord Edward: The Community of the Realm in the Thirteenth Century* (2 vols.; Oxford, 1947) is fundamental. Old but still useful is Kate Norgate, *The Minority of Henry III* (London, 1912). Also valuable are those sections in Bertie Wilkinson, *The Constitutional History of England 1216–1399* (3 vols.; London, 1948–1958) that deal with Henry III's minority and early personal rule. A useful article is Mabel H. Mills, "The Reforms at the Exchequer (1232–1242)," *Transactions of the Royal Historical Society*, ser. 4, X (1927), 111–133, treating administrative reforms during Henry's early personal rule. Donald W. Sutherland, in *Quo Warranto Proceedings in the Reign of Edward I, 1278–1294* (Oxford, 1963), considers the origin of this royal instrument in the time of Henry III.

One aspect of the king's relationship with his courts that cannot be overlooked is his theoretical position as source of all justice. The basic work in medieval political thought is R. W. and A. J. Carlyle, *A History of Mediaeval Political Theory in the West* (6 vols.; New York and London, 1903–1936). A brief but important work is Fritz Kern, *Kingship and Law in the Middle Ages,* ed. and trans. S. B. Chrimes (Oxford, 1939). C. H. McIlwain has written two general histories of political theory that contain chapters concerning medieval English doctrines, particularly Bracton's. They are *Constitutionalism: Ancient and Modern* (rev. ed.; Ithaca, N.Y., 1958) and *The Growth of Political Thought in the West* (New York, 1932). Ernst H. Kantorowicz, *The King's Two Bodies: A Study in Mediaeval Political Theology* (Princeton, 1957), is more general than the title indicates; it contains accounts of the views on kingship held by John of Salisbury and Bracton. Another consideration of John of Salisbury's political thought is John Dickinson's introduction to his translation of the *Policraticus,* which has also appeared as an article, "The Medieval Conception of Kingship and Some of Its Limitations, As Developed in the *Policraticus* of John of Salisbury," *Speculum,* I (1926), 308–337. Twelfth-century theocratic ideas of kingship are treated in R. W. Southern, *The Making of the Middle Ages* (London, 1956). Medieval English kingship in both theory and practice is considered in Percy Ernst Schramm, *A History of the English Coronation,* trans. L. G. Wickham Legg (Oxford, 1937).

J. E. A. Jolliffe also deals with both theory and practice in his *Angevin Kingship*, particularly the feudal principles utilized by Henry II and his sons to expand their power. F. M. Powicke in *Stephen Langon* (Oxford, 1928) and J. C. Holt in his article "The Barons and the Great Charter" treat conceptions of kingship held by the English barons and churchmen in the early thirteenth century.

In *Early English Legal Literature* (Cambridge Studies in English Legal History; Cambridge, 1958), T. F. T. Plucknett has considered the views of English medieval legal writers from the author of the *Leges Henrici Primi* to Bracton. This work provides a helpful statement of "the Bractonian problem," the questions of the texts of Bracton's treatise and of Bracton's training in Roman law. These questions were raised by Hermann Kantorowicz in *Bractionian Problems* (Glasgow, 1941), and they have resulted in much scholarly controversy. A detailed discussion of the question is found in H. G. Richardson, *Bracton: The Problem of His Text* (Selden Society, supp. ser., Vol. II; London, 1966). Articles dealing with "the Bractonian problem" include: C. H. McIlwain, "The Present Status of the Problem of the Bracton Text," *Harvard Law Review*, LVII (1943), 220–240; Fritz Schulz, "Critical Studies on Bracton's Treatise," *Law Quarterly Review*, XLIX (1943), 172–180; G. E. Woodbine's review of *Bractonian Problems* in *Yale Law Journal*, LII (1943), 428–444; H. G. Richardson, "Azo, Drogheda, and Bracton," *English Historical Review*, LIX (1944), 22–47; and Gaillard Lapsley, "Bracton and the Authorship of the 'Addicio de Cartis,'" *English Historical Review*, LXII (1947), 1–19. Articles discussing Bracton's conception of the royal power include Fritz Schulz, "Bracton on Kingship," *English Historical Review*, LX (1945), 136–176; S. J. T. Miller, "The Position of the King in Bracton and Beaumanoir," *Speculum*, XXXI (1956), 263–296; Brian Tierney, "Bracton on Government," *Speculum*, XXXVIII (1963), 275–317; and Ewart Lewis, "King above Law? 'Quod Principi Placuit' in Bracton," *Speculum*, XXXIX (1964), 240–269. Richardson's *Bracton*, his article "Azo, Drogheda, and Bracton," and Doris M. Stenton's introduction to *Rolls for Lincolnshire and Worcestershire* give good accounts of Bracton's life, training, and work as a judge.

Index